Seeing Is Disbelieving

Factual misinformation is spread in conflict zones around the world, often with dire consequences. But when is this misinformation actually believed, and when is it not? *Seeing Is Disbelieving* examines the appeal and limits of dangerous misinformation in war and is the go-to text for understanding false beliefs and their impact in modern armed conflict. Daniel Silverman extends the burgeoning study of factual misinformation, conspiracy theories, and fake news in social and political life into a crucial new domain, while providing a powerful new argument about the limits of misinformation in high-stakes situations. Rich evidence from the US drone campaign in Pakistan, the counterinsurgency against ISIL in Iraq, and the Syrian civil war provide the backdrop for practical lessons in promoting peace, fighting wars, managing conflict, and countering misinformation more effectively.

DANIEL SILVERMAN is Assistant Professor of Political Science in the Carnegie Mellon Institute for Strategy and Technology (CMIST) at Carnegie Mellon University. He has published articles on international security, peace, and conflict in a number of leading scholarly journals including *International Organization*, *International Studies Quarterly*, the *Journal of Conflict Resolution*, and *Journal of Peace Research*, along with public-facing outlets such as *The Washington Post*, *Chicago Tribune*, *National Interest*, and *Political Violence at a Glance*.

Seeing Is Disbelieving

Why People Believe Misinformation in
War, and When They Know Better

DANIEL SILVERMAN
Carnegie Mellon University

CAMBRIDGE
UNIVERSITY PRESS

CAMBRIDGE
UNIVERSITY PRESS

Shaftesbury Road, Cambridge CB2 8EA, United Kingdom

One Liberty Plaza, 20th Floor, New York, NY 10006, USA

477 Williamstown Road, Port Melbourne, VIC 3207, Australia

314–321, 3rd Floor, Plot 3, Splendor Forum, Jasola District Centre,
New Delhi – 110025, India

103 Penang Road, #05–06/07, Visioncrest Commercial, Singapore 238467

Cambridge University Press is part of Cambridge University Press & Assessment,
a department of the University of Cambridge.

We share the University's mission to contribute to society through the pursuit of
education, learning and research at the highest international levels of excellence.

www.cambridge.org
Information on this title: www.cambridge.org/9781009523578

DOI: 10.1017/9781009523561

When citing this work, please include a reference to the
DOI 10.1017/9781009523561

First published 2024

A catalogue record for this publication is available from the British Library

*A Cataloging-in-Publication data record for this book is available from the
Library of Congress*

ISBN 978-1-009-52357-8 Hardback
ISBN 978-1-009-52358-5 Paperback

To my grandmother Lila Price Margolis (1930–2022), and all those of the Greatest Generation, who taught me that motivation is the most powerful force in the social world.

Contents

Figures

Tables

Preface and Acknowledgments

This book started due to a confluence of several unexpected influences in my life. The seed was first planted when I watched an online debate in the summer of 2013 by the live debating organization *Intelligence Squared*. The title of the debate was "The US Drone Program Is Fatally Flawed." As a young doctoral student deeply interested in issues of international security, as well as political psychology and the politics of the Middle East and broader Islamic world, I was struck by the competing claims about how people in societies such as Pakistan understood and reacted to the US drone campaign there. This spurred my interest, and deeper investigation confirmed that there was wide variation in public perceptions of drone strikes in the country. The first fuzzy outlines of a project about understanding and unpacking variation in people's perceptions of wartime violence were beginning to emerge.

The budding project was aided greatly by two fortuitous factors early on. One was the US State Department's Professional Fellows Program (PFP), an exchange program that brings groups of emerging leaders from foreign countries to the US and places them into a relevant government or corporate office in an American city for 5–6 weeks. It so happened that a PFP delegation from Pakistan was sent to Columbus, OH, while I was in the early stages of my PhD at The Ohio State University (OSU), and I was able to meet dozens of young dynamic Pakistanis, learn much more about Pakistani society and politics from them, and probe some of the ideas that were swimming around in my head about the disagreements around drones in the country. Based on this and other networking that I was able to do at OSU, it began to be clear that the most interesting and dramatic variation in Pakistani perceptions of drones was between people who were from the targeted areas and those who lived elsewhere – and that these audiences had not only very different opinions but also very different factual understandings of the campaign. The project thus

shifted to focus more on people's factual perceptions and misperceptions in war, with an emerging idea that proximity to or removal from
the actual events in question was the critical part of the story.

The other key development around this time was meeting Mujtaba
Ali Isani, a doctoral student in the same program as me at OSU who
would go on to become a close friend and collaborator. Muj would
help me not only better refine my ideas about Pakistan but also conduct field and survey research there during the winter of 2014–15.
My success on that front owes thanks to many people, including
Muj's brothers and broader family, Tariq Junaid and the Institute for
Public Opinion Research in Islamabad for an excellent introduction
into the world of working with survey research firms, and the many
generous Pakistanis I had met from the PFP group and at OSU such
as Waseem Qureshi, Rashid Kazmi, Riaz Akbar, Zeesha Khawaja,
Farooq Afridi, and Muhammad Ali Paracha who showed me around
the country. From a scholarly perspective, my exploratory fieldwork
in Pakistan and experience studying the Pakistani case were tremendously illuminating. They helped me provide hard evidence about
several things related to the spread and influence of factual misperceptions in conflict. However, because the tribal regions of the country – where the strikes overwhelmingly occur – were not open to
large-scale attitudinal data collection at the time, I realized I would
need to turn to other cases to more fully and rigorously test crucial
parts of the argument.

In that regard, I was fortunate to forge a relationship toward the
end of my time as a PhD student at OSU with Karl Kaltenthaler of
the University of Akron and Munqith Dagher of IIACSS Research
Group in Iraq. Karl and Munqith had been working as a team to pub-
lish academic studies and policy briefings using data collected from
Munqith's survey research firm in Iraq, and I began to contribute to
some of this work. The connection was due completely to happen-
stance, as I asked Karl a question during a panel on which he was
presenting at a major political science conference and then struck up
a discussion with him afterward. A reminder that conference-based
networking can be extremely fruitful and meaningful! I soon realized
that a survey of Iraqis that Munqith had fielded for an unrelated pur-
pose offered an excellent opportunity to further test my argument
about factual misperception and misinformation in conflict. After
obtaining Institutional Review Board (IRB) approval, I analyzed the

data and wrote up the results with support from Munqith and Karl, finding evidence that those who had lived in areas targeted by anti-ISIL airstrikes were *less* likely to believe falsehoods about them. In addition, I was able to obtain data from the non-governmental organization (NGO) Airwars on the airstrikes themselves, and used this in combination with the survey data to provide added rigor to the findings. The results of this study were crucial for the continued development of the project, as they departed from the case in which the theory was originally developed (Pakistan) and confirmed its validity in a wholly new context (Iraq) for the first time. I am immensely grateful to Karl and Munqith for encouraging me to draw on portions of this article for Chapter 4 of the book. I am also thankful to Christopher Woods and his colleagues at Airwars for sharing their data for that research.

A third major layer of evidence for the book also came to me in a fortuitous way. Notably, as a postdoctoral fellow at Carnegie Mellon University (CMU), I began to collaborate with Justin Schon, a thoughtful junior-level scholar who was then at the University of Florida. Justin had recently published a book on the Syrian civil war entitled *Surviving the War in Syria*. As I became more familiar with Justin's work, and he with mine, I realized that the rich interviews he had done for the project with Syrian refugees could be very useful in providing another major test of my argument because they dealt at some length with civilians' engagement with new information during the war. Thankfully, Justin generously agreed to share the de-identified interview transcripts with me. Working with an excellent research assistant named Yousef Khanfar from Carnegie Mellon University-Qatar (CMU-Q), I then coded up a number of new variables from the interviews for quantitative analysis and mined them qualitatively in new ways with an eye toward my theory. The results helped further substantiate and support the book's central argument, while pushing it into new terrain in a number of different ways (including with a substantial and welcome infusion of qualitative evidence).

Several other important things that helped incubate the book must be acknowledged here. To begin with, this book grew out of a dissertation I completed in the Political Science Department at The Ohio State University, and I am tremendously grateful for all of the support I received there. My supremely patient and thoughtful dissertation advisor Chris Gelpi helped me hone and shape my initially fuzzy ideas into a real contribution. Rick Herrmann, Jan Pierskalla, and Jake Shapiro rounded out a fantastic dissertation committee that continuously challenged me to improve the project but did so from a solid foundation of support and encouragement. Other faculty such as the brilliant Bear Braumoeller played key secondary roles, and trusted peers such as Kyle Larson, Vittorio Merola, Reed Kurtz, and Marzia Oceno all helped in important and distinct ways as well. I am lucky to have had continuing support from excellent senior mentors at CMU, including Baruch Fischhoff, Kiron Skinner, Mark Kamlet, and Audrey Kurth Cronin. A strong group of junior faculty members and postdoctoral fellows at CMU including John Chin, Ignacio Arana, Daniel Hansen, Dani Nedal, Takiyah Harper-Shipman, Giorleny Altamirano Rayo, Dov Levin, Pearce Edwards, Ben Helms, and other participants in the Politics and Strategy Research Workshop/Political Science Research Workshop (PSRW) offered immensely valuable feedback about parts of the research. I am also grateful to John Haslam, Carrie Parkinson, and others at Cambridge University Press for their steady support of the project, as well as several unusually comprehensive peer reviewers that pushed me to significantly add to and reorganize the manuscript in ways that produced a much stronger and tighter final product. I am also very appreciative of Ben Schachter's excellent and patient work on the book's cover art, which brought the book's thesis to life in a visually elegant way.

Finally, on a personal level, I am deeply indebted to my wife, Ruth Silverman, for her constant love and support as well as her encouragement of my writing time; our baby boy, Levi Silverman, for filling my life with joy and excitement as I pursued the latter stages of this project, and for taking so many naps in his first half year of life that I could finish my revisions; my parents Fern and Barry for being unwavering supporters, useful sounding boards, and ruthless editors; and my friends – those of the lifelong hometown variety and many others whom I have gained more recently – for their positive roles in my lives and for their support and encouragement.

Ultimately, as I worked on preparing the book over the last couple of years, two major wars of world historical impact broke out: one when Russia invaded Ukraine in February of 2022 and the other when Hamas attacked Israel in October of 2023. The latter conflict in particular hit home to me due to my extensive connections to people in both communities, and in fact has made me understand the dangerous dynamics of wartime misinformation better than ever before. I have watched up close as a deluge of fake news, conspiracy theories, and rumormongering has flooded social media during the dispute – and as many figures I recognize from the public sphere and even from the ranks of academia have embraced or fallen for such claims. Indeed, the war has deepened my understanding of the *power* of misinformation in conflict, its strategic *utility* in inciting anger, denying harm, and concealing misdeeds, and the *ease* with which it can ripple through potentially sympathetic communities. Yet at the same time, both of these conflicts show dynamics consistent with the book's central thesis about the *limits* of wartime misinformation, and the complex, painful, powerful leaning process that enables communities on the front lines to see through its false allure. Whether this has made me more optimistic about the book's core argument and the extent to which it can be harnessed for prosocial purposes are unclear. I now understand the politics arrayed against the amplification of local accurate voices from the front lines of war better than ever before. But I also understand the forces that actively work to do that amplification and the powerful credibility of those voices when they are able to be widely shared and heard. Perhaps I am ever the optimist, but I believe that – while the problem of factual misinformation and manipulation in war may only have metastasized in recent conflicts – there is significant potential to push in a positive direction when people are properly armed with deep ideas and insights about the problem.

1 | *Introduction*
The Problem of Factual Misinformation and Misperception in War

The first casualty when war comes is truth.

– US Senator Hiram Johnson, 1917

On April 6, 2017, two days after the Syrian regime's infamous chemical weapons attack against the rebel-held town of Khan Shaykhun – which killed dozens of innocent Syrian civilians and left hundreds more burned and disfigured, prompting widespread international condemnation – Syria's Foreign Minister Walid Muallem held a defiant press conference outside of the Ministry of Foreign Affairs in Damascus. The Syrian government, Muallem said, "has not used and will not use" chemical weapons. Instead, the army had "attacked an arms depot belonging to the Al-Nusra Front which contained chemical weapons." Moreover, the allegation that the event was a sarin gas attack by the government, Muallem stated, had been *fabricated* by Al-Nusra as a desperate attempt to provoke Western military intervention in the conflict.[1] These statements are typical of those that have been made by the Syrian government and its Iranian and Russian backers following atrocities in the country's ongoing civil war.

There is just one problem, of course, with Muallem's claims – they are unequivocally false, a clear example of factual misinformation[2]

---

[1] See "LIVE: Syrian FM Walid al-Muallem holds press conference in Damascus." *Ruptly Video News Agency.* Available at www.youtube.com/watch?v=AcaF1vC8SPA.

[2] I follow a number of existing studies and define misinformation as false information that is conveyed with or without the intent to deceive its targets (Vraga and Bode 2020), whereas disinformation is false information that is specifically intended to deceive its audience (as is fake news, see Tandoc, Lim, and Ling 2018). The argument in this book applies to both of these concepts as well as to related ones such as lies, rumors, and fake news, as it is not specific to the source (or intentionality) of the falsehood. I often default to the term misinformation in the book because it is the most general and inclusive concept, though I use other more specific terms when warranted as well.

1

in modern war. In this sense, however, they are actually unremarkable. Misinformation, lies, and fake news have long been with us in situations of war as well as peace. From false stories about German atrocities – such as the mutilation of Belgian babies and the industrial processing of corpses by the German government – that proliferated in World War I (WWI) to fake reports about the crucifixion of Russian-speaking civilians and North Atlantic Treaty Organization (NATO) attacks against Russia during its occupation of Ukraine,[3] these phenomena have been a longstanding feature of violent conflict.

But to what extent are such lies actually believed? Do Syrians buy the regime's fabrications about events at Khan Shaykhun? More broadly, do civilian populations[4] really know what is going on in war, or do they form false beliefs about it? These questions are vitally important because of the dangers that such factual misinformation and misperception can present. For one thing, if it is embraced, misinformation in war-torn or otherwise fragile contexts can incite or escalate violence. For example, a flood of fake news about attacks by the Rohingya minority in Myanmar has fueled a brutal military crackdown against the community since 2017, sending over half a million people fleeing to neighboring Bangladesh.[5] Similarly, evidence suggests that some of the incendiary radio stations that were active in Rwanda in the 1990s – which contained rampant misinformation about Tutsi behaviors – played a significant role in fueling the tragic violence of the Rwandan genocide (Yanagizawa-Drott 2014).

In addition, wartime misinformation can undermine the possibility of peace. For instance, for Syrians who come to think that chemical attacks in places such as Khan Shaykhun were perpetrated by the rebels, the idea of reconciling with these groups becomes even more unlikely. And in World War II (WWII), lies by the Nazis about their continued successes late into the war helped sustain German war support rather than allowing for a greater acceptance of reality and

---

[3] See, for example, Arkady Ostrovsky, "Putin's Ukraine Unreality Show." *The Wall Street Journal*, July 28, 2014.

[4] By "civilian" this text refers to people in armed conflicts who are not "members of State armed forces or organized armed groups" and do not otherwise "take a direct part in hostilities" (ICRC 2009, 16).

[5] See, for example, Annie Gowen and Max Bearak, "Fake News on Facebook Fans the Flames of Hate against the Rohingya in Burma." *Washington Post*, December 8, 2017.

readiness to end the conflict (USSBS 1947). In sum, factual misinformation and misperception in war can spark more violence, and they can spoil and undermine the potential for peace. If we care about seeing violent conflicts de-escalated and resolved, we thus need a comprehensive understanding of misinformation and its appeal in war. That is the task taken up for the first time in this book.

1.1 The Neglect of Misinformation and Its Appeal in War

This book sits at the intersection of two major bodies of scholarship that have to date had remarkably little interaction. On the one hand, there has been growing attention in security, peace, and conflict studies in recent years to the "micro-dynamics" of conflicts – that is, to understanding how groups and individuals think and behave "on the ground" in violent conflict (e.g., Lyall 2010, Shapiro 2013, Toft and Zhukov 2015, Balcells 2017, Kaplan 2017, Hoover Green 2018, Krause 2018). This research has produced insights on everything from the patterns of violence that occur in civil wars (Kalyvas 2006) to the recruitment and management strategies of rebel organizations (Weinstein 2006) to the ways in which civilian populations mobilize and organize to resist armed actors (Arjona 2016). On the other hand, there has also been an explosion of research in the social sciences on lies, misinformation, conspiracy theories, and other related phenomena in social and political life (e.g., Nyhan and Reifler 2010, Uscinski and Parent 2014, Jolley and Douglas 2015, Druckman and McGrath 2019, Guess et al. 2020, Vraga and Bode 2020, Greene and Murphy 2021). This information helped us understand the spread, appeal, and consequences of misinformation in various social arenas, from election fraud (Berlinski et al. 2021) to climate change (Tesler 2018) to public health (Roozenbeek et al. 2020) and beyond.

Yet the area where these two substantial literatures would naturally bump into each other – that is, understanding misinformation in war and conflict – has received little scholarly attention. This is surprising from both perspectives. From the perspective of conflict studies, it is surprising that there has been much attention to individual-level behaviors and attitudes in war in recent years, yet little to people's factual beliefs – even though those beliefs can shape attitudes and behaviors. That is, *what people think is going on in war* can shape whom they support and what they do. From the perspective of misinformation research, it is equally surprising that while scholars have studied misinformation and lies in so many other areas of public life, its dynamics in situations of war and conflict have remained relatively unexplored. As contemporary, high-profile wars such as Russia's invasion and occupation of Ukraine and the conflict between Israel and Hamas have made quite clear, these two phenomena are deeply connected – war has become one of the main arenas of misinformation today, and misinformation has become one of the primary battlefronts in war. This book aims to rectify this gap and ultimately will have something important to say to both of these bodies of scholarship. It will show how influential models of civilian attitudes and behaviors in war should be modified based on people's varying latitude for believing misinformation and how our existing understanding of factual misinformation in other areas of social and political lives changes when it crashes on the jagged rocks of violent conflict.

Moreover, in addition to the sheer dearth of research at the intersection of these two areas, there are strong conceptual reasons why extending our understanding of belief in misinformation to consider situations such as war is critically important. In particular, while the existing literature has identified a wide variety of factors that shape people's susceptibility to embracing misinformation, its focus is overwhelmingly on *individual differences*. Factors such as ideological motivated reasoning (Nyhan and Reifler 2010), animosity toward partisan opponents (Osmundsen et al. 2021), a desire for group belonging (Rathje et al. 2023), weak critical reasoning skills (Pennycook and Rand 2019), low generalized social trust (Miller, Saunders, and Farhart 2016), and prior exposure to the claim (Pennycook, Cannon, and Rand 2019) among others have been credibly linked to people's receptivity to false and unsubstantiated information. Yet all of these factors focus on variation across individuals – the extent to which they hold certain preferences, possess certain capabilities, or have consumed certain information – and not variation in the *situations in which they find themselves*. This is surprising given that both "the person" and "the situation" are powerful drivers of human psychology (e.g., Ross and Nisbett 1991), and we might expect that extreme situations such as war are especially influential in shaping how people think and process new information. This text aims to fill this gap in our knowledge and will reckon with how the situational dynamics of war shape people's political psychology and their ability to discern true information from false information.

1.2 The Argument in Brief: How Proximity Constrains Credulity in War

This book explores the question of when people can sort truth from lies in war and form accurate beliefs about what is going on around them. It argues that much of the answer lies in their degree of proximity and exposure to the conflict events or dynamics in question. The punchline is that lies are pervasive in conflict, but they can be punctured when people are close to the "action" over time – in short, that seeing is the key to disbelieving in war.

The logic behind this conclusion is straightforward. In particular, it is premised on the idea that factual beliefs in war hinge critically on two key factors: (1) the *information* that people have about the relevant events and (2) their *motivation* to understand that information accurately or not. Indeed, drawing on research from social psychology, the argument begins with the fact that people often indulge in "motivated reasoning" about events around them, developing factual beliefs about their environments that fit their existing worldviews. In war, this means that people will often form beliefs about the nature of conflict events based on what they already think about the groups that are fighting. If, for example, an airstrike is conducted by the USA, and they dislike and distrust the USA, they will probably come to think the attack was indiscriminate in nature – as that matches the motives they think the Americans possess. Yet, not everyone has the luxury of allowing their worldviews to dictate their beliefs. For those who are sufficiently near the action – for those who see it and are directly affected by it – these "directional biases" will take a backseat to an "accuracy motive" (Kunda 1990), as getting it right or wrong may be a matter of life or death. In these cases, people's tendencies to form self-serving, biased beliefs about their environments are "disciplined" by the need to understand the risks and dangers around them in order to survive. Thus, if civilians live in a community that is under regular American bombardment – even if they dislike the USA – they are strongly incentivized to know who exactly is targeted and what exactly the dynamics of the bombing are for their own survival.

Meanwhile, a parallel process unfolds in the informational arena. Drawing on key ideas in communications, the argument advanced in the book builds on the fact that people's "information diets" have a strong effect on their beliefs as well, with distinct information sources varying widely in their representations of the world. The media in conflict environments are particularly prone to these dynamics, fueling factual biases among different audiences. For example, during the Israeli invasion of southern Lebanon in 2006, Lebanese civilians who got their news from *Al Jazeera* or Hezbollah's *Al-Manar TV* were treated to a very different depiction of what was happening on the ground – who was winning and losing, what was being bombed, and to what effects – than civilians who followed the *BBC* (Kalb and Saivetz 2007). Yet, as discussed earlier, not everyone is equally vulnerable to such biases – communities that are more exposed to the relevant events will resist or reject biased media narratives due to their superior local information about what is going on. In other words, for Lebanese civilians who were living on or near the front lines in towns such as Qana or Bint Jbeil, their beliefs about the nature of events in the war were sharply constrained by what they themselves and those around them actually experienced in the fighting. In this way, too, proximity to reality can be a powerful check on misinformation.

Table 1.1 sums up the theory. The overall picture is clear: Communities who are distant or removed from the relevant events will tend to form false beliefs and be easily misled about them, whereas those who are proximate and exposed to the events in question – for both informational and motivational reasons – will tend to form more accurate perceptions about them and to know better. This

Table 1.1 *Summarizing the model of people's factual beliefs in war*

Types of individuals	Information	Motivation	Result
Proximate/ exposed to the relevant events	→ Local knowledge +	Accuracy motive =	↑ Belief accuracy ↓ Misinformation vulnerability
Distant/removed from the relevant events	→ Partisan media +	Directional biases =	↓ Belief accuracy ↑ Misinformation vulnerability

conclusion is a powerful one from multiple perspectives. From a conflict perspective, we will see how it knits together existing disparate understandings about how civilian communities think in war into a more coherent whole. And from a misinformation point of view, we will see how it adds to existing ideas about people's biases and other individual differences fostering false beliefs and shows how these can be constrained by the power of high-stakes situations.

1.3 Empirical Approach to Analyzing Factual Beliefs and Biases in War

Broadly speaking, this book's methodological approach is to use a range of evidence about what people actually think in violent conflicts in order to test its claims. Indeed, studying people's susceptibility to wartime misinformation requires examining what people believe is happening in war and why they believe it. This requires looking carefully at what is "in people's heads" as they navigate violent conflicts – their attitudes, beliefs, and perceptions. The empirical core of the text thus contains a wealth of "micro-level" evidence from different wars.

Within this context, the book marshals several different types of micro-level information. This reflects a view that combining diverse types and sources of evidence is beneficial when testing an argument. One key source of data that is used is public opinion surveys, including both widely available public opinion polls conducted by large organizations such as the *Pew Research Center* in conflict environments and more specialized surveys obtained specifically to study the issues in this book. Surveys allow us to examine broad patterns in public perceptions and the factors driving them, and they are amply used – albeit in somewhat different ways – in both Chapter 3 on Pakistan and Chapter 4 on Iraq.

Another major source of data presented in the book is violent event data. Violent event data does not directly tap into people's thinking in war. However, it is highly useful in multiple ways. First, violent event data helps us benchmark baseline realities in armed conflicts, especially when we can triangulate across multiple sources of data and complement them with detailed qualitative and contextual understanding. Second, violent event data can be combined with public opinion surveys in novel ways to examine how people's beliefs and attitudes shift with proximity to wartime events in either space or time. Indeed, this is a strategy that is used extensively in Chapter 4.

A third key type of data used in the book is interview data. Interviews are often conducted on smaller samples than large-n public opinion surveys, but they can provide deep knowledge of people's thinking and decision-making in situations such as wars because they can capture and convey their personal narratives and experiences robustly. In this sense, they are an important complement to the use of large-scale public opinion surveys and violent event data referenced earlier. The book analyzes a sizable batch of semi-structured interviews with refugees from Syria both quantitatively and qualitatively in Chapter 5.

Finally, the content in this text is informed by exploratory fieldwork that was conducted in Karachi, Lahore, and Islamabad, Pakistan, in the winter of 2014–15, and in Amman, Jordan, in the summer of 2017. While this fieldwork was conducted early on in the research process and aimed to interface with local survey firm administrators as much as to personally collect data, it included considerable "soaking and poking" that informs the treatment of the cases in the book. In Pakistan, especially, information was gleaned from direct conversations with numerous journalists, experts, political elites, and ordinary civilians about the fighting in the country's northwest and the politics around it, yielding important contextual knowledge about the conflict and public perceptions of it by people both from the tribal areas and from elsewhere in the country.

1.4 Conceptual Ground Clearing

It is also important to do some conceptual ground clearing and flesh out a few key concepts and scope conditions before proceeding. First, a word on the types of violent conflict to which the book applies. While many important works on the dynamics of conflict in recent years restrict their focus to a specific type of war – such as interstate war, civil war, or insurgency – to facilitate clear theory building, the dynamics outlined here apply widely across different types of violent disputes. The primary argument in the book is applicable to any form of organized violence, be it intrastate or interstate, asymmetric or symmetric, ethnic or nonethnic, or criminal or political in nature. This is because the assumptions required for it to hold are simply that (1) civilians in the dispute have some prior preferences or allegiances toward the belligerents involved – that is, they are not simply all neutral and impartial – and (2) media outlets do not all report events in the dispute with perfect agreement and accuracy. If these two minimal conditions are met, and one can argue that they are in all violent conflicts, the central argument of the book – that civilians removed from events will tend to form factually biased beliefs about them, whereas those in the line of fire will tend to be more accurate in their perceptions and be less easily misled – will be applicable.[6]

There is also the question of the types of beliefs to which this text applies. Here it is worth stressing that the book studies the accuracy of people's *factual or empirical* beliefs about conflict, and not their *moral or normative* beliefs about it. Thus, questions about who is winning and losing, who is fighting and not fighting, who is being targeted and not being targeted, and what tactics are being used and not being used are all subject to the central argument. In contrast, judgments about whose cause is just and unjust, who is the victim and who the oppressor, and who deserves to win and lose are not within our purview. In fact, this distinction parallels the words of one scholar and ex-war correspondent, who noted aptly that "wartime news breaks down into two main sections – news of the fighting and the justification for it" (Knightley 2004: 502). The book tackles the former and not the latter. No claims are made about the extent to which people's normative beliefs about the conflict change with their degree of exposure to the events in question, except insofar as they are influenced by new information learned about what is taking place on the ground.[7]

---

[6] Now, when the different civilian communities and media outlets in the dispute are *more* polarized, the gap between proximate and distant civilians may be *larger*, but the basic argument requires only that there be some distribution of popular preferences and media coverage in the dispute.

[7] One further caveat is that we must focus on factual beliefs about the past or present as opposed to the future. People's predictions or expectations about the future course of a war are not falsifiable, no matter their content (e.g., "we *will* win" may yet turn out to be true even if one is currently losing), whereas those about the present or past may be judged against the facts on the ground (e.g., "we *are* winning" or "we *have* won" is false if your side is losing or it has lost).

1.5 A Note on Sorting Fact from Fake

One practical question that should be addressed here is what is meant by terms such as "fake," "false," and "misperception" – that is, how one can identify a particular factual belief as incorrect or inaccurate. In fact, this is a critical question not just for this book but for all research about fake news, misinformation, and other related phenomena. Following influential studies in the literature, this book treats as inaccurate any belief that is either: (1) demonstrably false or (2) not supported by or at odds with the weight of existing evidence – in other words, that is *false* or *unsubstantiated* (Nyhan and Reifler 2010). Such definitions can be best clarified in concrete terms. For example, if I hold up a blue pen and say, "this pen is red," my statement is demonstrably false. Similarly, if there is an attack in war that is extremely precise and causes no collateral damage, and someone believes that it killed all civilians, that belief would also be inaccurate.

Since it is easy to get lost in the definitional "weeds," it is important here to step back and recall that wars are generally deeply politicized contexts awash in blatant combatant propaganda. Many beliefs that arise in war are either the result of stories that were fabricated and manipulated (sometimes even admittedly) by one "side" or another, or are so plainly false to those outside the passions and prejudices of the conflict as to be almost absurd. In other words, there are many bald lies in war. For example, infamous pieces of atrocity propaganda such as the German corpse factory story in WWI (Knightley 2004, Ch. 5), the accounts of Israeli rape at Deir Yassin in 1948 (Morris 2005), or the Kuwaiti "incubator babies" story in the Gulf War (Marlin 2002, Ch. 5) were all later acknowledged as at least partially false by those who created or spread them. Moreover, the release of private correspondence from participants such as combatants, censors, editors, and correspondents has made clear the suppression of news about major developments in numerous violent conflicts, from the British concentration camps during the Boer War (Knightley 2004, Ch. 4) to the carpet bombing of Laos and Cambodia by the USA during the war in Vietnam (Knightley 2004, Ch. 16). While hindsight often provides the clearest indications of such manipulation, the revelations from WikiLeaks and other major "document dumps" that occur today give us windows into the private views of participants about campaigns such as the US drone program in Pakistan.

In addition to public admissions and revelations of lying, factual statements and beliefs can be judged against evidence about what is actually happening on the ground. For example, one false belief explored in Chapter 4 is that the international anti-Islamic State of Iraq and the Levant (ISIL) Coalition during the administration of President Barack Obama was "mainly targeting" the Popular Mobilization Forces (PMF) – a collection of Shi'a-led militias with whom it was nominally allied – rather than ISIL in Iraq. Leaving aside the fact that this claim was outlandish on its face, *Airwars* – an independent organization that tracks air campaigns around the world – found only a few dozen credible "friendly fire" claims out of more than 10,000 airstrikes conducted by Coalition forces in Iraq (Airwars 2017). Regardless of the intentionality of such incidents, the claim that the Coalition is *mainly targeting* the PMF is thus clearly not supported by the evidence. Similarly, organizations such as Bellingcat have used open-source evidence to expose a variety of false claims in conflict. For instance, in the face of Russia's claims that none of its troops fought in Ukraine in 2014, Bellingcat found Russian social media posts that included "selfies" by Russian soldiers with their platoons in Ukrainian territory, which exposed this as a lie (Bellingcat 2014a). Meanwhile, it also retraced the transit of a surface-to-air missile across Ukraine using ground-level and satellite photos to reveal that the Malaysian passenger jet (MH17) that crashed in Ukraine in 2014 was in fact downed by Russian-backed militants (Bellingcat 2014b). In sum, academic and NGO conflict event datasets, analyses by conflict-monitoring groups such as Bellingcat, and other types of high-quality information can offer crucial "reality checks" about factual claims in war.

Ultimately, however, the approach taken in this book for factual claims in ongoing conflicts (for which there is generally no single "silver bullet" piece of evidence like an admission of lying) is to rely on multiple different types and sources of independent evidence to establish falsehood. Pursuant to this end, the book triangulates between not just quantitative evidence such as violent event databases but also qualitative evidence such as journalistic and academic interview-based investigations, leaked combatant reports and statements via WikiLeaks, and other sources of reliable information about events on the ground. Moreover, given the relatively high-profile nature of the three primary cases in the book, there is often a wealth of evidence available – including a number of databases monitoring events that can be compared. If all of the data sources point in the same direction, that is telling. For example, as discussed in Chapter 3, the fact that all three leading US drone strike-tracking databases – despite their distinctive methodologies – indicate that the US drone campaign in Pakistan is *not* primarily killing civilians is significant. When combined with diverse qualitative evidence such as eyewitness testimonies, quality investigative reporting, interview-based scholarly research, and candid official statements that all tell the same story, this allows us to be confident that claims about the American drone campaign in Pakistan being indiscriminate are false. Finally, the aforementioned exploratory fieldwork that was conducted in Pakistan and Jordan, during which informal conversations took place with a number of people who had personally lived through the conflicts of interest, has only added further confirmation to the selection and treatment of the cases of misinformation that are examined in this text.

1.6 Major Implications of the Book for Theory and Policy

The argument advanced here has a number of key implications for scholars, policymakers, journalists, and engaged citizens. This section sketches out a few of the most important takeaways – a more extensive discussion can be found in the book's conclusion.

First, the book shows where factual misinformation and misperception is – and critically, is not – a threat in war. For both informational and psychological reasons, people near the "action" in war typically know what is happening in conflict, while those more removed from the front lines are more vulnerable to lies and misinformation about what is going on. Counter to alarmist views of misinformation and propaganda by states like Russia as unstoppable and overpowering in war, this reveals how its impact is quite constrained by and conditional on people's actual exposure to the fighting. It is chiefly communities who are *partisan about but removed from* the actual fighting that are most susceptible to falsehood – for example, this may include urbanites in a country with a rural insurgency, citizens of a powerful state intervening in another country or fighting abroad, or those in diasporas with resistance organizations that aim to represent them and exploit their grievances. In the words of one Somali community advocate based in the USA, Abdirizak Bihi, "the Somalis inside Somalia knew that al-Shabab was bad ... [w]e were concerned about the Somalis in the diaspora ... who never really knew the facts and were always manipulated and misled."[8] This project helps build on these anecdotes and provide a systematic framework for thinking about where we should expect to see this problem of dangerous factual misperceptions flourish the most (and least) in armed conflicts. Using this framework, the book also builds on bargaining models of war and extracts implications for where wars are likely to be the most enduring and peace the most elusive.

Second, this book helps deepen our understanding of civilian populations and what makes them "tick" in war zones more broadly. Research and writing on civilians has been split between two camps: A "rationalist" view in which they are seen as pragmatic actors who recognize and react to combatant rewards and punishments in ways that maximize their odds of survival (Popkin 1979, Kalyvas 2006), and an "identitarian" view in which they are seen as harboring powerful in-group vs. out-group loyalties that strongly condition their attitudes and behavior (Lyall 2010, Lyall, Blair, and Imai 2013). The book suggests that both of these views are partially right, and partially wrong. Specifically, it reveals that civilians living directly in the "line of fire" fit the pragmatic model well – their biases are "disciplined" by survival concerns – but the majority of civilians living elsewhere in conflict settings do not. In this sense, the project has a deeply *unifying* effect on different strands of scholarship about civilian populations, showing how they coexist at different levels of removal from events on the ground. As discussed more fully in subsequent chapters, this helps explain why we see such differential responses locally vs. nationally to something like the US drone campaign in Pakistan, and it sounds an important note of caution about the efficacy and scalability of many of the "population-centric" tactics at the heart of modern counterinsurgency practice.

Third, this volume should also be of interest to political psychology and behavior scholars more generally. In recent years, there has been a surge of behavioral research on the abundance of lies, conspiracy theories, false perceptions, rumors, and "fake news" in mainstream politics (e.g., Wood and Oliver 2014, Jolley and Douglas 2015, Miller, Saunders, and Farhart 2016, Vraga and Bode 2020). While

[8] See "'Most Wanted' American Jihadist Rapper Killed in Somalia." *Associated Press*, September 12, 2013.

debates continue to rage about the strength of these beliefs, there is a creeping image in the mass public and commentariat that we are mired in a "post-truth era" in which facts exert little impact on how people form beliefs and opinions. Misinformation scholars tend to hold more nuanced views than this, recognizing that the prevalence of misperceptions on an issue hinges on a variety of factors such as people's identities (Kahan 2017), their cognitive biases (Pennycook and Rand 2021), and the information they consume from the media (Nyhan 2021). Yet they leave little room for the *real-world situations* that surround people to shape and constrain their beliefs. This book shows that, while rumors and lies are pervasive in wars, there are also clear situational limits to their appeal. In fact, it suggests that exposure to high-stakes stimuli is an antidote to lies and misinformation: Civilians who witness events and have to make good choices to survive seek out the facts and cut through the lies. In this sense, the study offers a note of qualified optimism in the often-gloomy debates about facts in politics. When people have enough "skin in the game" and can see the relevant events, they tend to get it right regardless of their prior attitudes and identities. At the same time, it also raises the question: Who else in social and political life – from those near violent crime to natural disasters to outbreaks of disease – thinks like local civilians near the front lines of war? In the conclusion, crucial implications are extracted about the generalizability of the book's findings for our understanding of when people learn beyond situations of war and conflict, implications which should be of great interest to behavioral social scientists more broadly.

Finally, the project also contains key implications for policymakers. For those who wish to mitigate or manage violent conflicts, it suggests that encouraging combatants to exercise restraint, aid civilians, participate in peace negotiations, or undertake any number of other prescribed actions within a given conflict zone is necessary but not sufficient. For instance, did ordinary Colombians *believe* that the FARC was actually demobilizing as part of their society's peace process or not? Without challenging disinformation (and the psychological and informational biases that underpin it), such deeds may fall on deaf ears – or even have an exacerbating impact – on the vast majority of the population. In this sense, actors like the United Nations who wish to mitigate or de-escalate wars must consider not only which actions are taken by combatants, but also – or even especially – which actions civilians *think* are being taken by them. Waging information campaigns to counter influential lies should thus be a standard part of the peace-making toolkit. In the book's conclusion, other novel solutions to these issues are considered, including methods that social media platforms like Twitter and Facebook could use to amplify the voices of local communities near the front lines in conflict settings over their more distant counterparts in order to inject more truth into what we read, hear, and see from armed conflict settings. Ultimately, it is up to us as scholars, policymakers, and citizens to help translate the new insights revealed in this text into social and political actions that can challenge the influence of dangerous wartime lies and misinformation.

1.7 Outline of the Book

This book consists of six chapters. Chapter 2 builds the theory about how civilians develop factual beliefs in war. This chapter walks through the two major factors that power the theoretical engine behind the book's argument. First, it explores the role of people's psychological *motivation* in how they think about the world, and its application to belief formation in war zones. In general, people will be motivated to interpret events in a way that fits their prior worldviews in the dispute, but not everyone will do so: for those who are closer to the action, such biases are outweighed by an "accuracy motive" and the need to get it right. Then, it discusses the role of people's *information* sources in shaping their factual beliefs. The media in conflict zones is particularly prone to fueling factual biases, but not everyone is equally vulnerable: Those more directly exposed to the relevant events will often reject biased narratives due to their community's local information about what is actually taking place. Ultimately, the chapter weaves these two factors together, showing how they jointly ensure that fake news spreads widely in war, but those who are close enough to the action are generally less vulnerable to it and often know better.

Chapter 3 examines these issues in the case of the US drone campaign in the tribal regions of Pakistan. It first shows that, while the drone campaign is empirically quite precise and targeted, it is largely seen as indiscriminate throughout Pakistani society. In other words, there is a pervasive *factual misperception* about the nature of the drone strikes in Pakistan. Second, the chapter shows that this misperception is consequential. Notably, it shows that Pakistani perceptions of the inflated civilian casualties associated with the strikes are among the strongest drivers of opposition to them in the country. It also provides evidence which suggests that this anti-drone backlash fuels broader political alienation and violence in Pakistan. Finally, the chapter shows that these misbeliefs about drones (and the reactions they inspire) are not shared by local civilians living within the tribal areas where the incidents occur. In sum, the chapter demonstrates that factual misperceptions about US drone strikes in Northwest Pakistan are generally widespread and consequential in the country, but not in the areas that actually directly experience the violence.

Chapter 4 shifts to the Coalition air war against ISIL in Iraq. In particular, it investigates a unique nationwide survey of contemporary Iraq that measures Iraqis' factual perceptions about the Coalition airstrikes against ISIL, as well as whether they have lived under ISIL rule where the vast majority of strikes actually occurred. Moreover, this survey is paired with geo-located event data on the Coalition airstrikes themselves obtained from *Airwars* in order to measure the respondents' proximity to the events more directly. Overall, the results reveal that Iraqis' factual misperceptions about Coalition actions are widespread – fueled by both their own preexisting political orientations and streams of information in the dispute – but that civilians with greater personal exposure to the campaign are much less likely to embrace these falsehoods. Indeed, both experience living under ISIL control and proximity to the airstrikes themselves significantly reduce factual misperceptions about the Coalition's aerial campaign, including false claims about its targeting of Shiʿa Arab-led militias and its strategic benefits to ISIL.

Chapter 5 investigates these dynamics in the context of the Syrian civil war. In particular, it plumbs a rich batch of semi-structured interviews conducted with Syrian refugees in Turkey that was generously shared with me by Schon (2020) for this book. These interviews measure people's confidence in their truth discernment ability – their ability to distinguish true vs. false information – during the war, along with detailed information on what they heard and experienced while they were in Syria. The chapter analyzes these interviews with a mixed-methods approach. Quantitative analyses show that those who spent longer in Syria, witnessed a wider range of events in the war, and explicitly rely on personal experience to assess new information are much more confident in their truth discernment ability. This is supported by ample qualitative material from the interviews, which demonstrates how Syrian refugees put stock in many of these same factors and drew many of these same connections themselves when discussing informational dynamics, lies, and learning in the war.

Chapter 6 concludes and considers the book's major theoretical and practical implications. As alluded to above, the book pushes us to think about fake news and factual misperceptions as an important "layer" of war – a layer that has been largely neglected despite the burgeoning attention to these issues in other domains. This final chapter examines what the book's findings tell us about such topics as the psychology and behavior of civilian populations, the duration of armed conflicts, the feasibility of prevailing counterinsurgency models, and the depths and limits of misperceptions more broadly in social and political life. It also engages with the practical implications of the book for policymakers, journalists, activists, and ordinary politically engaged citizens in greater depth, exploring how the problems outlined in the research might also be their own solutions. Ultimately, this book has something to offer to anyone who is interested in the dynamics of truth and falsehood in violent conflicts (and beyond) – and perhaps the beginnings of a framework for those who would like to cultivate more truth.

2 | *A Theory of People's Factual Beliefs and Credulity in War*

The truth is not half so important as what people think to be true.

– Napoleon

Why do people believe misinformation in war, such as the claims of the Syrian regime that chemical weapons attacks in places like Ghouta and Khan Shakyhun were conducted by the rebels? This chapter offers an answer to this question, blending ideas from psychology, communications, and conflict studies to build a theoretical framework about the formation of factual beliefs in war. The punchline of this framework is that proximity and exposure are *antidotes* to misinformation. Indeed, the framework distinguishes between people who live in areas that are directly exposed to events at the center of a misinformation narrative – who tend to have both better local information about those events as well as an incentive to use it more carefully – and people who live elsewhere in the conflict environment, whose beliefs can be distorted and manipulated much more easily by motivated biases and media narratives in the dispute.

In order to build this framework, the chapter first takes stock of the existing literature about people's belief in misinformation in war, which provides a useful starting point for the argument. Then, it walks through the two critical factors of *information* and *motivation* that powerfully shape people's factual beliefs in conflict situations, in turn, and explains how they diverge between those who are proximate to and those who are removed from the fighting. Finally, it puts the two pieces of the argument together to form a coherent whole, illuminating how the theory operates in practice with illustrative examples from the 1948 Arab-Israeli War, WWII Germany, and the contemporary Russian invasion and occupation of Ukraine.

2.1 Existing Scholarship and the Neglect of the War-Misinformation Nexus

Imagine that an improvised explosive device (IED) erupts on a dusty dirt road in southern Afghanistan, an Israeli bulldozer smashes a house in Gaza, or a band of rebels raids a small village in Liberia. How do civilians – both within the immediate areas and beyond – form factual beliefs about what happened in these routine acts of violence? How susceptible are they to distortions and manipulations of these facts in the form of misinformation narratives? As suggested in Chapter 1, such questions are critically important. Misinformation in war can have stark implications, inciting and exacerbating violence by planting false and incendiary ideas in the heads of millions of people – as in the case of the flood of propaganda fostering the crackdown on the Rohingya in Myanmar. So too can it upset and undermine efforts to achieve peace and reconciliation in ongoing disputes, as with some of the rumors in Colombia that swirled around the peace process with the FARC.[1]

So how do civilians decide whether to believe such misinformation and how do they form factual beliefs in armed conflict more broadly? Overall, there has been relatively limited attention to date on this question, which is surprising given that it represents the place where two of the most vibrant research enterprises in the entire social sciences should naturally intersect with each other. On the one hand, there has been a significant surge of research in political science, economics, and other related fields on the "micro-level" dynamics of conflict – a shift away from investigating the cross-national factors that make violent conflict more likely toward the behaviors and attitudes of groups and individuals on the ground within conflict settings (e.g., Kalyvas 2006, Weinstein 2006, Schutte 2015, Zhukov 2017, Berman, Felter, and Shapiro 2018, Revkin 2021, Silverman 2020, Knuppe 2024). This scholarship has harnessed an explosion of new microlevel data from conflict zones and yielded impressive results, helping advance our knowledge of the dynamics of wartime violence (Kalyvas 2006, Cohen 2016), the structure and decision-making of violent nonstate

---

[1] See, for example, Gwen Burnyeat, "Government Peace Pedagogy in Colombia." *Anthropology News*, April 13, 2021. Available at www.anthropology-news .org/articles/government-peace-pedagogy-in-colombia/.

actors (Weinstein 2006, Arjona 2016), and the loyalties and attitudes of civilians in conflict (Getmansky and Zeitzoff 2014, Matanock and Garbiras-Díaz 2018). While initially, this attention tended to focus most on wartime *behaviors*, over the past decade there has been a growing body of research on wartime *attitudes* as well, focusing on outcomes like attitudes toward combatants in the conflict (Lyall, Imai, and Blair 2013, Akcinaroglu and Tokdemir 2020), attitudes toward the social groups that are involved in the dispute (Peffley, Hutchinson, and Shamir 2022), and attitudes toward peace settlements and the resolution of conflict (Tellez 2019). While all of this is deeply important, there has been very little attention to people's *beliefs about what is even happening in armed conflicts*. This is notable given that what individuals believe is taking place can influence whom they support and what they do. And the very fact that conflict actors expend considerable resources trying to shape those beliefs underscores their importance. For instance, the media strategies of the different belligerents in the Syrian civil war have been described as attempts to "assign blame and, through images and rhetoric, present a distribution of pain and suffering that warrants their actions" (Powers and O'Loughlin 2015). Why waste resources doing this unless you think civilians' factual beliefs about what is happening in conflict are important, as well as malleable?

On the other hand, another of the greatest growth areas in the social sciences in recent years has been the study of misinformation, fake news, conspiracy theories, and related phenomena (e.g., Nyhan and Reifler 2010, Oliver and Wood 2014, Miller, Saunders, and Farhart 2016, Williamson 2018, Hughes and Waismel-Manor 2021, Pennycook and Rand 2021, Radnitz 2021, Badrinathan 2021). Spurred on by salient real-world events – prominent among them Russia's disinformation in the 2016 US presidential election, the surge of anti-vaccine misinformation worldwide during the COVID-19 pandemic, and the 2021 insurrection fueled by misinformation at the US Capitol – research in this area has veritably exploded over time. Scholars across a wide range of disciplines, including communications, political science, psychology, economics, and computer science, have increasingly examined the phenomenon of misinformation, yielding insights about its prevalence, sources, and appeal in political life on issues ranging from climate change to vaccines to election fraud (Tesler 2018, Vraga and Bode 2020, Ryan et al. 2020, Graham and Yair 2022). Yet, there has been strikingly little attention to how it operates in situations of violent conflict, even though this is one of its top domains today. Conflicts like those in Israel-Palestine, Syria, Ethiopia, and Ukraine are awash in misinformation about what is happening on the ground when the fighting flares up. Is such misinformation effective? Does it work the same way in war as it does elsewhere? In fact, this book will show that the answer to these questions is both yes and no.

In sum, the place where the extensive literatures on belief in misinformation and the micro-dynamics of conflict should meet is surprisingly uncharted scholarly terrain.[2] In addition to this, there are strong *conceptual* reasons to think that exploring this terrain will be particularly fruitful. Notably, while the rapidly-growing body of research on misinformation has highlighted numerous explanations for its appeal, from partisan polarization (Osmundsen et al. 2021) to a lack of critical thinking (Pennycook and Rand 2021) to personality traits (Petersen, Osmundsen, and Arceneaux 2023), the overwhelming emphasis is on *individual differences* – to the exclusion of situational constraints. In other words, with few exceptions, explanations for why people believe or reject misinformation in the literature highlight variation in their biases, worldviews, cognitive abilities, information habits, and the like – and not variation in the situations or contexts in which they find themselves. This clashes with longstanding traditions in psychology which treat both "the person" and "the situation" as critical inputs into how individuals think about the world (e.g., Kenrick and Funder 1988, Fleeson 2004, Stewart and Barrick 2004, Furr and Funder 2021). And war is, to put it mildly, an extreme situation. Surely, the life-and-death realities and survival imperatives of war will constrain people's thinking about their surroundings to some extent. By investigating how the situation of war and exposure to it influences people's credulity about what is happening in their

---

[2] There are a couple of notable exceptions to this lack of research on belief in wartime misinformation that should be referenced – in particular, studies by Greenhill and Oppenheim (2017) and Schon (2020). Greenhill and Oppenheim (2017) use a pair of surveys to explore belief in unsubstantiated rumors in conflict settings in Southeast Asia. Schon (2020) investigates belief in rumors among Syrian refugees with semi-structured interviews. While these studies are valuable building blocks, highlighting individual biases and strategies that influence vulnerability to misinformation in war, they exhibit the same focus on individual-level variation and neglect of situational differences as the broader literature on misinformation belief.

environment, this book takes a crucial step toward addressing this neglect of situational dynamics and differences in our broader understanding of people's belief in misinformation.

Meanwhile, the most relevant literature in the microlevel study of conflict – the literature on civilian populations in war – is similarly ripe for the kind of theoretical intervention made in this book. Indeed, scholarship on civilian populations in war has largely been caught between two dueling perspectives. In one, which we might call a "rationalist model," civilians are seen as highly rational actors who react carefully and strategically to combatants' behaviors in war in an attempt to maximize their chances of survival (Kalyvas 2006). This view is reflected in notions of civilians as so-called "rational peasants" (Popkin 1979) and undergirds findings in which civilians' support is highly sensitive to how they are treated, such as whether combatants avoid collateral damage or give aid in their communities (e.g., Condra and Shapiro 2012, Berman, Felter, and Shapiro 2018). In the other view, which we might call an "identitarian model," civilians are seen as entrenched in their in-group identities, reacting to events in war based on *who* they involve rather than *what* they entail (e.g., Lyall 2010, Lyall, Blair, and Imai 2013). Findings that civilians treat harm by in-group and out-group actors differently, or that they are insensitive to combatant signals more broadly are consistent with this line of thinking (Lyall, Blair, and Imai 2013, Sexton and Zurcher 2023). While these perspectives have proven tremendously useful in capturing aspects of civilian behavior, the debate they comprise neglects the role of situational dynamics – how the contexts civilians are in might systematically push them toward thinking in one way or the other. This neglect leaves room for an integrative understanding which allows for both rationalist and identitarian ideas of civilian decision-making to coexist based on where people are situated in a conflict.

2.2 Motivation and Information: How People Form Factual Beliefs in War

This chapter now turns to the task of laying out the logic of the book's theoretical argument, walking through both the *motivational* and *informational* forces that drive factual belief formation in war. One question that may arise here is why the book focuses on people's factual beliefs in war in general rather than their vulnerability to misinformation in war in particular. To be sure, people can form false beliefs in war for reasons aside from misinformation, including cognitive errors and self-delusion about the facts rather than top-down informational pressures. Yet the wider focus has two major justifications. First, while the book's main goal is understanding the appeal and spread of factual misinformation in war, the broader phenomenon of factual misperceptions arising from self-deception and other factors is also substantively important and of tremendous interest. Factual misperceptions in conflicts of all types share many features, tend to occur in similar situations (as seen throughout this book), and can have similarly disruptive effects. Second, understanding the landscape and the causal drivers of factual beliefs overall is critical to grasping when and where misinformation is likely to flourish. Where people have the means and motives to form accurate beliefs about war, misinformation will gain little traction. And on the contrary, where they tend to form biased beliefs aligning with their preexisting identities and information diets, misinformation will find fertile ground. So, developing a general theory of factual belief formation in war is crucial both to understanding the broader phenomenon of false perceptions in conflict and the appeal and penetration of wartime misinformation more specifically.

2.2.1 *The Role of Psychological Motivation*

The first key factor that shapes how civilians form beliefs about what is happening in war is their psychological motivation when interpreting it. Decades of research from psychology show that people often process new information in ways that uphold their prior attitudes and attachments. Specifically, they frequently indulge in "motivated reasoning": Reasoning directed toward reaching conclusions that satisfy their emotional and psychological goals rather than those that are accurate or defensible by any objective standard (e.g., Kunda 1990, Taber and Lodge 2006). Scholars have emphasized different types of emotional goals that can be prioritized in this process, including the defense of group identities (Kahan 2017), political ideologies (Miller, Saunders, and Farhart 2016), or prior worldviews more broadly (Greenhill and Oppenheim 2017). In any of these cases, the key point is that an individual seeks congruence with his or her existing attitudes, beliefs, or identities when processing new information rather than seeking to maximize accurate conclusions about the world. Indeed, studies reveal that when people hold these strong "directional biases," they not only tend to reach more self-serving and biased conclusions, but they actually tend to access and process information differently when doing so. These dynamics are found in a variety of social, economic, and political settings, from legal disputes (Braman and Nelson 2007) to political campaigns (Taber and Lodge 2006) to economic markets (Benabou 2013) and even to beliefs about potentially life-threatening issues like crime and gun control (Campbell and Kay 2014).

These tendencies should apply strongly to civilian communities in armed conflicts as well. While individual civilians may not all be microcosms of overarching "master cleavages" (Kalyvas 2006), neither are they just "blank slates" that all interpret battlefield dynamics in the same way. On the contrary, individuals often harbor strong preexisting attitudes and attachments toward the combatants in war which they will attempt to preserve when processing an incident of violence. For example, if a civilian holds deep animosity toward one of the combatants, he or she will "want to believe" that it was indifferent to any collateral damage that occurs during its use of force – or even that such harm was intentional. To do otherwise would be to threaten or challenge this deeply entrenched attitude, which would be cognitively and emotionally costly.

There is a rich history of this type of thinking in war. In fact, in his scathing critique of the propaganda in WWI, *Falsehood in War-Time* (1929), former British Member of Parliament Arthur Ponsonby contends that wartime manipulation is possible not only because of the lies and the liars, but because of the mass public's willingness to accept them. In wartime, he notes, citizens often "quite willingly delude themselves in order to justify their own actions. They are anxious to find an excuse for displaying their patriotism" (Ponsonby 1928: 2) In the infamous WWI account of "the Belgian baby without hands," in which a false report that a Belgian baby whose hands were cut off by German soldiers circulated widely in Allied nations, inflaming anti-German sentiment, Ponsonby's critique is telling: "No one paused to ask how long a baby would survive with its hands cut off unless expert surgical aid were at hand to tie up the arteries (the answer being a very few minutes). **Everyone wanted to believe the story,** and many went so far as to say they had seen the baby" [emphasis added].

Similar dynamics helped foster what is perhaps the most notorious piece of anti-German atrocity propaganda in WWI: the "German corpse factory" story. This was a fake report that Germany was industrially processing trainloads of its own dead soldiers in a factory to extract their oils, fats, and other useable materials for the war. Although it was probably the most "appalling atrocity story of the war" (Knightley 2004: 114), it nevertheless grew popular in Allied countries. One scholar links its appeal to the fact that "many people wanted to believe it. The war was well underway, with all its horrors and grief. To think that the enemy was the incarnation of evil helped the war effort" (Marlin 2002: 72). Thus, individuals with strong animosities toward a specific combatant or whose central group identities push them to view the combatant as an implacable adversary will be more willing to embrace negative and fictitious stories about its wartime behavior.

These kinds of dynamics are clear in contemporary conflict settings as well. For example, in one of the few existing studies on public belief in false and unsubstantiated information in armed conflict, Greenhill and Oppenheim (2017) show that holding a worldview that is compatible with the substance of a rumor is one of three factors that make it more likely to be believed. In particular, they find that those who distrust the army in two Southeast Asian conflicts are more likely to accept negative rumors about the government's behavior in each dispute. Similarly, in another such study, Schon (2020) finds that Syrian refugees' belief in rumors about events in Syria are at least to some extent shaped by whether they are pro- or anti-Assad in their politics (and the slant of the rumor).[3] Echoing results about misinformation and motivated reasoning more broadly, there is thus already evidence in the literature that people's prior orientations toward one "side" or another in war shape their likelihood of embracing false information about it.

2.2.1.1 Accuracy Motives and Wartime Survival

Yet people do not always or unconditionally hold self-serving beliefs. When the stakes are sufficiently high, they will approach new information more carefully and thoroughly in the pursuit of accuracy

---

[3] These two studies stand as notable exceptions to the scholarly neglect of people's belief in wartime misinformation, yet they are subject to the same critiques made earlier about focusing on individual biases and differences and ignoring the role of situational constraints and the factors that "discipline" people's biases in conflict.

(Kunda 1990). Indeed, researchers have induced such an "accuracy motive" in subjects by increasing the payoffs or the stated importance of tasks (McAllister et al. 1979) or making people publicly defend their conclusions (Tetlock 1983). In these contexts, individuals tend to take longer, use fewer cognitive shortcuts and heuristics such as outgroup stereotypes, and reach more accurate and unbiased conclusions about the situations or issues at hand.

While these studies use economic incentives or social pressure to motivate people, there is no more powerful "accuracy motive" than physical survival. When people think strongly that they (or their loved ones) could be killed – when their lives are actually "on the line" – they will expend much more time and energy than they would under normal circumstances to process information about the threat, adjusting (or abandoning) their preexisting attitudes and attachments as needed. While this process may be cognitively and emotionally costly, such cognitive effort or discomfort is vastly overshadowed by the motive to survive. In fact, studies show that the process of learning, updating, and adjusting preexisting beliefs is deeply linked to anxiety (Redlawsk et al. 2010), which is something in ample supply in such life-and-death circumstances.

Examples of this intense motivation for survival and careful attention to threats in conflict situations abound. Consider the ongoing US drone campaign in Pakistan, which – as explored far more deeply in Chapter 3 – has been quite targeted and precise in nature despite the popular claims to the contrary (Plaw and Fricker 2012). While there is a widespread belief throughout "Pakistan proper" that the drone attacks are indiscriminate (Silverman 2019), those living in the tribal regions – where they actually take place – tend to know better. Indeed, one Pakistani journalist writing on the topic notes that the targets and results of the strikes are well understood in these areas because "for those who live the closest to the strike zones, drones *are not just some abstract talking point. Just getting through the day has become a high-stakes game*" (emphasis added).[4] In other words, the stakes of the situation are very different for people who have to make choices which could put them or their loved ones in danger depending on the nature of the violence they face. In this sense, civilians who actually live in

---

[4] Naheed Mustafa, "Drone Lands Dispatch: Letter from Pakistan." *Foreign Affairs*, December 9, 2013.

or near the line of fire have a powerful accuracy motive to understand what is going on around them; they have to "get it right" in order to survive, regardless of how it makes them feel or its alignment with their prior identities and worldviews.

Putting these pathways together, this book contends that civilians in societies experiencing war will be free to indulge in "directional biases" about the fighting unless they live in or around directly and repeatedly exposed areas – in which case they will be "disciplined" by their motivation for accuracy. In other words, they only need to think about conflict events carefully and unbiasedly when they themselves (or their families) are regularly exposed to them, or at least near enough to them to make the risks and dangers they represent real. This gap between the way in which "local" vs. "non-local" civilians think about war is quite clearly apparent again in the case of the US drone strikes in the tribal regions of Pakistan. In fact, one Pakistani reporter notes that the chief secretary of Khyber Pakhtunkhwa, a province adjacent to the tribal regions, "was of the view that the further away people were from the drone attacks, the more worked up they got about them."[5] In a similar vein, a scholar with family links to the tribal regions notes that the narrative of the US drone attacks violating Pakistani sovereignty – one of the primary moral critiques of the campaign – is a "luxury for those who enjoy the comforts of the big cities of Pakistan but it only extracts a wounded smile from the face of a tribesman."[6] Such quotes suggest that it is only people residing outside of the line of fire who can afford to use primarily an abstract moral lens to understand the violence, whereas those residing near (or in) it must approach the danger through a more personal and material lens. In fact, some observers have even lamented that – throughout the rest of Pakistan – there seems to be an "inability, *and sometimes unwillingness*, to consider the experience of those who actually live in the FATA" (emphasis added) with respect to the strikes.[7]

2.2.1.2 Other Potential Psychological Responses
While this book focuses on accuracy motives as the main psychological response to direct war exposure in this book, there are alternative

---

[5] Irfan Hussein, "View from Abroad: Mowing the Grass with Drones." *Dawn*, September 21, 2015.
[6] Muhammad Zubair, "View: Drone attacks – myth and reality." *The Daily Times*, June 4, 2012.
[7] Ibid.

psychological processes that merit consideration. First, terror management theory (TMT) suggests that the prospect of one's own mortality produces a fundamental, existential anxiety and resulting desire to invest life with greater meaning (Becker 1973). This, in turn, leads people to construct and rely more on systems of shared culture, identity, and religion (Greenberg, Solomon, and Pyszczynski 1986). In this vein, experimental studies about mortality salience show that priming people to think about death encourages them to adopt stronger religious beliefs, social identities, and other attitudes or behaviors which produce more self-esteem (Jessop et al. 2008, Heflick and Goldenberg 2012, Jong et al. 2012). This might imply that living in a context with a sustained risk of violent death like armed conflict would make people anchor more on their preexisting attitudes and identities and thus perceive conflict dynamics through *more* of a directionally biased lens.

Yet this thinking conflates an abstract and existential anxiety about death with an acute and immediate fear of survival, as when bombs are falling or bullets are flying in a war zone. As noted by evolutionary psychologists, distracting yourself from thoughts of death – which is the first step in the TMT process – would be highly maladaptive in actually deadly situations, as when you enter a cave and there is a predator awaiting you (Landau et al. 2007). In addition, TMT is easily induced in lab contexts when there is no immediate physical risk (Navarette and Fessler 2005). These facts suggest that it is something quite distinct from the response that people feel when they are in real physical danger. Moreover, the psychological processes that are at work in TMT are deeply at odds with those of people in violent conflicts or death occupations, who report a shutdown of emotions or "psychic numbing" as they focus on their personal survival and threats to it. In fact, one trauma scholar and veteran police officer explains that during "a profoundly threatening event or image, the survivor experiences a debilitating loss of the capacity to symbolize, and often the simultaneous loss of the capacity to fully experience emotion" (2005: 200). This response clashes sharply with the type of abstract, existential reaction that is at the core of TMT.

Another potential line of critique holds that, in situations of severe physical threat, people tend to just "freeze" or psychologically shut down. In fact, a strand of research on the psychology of human reactions to disasters, such as shipwrecks, plane crashes, and fires, shows that individuals often suffer from cognitive collapses such as losses in working memory and executive functioning during such episodes (e.g., Leach 1994, 2004, Robinson and Bridges 2011). There is a wealth of anecdotal evidence behind this contention, such as the fact that a substantial percentage of skydiver deaths are due to unopened parachutes (so-called "no-pull" fatalities), or that one of the top causes of death among firemen is unbuckled ambulance seatbelts. While we tend to focus on the examples of heroism and perseverance against all odds – the "Jon Krakauer" of the world – one scholar in this area estimates that about 75 percent of people in life-threatening situations are "unable to think clearly or plot their escape. They become mentally paralysed."[8] The primary implication of this literature for the question posed in this book is that people in war zones may fail to internalize any meaningful information about the fighting when bullets and bombs are whizzing around them, and thus not have a very accurate picture or perception of the dangers they face.

While this would indeed be a cause for concern, such responses apply mainly to people in their initial encounters with the extreme situation. The first time (or, even, the first few times) that someone is in a building that catches on fire or has a gun pointed at them, they may well "freeze" or "black out." Yet, over time, after sustained exposure to building fires or armed robberies, people learn what to expect from these situations. This is why – while rookie police officers and first-year medical students are often quite anxious about dealing with corpses – veteran officers and surgeons do so with relative ease (Henry 2004). Indeed, the entire point of disaster preparedness training is to make citizens anticipate their responses in a crisis so that they can act like they have been there before (Leach 2004). This is closely connected to work on "recognition-primed decision making," which examines how people like first responders make quick and effective decisions in extremely high-stress situations (Klein 1998).

The fundamental point for the purposes of this book is that people who survive a war zone for any extended stretch of time become like a veteran war reporter, and not like an ordinary citizen facing

[8] Michael Bond, "How to Survive a Disaster." *BBC Future*, January 28, 2015.

a gun for the first time. This adaptation is evident in the experience of Megan K. Stack, who cut her teeth as a young war reporter after being thrust into some of the hairiest wars in the Middle East in the 2000s. After several days in the 2006 Lebanon War, she reports that "the war no longer feels temporary. Now there is a hardening, an acceptance of this condition. Roads are death and sky is fear and people scurry down into the scorched earth like moles" (2010: 237). In other words, concerns about "freezing" and mental paralysis blocking people's ability to think and to learn may be relevant for their initial exposure to situations of violence but are less so for their reactions and perceptions after any protracted immersion in war.

Meanwhile, another concern is that civilians exposed to war might gain intimate knowledge of events they experience, but those intense experiences might make them view everything through a narrow lens and become blinded to or biased about the broader strategic picture. While this issue is worth grappling with, a couple of points must be noted. First, the logic of the survival motivation piece of the argument holds that exposure to the fighting in war stimulates demand for accurate information about it in order to boost one's chances of survival. This suggests that exposure should make civilians more discerning about broad strategic claims, provided they are not fully normative in nature and have at least some bearing on personal survival – as common empirical issues in war such as who is winning and losing and how each side is waging the fight certainly do. Second, just as broad social scientific theories have "observable implications" (e.g., King, Keohane, and Verba 1993), big picture narratives in war often have concrete, verifiable implications that allow civilians to evaluate their veracity. For instance, the idea that Nazi Germany was on an inevitable march to victory in WWII even late in the war was a broad strategic propaganda narrative, but civilians in German cities that were being bombed ferociously by Allied warplanes could directly see evidence that made them question it. Likewise, the overarching strategic narrative that Russia was liberating Ukraine from a "Nazi junta" in 2022 was belied for some Russian soldiers by the visible evidence they encountered of Ukrainians' bristling hostility toward their presence. Thus, civilians immersed in war can often learn things locally that bear strongly on the broader empirical picture. Ultimately, this suggests that people exposed to the fighting have the incentives as well as the opportunities to be, if anything, *less* biased about big picture factual issues in war.

Finally, some may accept that civilians are indeed driven by a survival motive, but wonder if that always pushes them toward accuracy. In particular, one worry might be that survival-seeking civilians could be incentivized to adopt a risk-averse or overly cautious understanding of potential threats in war rather than a strictly accurate one. In other words, they might embrace the maxim of the trigger-happy soldier to "shoot first, ask questions later." Of course, since we are talking about civilians and not combatants, they cannot simply neutralize all oncoming threats through violence. A civilian equivalent might be to flee first and ask questions later or to inform on potential enemy collaborators first and ask questions later.

While this is a logical concern, the issue is that all of the strategies or options available to civilians have risks. Consider migration, which might be seen as the quintessential way to "escape" the perils of conflict. Civilians can flee from war, but this in and of itself entails considerable risk. Indeed, migration out of a conflict setting can be quite dangerous, as civilians must often be guided by people-smugglers, cross checkpoints controlled by unknown combatants, and traverse areas of fighting or potential fighting to do so. As stated by Schon (2020: 155), "migration is one of the least desirable survival strategies because it imposes high costs and dangerous risks upon civilians." Informing on possible enemy collaborators also carries risk, given that targeting suspected informants in war is common (Bauer, Reese, and Ruby 2021). This is why information provision in war is often done in secret and with "code words" (Schon 2020: 146–49). While the risks of each of these options vary, the broader point is that all strategies for civilians – including staying put, fleeing, collaborating, and organizing a self-defense militia, as well as the many fine-grained tactical choices within each of these broad categories – involve serious risks to survival. This is precisely the problem that acquiring accurate information helps solve. As a British intelligence report noted of the British public during German bombing campaigns known as "The Blitz" during WWII (Jones et al. 2004: 473), "people in target areas, and elsewhere, are critical of official and press accounts which appear to tone down the raids and the damage they cause. People ask for 'less secrecy and *more true information*'" (emphasis added).

2.2.2 The Role of Information Channels

On top of motivation, the other key variable affecting how civilians perceive the nature of war is the information they consume about it. Ample research shows that the political information "diet" that people absorb shapes their attitudes and beliefs in a variety of areas, from foreign policy opinions (Baum 2013) to economic perceptions (Soroka, Stecula, and Wlezien 2015) to voting intentions (Lelkes et al. 2016). Different streams of news and information change what audiences see in two core ways: (1) selection bias, which refers to *which* events they elect to report and (2) description bias, which refers to *how* they choose to report or frame them (McCarthy et al. 1996). Indeed, empirical studies show broad variation in which events attract the attention of different news sources (e.g., Danzger 1975, McCarthy et al. 1996, Mueller 1997), and, of course, there is a large body of research on the divergent framing of events across distinct media sources, such as the dueling cable news networks Fox, MSNBC, and CNN in the American media landscape – to pick just one classic, well-studied example (e.g., Morris 2005, Feldman et al. 2011, Hyun and Moon 2016). Such variation may arise from a mixture of different resources and constraints as well as different interests and agendas. Additionally, people can also acquire "local information" through their social networks which pushes back against these broader top-down frames and narratives (Druckman and Nelson 2003). Thus, the information diets to which individuals are exposed – through both vertical information streams as well as horizontal social networks – can heavily influence their factual understandings about what is happening in social and political life.

These dynamics apply in armed conflicts as well. After most significant clashes or battles that take place in a violent conflict, there is an inevitable contest between the two (or more) "sides" to control how they are represented by the media in the conflict zone (Tugwell 1986). In the words of one researcher, "each violent event creates an 'opportunity space' into which both insurgent and state seek to inject their narrative" (Stevens 2013: 93). Consider the following example – used by the conflict scholar Philip Schrodt and his colleagues to illustrate the inherent challenges in coding violent event data – of how states vs. insurgents can "spin" the exact same violent event:

State: Terrorists slaughtered innocent civilians in the town of Ocho Rios
before being driven off by government troops.

Insurgent: Liberation forces battled occupying forces in the town of Ocho
Rios, causing several casualties before retreating.

While these headlines describe the same attack, their audiences
would likely draw quite divergent conclusions about what occurred.
Moreover, this is just an example of description bias and ignores the
potential for selection bias – that the event might not be reported at
all in many sources. In fact, tales of wartime horrors can be entirely
fabricated by one side in an effort to smear the reputation of the
adversary, a shamefully common practice that philosophy scholar
Randal Marlin has termed "atrocity propaganda" (2002). While
some of these issues have been examined as methodological challenges that may affect the content of armed conflict datasets, such as
the *Uppsala/PRIO Armed Conflict Dataset* (Gerner et al. 1994, Otto
2013, Weidmann 2015), their implications have not yet been considered for ordinary people living in conflict zones. If these issues affect
teams of scholars trying to understand what happened years after an
incident of violence, should they not be expected to do the same for
civilians trying to learn what is taking place around them in real time
and while shrouded in the proverbial "fog of war"?

2.2.2.1 The Weaponization of Wartime Media
Conditions common to conflict settings make the problem of media
bias especially severe. First, much of the media in war is actually
owned by combatants themselves. For instance, a World Bank
report on patterns of global media ownership found that the state
owns on average 29 percent of the top five newspapers, 60 percent of the top five TV channels, and 72 percent of the five radio
stations in its territory around the world (Djankov et al. 2003).
Moreover, these figures grow even larger in the regions that suffer
from the most endemic war and conflict, like Africa and the Middle
East. Since the state is itself a combatant in all civil as well as interstate wars, this already implies a large degree of direct media control for combatants in armed conflict. But in addition, most major
insurgent organizations have their own media arms or outfits (e.g.,
Hezbollah's *Al-Manar TV*, Al-Shabaab's *Radio Andalus*, or ISIL's
"Voice of the Caliphate" radio) that broadcast their messages as

well. Thus, much of the media channels in war are directly owned by combatants themselves and are thus little more than a propaganda vehicle in armed conflicts.

Second, the media landscape in wartorn societies tends to naturally polarize along the lines of the war. Media channels often represent distinct constituencies or communities engaged in the fighting, like Shiʿa Arab, Sunni Arab, and Kurd in Iraq, or Croat, Serb, and Bosnian in the Balkans, and have strategic (*viewership*) and sincere (*partisanship*) incentives to pander to their audiences. For example, the media in post-2003 Iraq has often been sharply polarized between pro-Shiʿa Arab channels like *Al-Iraqiyya TV* vs. pro-Sunni Arab ones like *Al-Baghdadiyya TV* (Amos 2010). This polarization has been readily apparent in Iraqi media coverage of ISIL, with some of the networks aligned more with Sunni Arab perspectives initially presenting the group as "tribal revolutionaries" while some of those catering more to Shiʿa Arab constituencies have employed far more nefarious terms such as "terrorist gangs."[9]

Finally, if a media source is not biased by its ownership or audience, combatants can still influence and control it in a number of ways. To begin with, censorship is pervasive in war. Indeed, reporters have been banned from the front lines of many wars, from Korea to Grenada to Sri Lanka, for long periods (Knightley 1975, Oberg and Sollenberg 2011). And sources that are seen as hostile to a belligerent and its interests – such as *Al-Baghdadiya TV* in Iraq or *Al-Aqsa TV* in Gaza – have sometimes been completely shut down. At the extreme, belligerents can employ violence to silence hostile media. The number of journalists killed in conflict has risen drastically over time, from two in WWI to 66 in Vietnam to 127 in Iraq – often by assassination (Liosky and Henrichsen 2009). In some cases, armies have even intentionally attacked and destroyed news facilities, as in NATO's bombing of *Radio Television of Serbia* (RTS) in the Balkans or Israel's bombing of *Al-Aqsa TV* in Gaza during Israeli-Palestinian armed confrontations.[10] Yet violence is not the only tool available to combatants, and

---

[9] Mohammed Salih, "Iraqi Media Divided in Coverage of IS Conflict." *Al-Monitor*, September 4, 2008.

[10] On the NATO bombing of RTS, see "Serb TV Station was Legitimate Target, Says Blair." *The Guardian*, April 23, 1999. On the *Al-Aqsa TV* bombings, see, for example, "Israel Bombs Hamas Local Radio and TV Stations in Gaza." *Middle East Monitor*, July 29, 2014.

many subtler tactics – from applying social and economic pressure to providing "information subsidies" and embedding reporters within one's own forces – are used to control the media's coverage in times of war as well. As summarized in one article:

It is not uncommon for governments even in countries with relatively high levels of press freedom to impose censorship on particular types of reports, for instance on military operations, or to ban journalists from areas of combat ... Even in the freest countries where there is no censorship of the news media, governments and military authorities still attempt to control or influence the flow of information. They do this for example by arranging press conferences, providing video material or privileged access, or embedding reporters with their own troops.

In brief, most media in wartime are not independent: Combatants tend to perceive the media not as impartial observers, but as critical tools and potential "weapons" in their armed struggle (Kalb and Saivetz 2007: 43). One quantitative analysis shows that societies experiencing conflict have much lower press freedom scores even after accounting for other relevant variables, leading its author to declare that – if "truth is the first casualty of war" – a free press is the second (Vultee 2009). Or, in the words of a *New York Times* correspondent covering Algeria's War of Independence in 1957, "all information in Algeria is controlled by the French" (Knightley 1975: 371).[11]

2.2.2.2 The History of Factually Biased News in War

Unsurprisingly, given this weaponization of information in armed conflict, there is a long and rich history of factually biased news coverage of war. As documented by Phillip Knightley in *The First Casualty: From the Crimea to Vietnam, the War Correspondent as Hero, Propagandist, and Myth-Maker* (1975), these issues were widespread from even the earliest days of professional war reporting in the nineteenth century. In news coverage of the American Civil War, for example, Knightley explains that:

---

[11] Of course, this is not to deny that there is variation in the extent to which individual media sources are biased in wars, and that more accurate and credible – and less propagandistic or partisan – channels are a valuable resource. Rather, the claim is simply that there is an ample *supply* of biased media and information channels in conflict, and that these channels tend to exert a generally biasing influence on their respective audiences.

Accuracy became a minor consideration. Casualties were grossly under-estimated; generals listed as killed lived on to die of old age; battles were reported on days when there was no action at all; at times the whole Southern army was reported to be marching on Washington. Atlanta was reported captured a week before the battle for the town took place. It was but a small step from ignoring accuracy to faking whole reports. Julius Browne of the New York Tribune collected from officers [sic] details of the Battle of Pea Ridge (March 1862) and wrote a brilliant, but entirely imaginary, eye-witness report ... The Battle of Shiloh (April 1862) caught correspondents by surprise, so they dashed off dispatches about desperate hand-to-hand fighting that had never occurred, a mass effort of faking reports that led to a cynical acceptance of the practice. Even war artists were not above faking their sketches...

Likewise, in one infamous (and perhaps apocryphal) exchange symbolic of journalistic practice in this period, a war illustrator working for William Randolph Hearst's *New York Journal* in Spanish Cuba cabled back to Hearst in 1897 that there was no conflict to cover, to which Hearst allegedly retorted "You furnish pictures. I'll furnish war."[12] And, in fact, the sensationalized reporting of the sinking of the USS Maine by Hearst's *Journal* – which printed the headline *"CRISIS IS AT HAND: SPANISH TREACHERY"* despite Spain's fervent denials of involvement – along with that of other American newspapers, helped spark the Spanish-American War and the dawn of American empire (Knightley 2004: 58).

It was WWI, however, that helped elevate these black arts to new heights. As noted earlier, the Allied press churned out a steady stream of anti-German atrocity propaganda reports in order to sustain public support for the war effort. These included not only the abovementioned accounts of the "Belgian baby without hands" and the "Germany corpse factory," but dozens of other stories of mutilation, humiliation, brutalization, and even crucifixion by German troops (Ponsonby 1928). While these tales often had the intended nationalist result, they were frequently fake (Marlin 2002). For example, five leading US correspondents penned the following open letter following the war, worth quoting here at length:

To let the truth be known, we unanimously declare the stories of German cruelties, from what we have been able to observe, were untrue. After

---

[12] See, for example, Milton (1989). The quotation is potentially apocryphal but still illustrative of early war reporting.

having been with the German Army for two weeks, and having accompanied the troops for over one hundred miles, we are not able to report one single case of undeserved punishment or measure of retribution. We are neither able to confirm any rumours as regards maltreatment of prisoners and non-combatants. Having been with the German troops through Landen, Brussels, Nivelles, Buissière, Haute-Wiherie, Merbes-le-Château, Sorle-sur-Sambre, Beaumont, we have not the slightest basis for making up a case of excess. We found numerous rumours after investigation to be without foundation … For the truth of the above we pledge our word of honour as journalists.

(Signed) Roger Lewis, Associated Press; Irwin Cobb, Saturday Evening Post, Philadelphia Public Ledger, Philadelphia; Harry Hansen, Chicago Daily News, Chicago; James, O'Donnell Bennett, Chicago Tribune; John T. McCutcheon, Chicago Tribune, Chicago.

Similar postwar denials were made by other witnesses who saw the front lines (Ponsonby 1928).[13] Ultimately, war reporting in WWI was perhaps best captured by Ernest Hemingway, who declared with trademark flair that "the last war, during the years of 1915, 1916, and 1917 was the most colossal, murderous, mismanaged butchery that has ever taken place on earth. Any writer who said otherwise lied. So the writers either wrote propaganda, shut up, or fought" (1942: 9).

These strong wartime media biases continued as the twentieth century wore on. During the Second Italo-Abyssinian War of 1935–36, veteran war reporter Herbert Matthews of the *New York Times* estimated that "of all the photographs published of the war, ninety-nine

---

[13] Of course, Germany did commit various atrocities in World War I, especially during the invasion and occupation of Belgium from 1914 to 1918 in which its army executed some 6,000 Belgian civilians and sent tens of thousands more back to Germany to serve as forced laborers. Yet careful historical analysis has shown that these atrocities were not exceptional by the standards of the behavior of other WWI combatants (e.g., Kramer 2009) nor were they of course anything like the extreme scope and brutality of what was perpetrated by Nazi Germany to its victims during World War II. More to the point, there was a broad category of extremely lurid and graphic claims about German behavior during the war – involving brutal allegations of things like Belgian nurses being mutilated with their breasts cut off, Belgian babies skewered on swords, and the idea of a German corpse factory – which were entirely false but played on themes of German barbarism and brutality and were spread in the Allied press to cultivate support for the war effort (see, e.g., Marlin 2002).

out of a hundred had been faked" (Knightley 1975: 186). The Spanish Civil War of 1936–39 was also rife with war propaganda, sparking George Orwell to note that "early in life I had noticed that no event is ever correctly reported in a newspaper but in Spain, for the first time, I saw newspaper reports which did not bear any relation to the facts, nor even the relationship which is implied in an ordinary lie" (1943: 4). Meanwhile, in WWII, there is a vast literature on the wartime propaganda and media bias by both Axis and Allies (see Short 1983, Koppes and Black 1990, Earhart 2008, Kallis 2008). Phillip Knightley observed that, in the Pacific Theatre, "neither side reported its own atrocities. Throughout the war, there was not a single mention in Japan of any atrocity by a Japanese soldier, and I have been unable to find any report in the Allied press of an atrocity committed by an Allied soldier. Both sides emphasised atrocities committed by the enemy" (1975: 294). And censorship, propaganda, and bias in war coverage persisted throughout the Cold War, from Korea to Algeria to Vietnam (Knightley 1975, Chs. 14–17, Carson 2015).[14] Nor have such biases abated in the post-Cold War era, from the false "incubator babies" claim that helped spark the First Gulf War (Marlin 2002) to the infamous *Radio Television Libre des Mille Collines* station whose incendiary propaganda fueled the Rwandan Genocide (Yanagizawa-Drott 2014) to the many media distortions that have plagued more recent violent conflicts like those in the Balkans (Thompson 1999), Iraq (Cioppa 2009), the US drone campaigns in Somalia, Yemen, and Pakistan (Sheets et al. 2015), and the Donbas War in Ukraine (Zhukov and Baum 2016), among others.

In sum, this brief overview of the historical record is not meant to condemn specific actors or events per se but to vividly convey the fact that the manipulation of the media in wartime – and particularly its reporting of violence by the different warring parties – is ubiquitous. Moreover, as stated earlier, even relatively independent media sources still diverge in subtle but important ways in what conflict events they report (*selection bias*) and how they frame and cover them (*description bias*) that shape their audiences' beliefs. In sum, how

---

[14] In Vietnam, for example, the real scope of the massive escalation of fighting into neighboring Laos and Cambodia was unreported until the "Pentagon Papers" leak by the *New York Times* in 1971. See, for example, "25 Years Later; Lessons from the Pentagon Papers." *New York Times*, June 23, 1996.

people perceive events on the ground in war is likely to be strongly influenced by the media sources they consume in the dispute.

2.2.2.3 The Informational Advantage of Local Experience

Yet, people do not always accept media narratives uncritically. In particular, people living in or near the areas directly implicated in a misinformation narrative have other means of learning what has happened. Specifically, people who reside in communities that are directly and repeatedly affected by a given type of conflict event or dynamic have an *informational advantage* in the form of local, experiential knowledge about it in their community. Such "locals" will not be swayed by broad top-down narratives if they clash with the experiences and accounts of their families, friends, and neighbors who actually witnessed relevant events or their aftermath. Moreover, this resistance to biased media streams will be aided by the "accuracy motive" discussed earlier, which will make local civilian populations seek out alternative (i.e., non-biased) channels of information about proximate violent events due to its importance for their survival.

The capability of this local "ground-level" information to puncture biased media narratives in conflict settings is often quite clear. One context in which this is apparent is in the observations of war reporters, and their tensions with their editors back home. Indeed, recall the letter from the US correspondents in WWI: "we unanimously declare the stories of German cruelties, *from what we have been able to observe,* were untrue" (emphasis added) (Ponsonby 1928: 76). Similarly, one American correspondent for the Chicago *Daily Chronicle* who was captured by Germans in WWI was then asked by his editors to write a story on the poor morale and living conditions in Germany, but declared that this "was simply not true, and he resigned" (Knightley 1975: 89). The experience of Herbert Matthews of the *New York Times* amid the Spanish Civil War, however, is perhaps the most telling. In 1937, Matthews visited the locale of a failed attack by General Francisco Franco's forces near Madrid and observed that the attacking force was Italian. Matthews – who knew Italian – spoke with the defeated soldiers and examined their equipment. This revelation was important, as it was the first evidence of the regime of Benito Mussolini supplying not only arms and advisors, but actual troops to aid the Nationalist cause. But his editor, who disliked the story, changed every appearance of the word "Italian" to "Insurgent." Matthews was furious at the changes, stating that "when an accredited correspondent tells his newspaper that he has seen something with his own eyes, the paper must believe [and] trust him more than it trusts his competitors *or his editors 3,000 miles away*" (Knightley 1975: 200) (emphasis added). This story echoes the propaganda by Russia to mask its incursion into Ukraine in 2014, which was exposed by reporters observing the uniforms and accents of troops in their interviews.[15] In these cases, war reporters acquired local, experiential knowledge that punctured a biased elite- or media-driven narrative.

Similar dynamics occur with civilians in wars as well. Davenport and Ball (2002) compare the quality of three sources of information on Guatemalan state violence from 1977 to 1995: Newspaper stories, human rights reports, and eyewitness testimony. While they find that all three sources have value, their analysis shows that civilians are often the best informed – at least on the events in their locales. Specifically, they write that interviewees tended to recall "the perpetrator who abused the victim(s) and specifically what was done during the violation. As a result, such sources are useful for identifying what happened and who did it within particular locales" (447). Civilians thus have an informational advantage on events within their communities, for which they can rely on local knowledge and experience. Likewise, in the case of the US drone campaign in Pakistan, the local communities in the tribal areas have always had the most knowledge of the strikes. As recounted by one local journalist, when the first American drone strike was conducted against local Taliban commander Nek Mohammed on June 18, 2004, "no one in the Pakistani public or media knew that it was a drone ... the villagers, however, supplied the explanation: they collected the fragments of the missile, on which was printed in black, 'Made in USA.'"[16] Another strike in 2005 fueled similar uncertainty until a journalist from a nearby village sifted through the debris and found the remains of a Hellfire missile.[17] Such revelations cast doubt upon the Pervez Musharraf regime's claims that Pakistani army forces had been behind the attacks.

[15] See, for example, Courtney Weaver, "Café Encounter Exposes Reality of Russian Soldiers in Ukraine." *Financial Times*, October 22, 2014.
[16] Pir Zubair Shah, "My Drone War." *Foreign Policy*, February 27, 2012.
[17] Ibid.

Table 2.1 *Summarizing the model of people's factual beliefs in war (reproduced)*

Types of individuals	Information		Motivation	Result
Proximate/ exposed to the relevant events	→ Local knowledge	+	Accuracy motive =	↑ Belief accuracy ↓ Misinformation vulnerability
Distant/removed from the relevant events	→ Partisan media	+	Directional biases =	↓ Belief accuracy ↑ Misinformation vulnerability

2.3 Summarizing and Illustrating the Theoretical Framework

This chapter outlined a simple but powerful framework in which people's factual beliefs – and their susceptibility to factual misinformation – in war hinge on two critical variables: (1) their information channels about the fighting and (2) their psychological motivations when processing that information. Based on this framework, it argued that if people live in or near areas that directly experience relevant events in a misinformation narrative, they will have both the information and the motivation to understand those events accurately. In contrast, if they live outside of the directly affected areas, their perceptions of events in the conflict will be shaped by their motivational biases – if they hold strong prior attitudes toward the perpetrator or target of an attack – and their exposure to different streams of media and information. Ultimately, this means that there is likely to be wide variation in people's recognition of the factual realities of conflict based on their removal from the fighting and their biases in the dispute. Table 2.1 (reproduced) sums up the theoretical framework, showing how the two central factors of information and motivation fit together to produce greater accuracy of beliefs and lower vulnerability to misinformation among more proximate and exposed civilian communities in war.[18]

---

[18] Note that the model does not imply that those removed from events will *automatically* embrace substantially more falsehood and misinformation about them, but simply that there is much greater scope for them to do so since they are free from the sharp constraints faced by local populations.

While the theoretical model is fairly intuitive and straightforward, it is worth underscoring the ways in which it is novel so that its contributions are clear. First, the primary axis of variation in the theory is situational and not individual. This means that it is powered not by how people are different – like most of the existing literature on misinformation, and in fact, much of the broader behavioral canon in recent years – but by how they are the same. We are all susceptible to believing misinformation about war that aligns with our biases, but the book argues that our ability to indulge in these biases is systematically shaped by the context we are in: The extent to which we are exposed to the front lines of a violent conflict or far removed from them.

Second, the theory highlights one critical set of conditions under which people organically overcome or "discipline" their biases. Indeed, bias has become a major focus of behavioral social science in recent years, with much attention both to how motivated – particularly partisan, but also racial and otherwise identity-driven – biases as well as cognitive biases influence people's thinking (Peffley, Hurwitz, and Sniderman 1997, Johnson and Levin 2009, Webster and Albertson 2022). This is no less true in the study of factual misinformation, in which automatic cognitive biases and motivated political ones are often framed as key alternate perspectives in the literature (e.g., Rand and Pennycook 2019). Of course, there *is* substantial misinformation research showing that people can learn despite these biases, but this generally involves interventions like digital literacy training, accuracy primes, and other top-down "corrections" or nudges (e.g., Wood and Porter 2019, Rand and Pennycook 2021). In contrast, there is little to no research on people overcoming

---

The actual extent to which their beliefs are biased will hinge on the strength of their directional motives, the extent to which the empirical reality of war cuts against those motives (the more it does so, the greater the misperceptions needed to reconcile it with their views), and the intensity of the misinformation to which they are exposed, among other factors. In practice, since most people in a conflict setting have at least some preferences if not loyalties in the dispute, and at least some elements of the conflict are likely to be "bad" for those preferences (e.g., not all events in the war make their preferred actors look successful and moral all of the time), we are likely to observe at least *some* factual bias in their beliefs. Thus, while there will be variation in degree across cases, those removed from the front lines represent the demographic terrain in war in which factual bias and misinformation can truly take root.

their biases due to the incentives and the opportunities that occur naturally in their surrounding environments. The theory in this book provides one set of conditions – exposure to high-stakes and highly-visible phenomena – under which this kind of strong, organic learning occurs. The conclusion of the book (Chapter 6) considers the degree to which these neglected processes might travel and inform a wider range of human beliefs and behaviors.

And third, the theoretical framework highlights when direct observation reliably translates into accurate perception. Indeed, the idea that directly observing events will provide more accurate and untainted information about them is perhaps the most intuitive part of the theory, and it builds on a small but vibrant literature on the informational value of "citizen witnessing" of conflicts and disasters in international affairs (Allan 2013, Nilsson 2019). To be sure, this witnessing mechanism has been far too absent from the literature on public belief in misinformation. Yet, the theory also highlights how the mechanisms of acquiring personal information and facing a survival motivation work in tandem. While both do promote accurate beliefs separately, it is when people are strongly motivated to understand an issue that seeing what is happening yields the greatest results. In other words, it is a combination of *means* (personal observations) and *motives* (survival motivation) that drives the powerful learning in war that is studied in this book. Such issues are also explored more in the conclusion, which considers the extent to which the mechanisms apply across different types of phenomena that vary based on the two mechanisms in the argument.

Two other points about the model should be clarified. First, the theory does not negate the potential for other types of psychological biases aside from the motivational ones described earlier. Cognitive biases in which people fall prey to judgment errors unintentionally based on their mental hardwiring and features of their environment – such as probability neglect, in which the frequency of salient events is overestimated (Sunstein 2003), or recency bias, in which recent events take on an outsized role in people's thinking (Baddeley and Hitch 1993) – may well impact the formation of factual beliefs in war too. This framework leaves ample room for these tendencies but contends that they will be subject to the same disciplining effect that comes with proximity to the front lines as their motivated counterparts. Recall that in laboratory studies, scholars find that individuals tend to take longer and use fewer cognitive shortcuts and heuristics such as stereotypes when the stakes of the task increase (e.g., McAllister et al. 1979, Tetlock 1983). In the same way, civilians may generally tend to overweight salient or recent attacks in forming wartime beliefs, but they will be pressured to shed or at least constrain these tendencies in situations where making judgment mistakes could lead to very serious and potentially even deadly consequences for them.[19]

Second, it is important to clarify that the informational side of the argument has an inclusive and encompassing cast as well. Prominent ideas from psychology such as the "illusory truth effect" (Fazio et al. 2015) – the idea that repeating information tends to boost people's familiarity with and acceptance of it – are well-accommodated by the theory too. The notion of information diets in the theory is conceptualized broadly, to include information received from any kinds of sources and which can vary in quantity and quality. The claim is simply that variation in these diets can lead to factual biases among civilian populations in conflict, which will be mitigated and diminished when people can rely on the accumulated local experience of their communities on the front lines as opposed to exposure to the "televised war" received via top-down media.

2.3.1 Illustrative Case Vignettes

The different components of the theory can perhaps be best integrated and communicated by making brief forays into illustrative cases. This section discusses three such cases, two historical (factual misinformation in WWII Germany and in a crucial episode in the 1948 Arab-Israeli War) and one contemporary (Russia's ongoing invasion and occupation of Ukraine) in order to illustrate how the theory comes together and functions in practice.

The 1948 Deir Yassin Massacre: The Deir Yassin massacre was a notable atrocity that occurred in the Arab-Israeli War of 1948. In the spring of 1948, Deir Yassin was a neutral Palestinian village close to

---

[19] That said, examining the potential impact of cognitive biases on wartime belief formation explicitly is considered further as a possible avenue for future research in Chapter 6, the conclusion.

Jerusalem – it had remained out of the fighting and was not initially a key Zionist strategic target. However, on April 9, 1948, the Zionist paramilitary groups Irgun and Lehi elected to attack the village. Encountering fiercer resistance from the town than they expected, the groups turned to indiscriminate tactics including destroying Palestinian homes with mortars or grenades to clear it. They also executed a number of Palestinian prisoners both during the fighting in the town and after it had ended in a nearby quarry (Gelber 2006: 311–12). Overall, about 110 Arabs were killed during the event, including many unarmed civilians and prisoners (Kan'ana and Zaytuni 1987: 5). Clearly, the attack was a shameful massacre.

Yet, Palestinian and Arab elites decided to exaggerate the scope and nature of the massacre in order to maximize popular support for Arab intervention in the conflict. As recounted by Hazem Nusseibeh, editor of the *Palestine Broadcasting Service* at the time: "I asked [Dr. Hussayn Khalidi] how we should cover the story. He said, 'We must make the most of this.' So he wrote a press release, stating that at Deir Yassin, children were murdered, pregnant women were raped, all sorts of atrocities."[20] These false accounts were subsequently transmitted to Palestinian and Arab radio stations in Cairo, over the protests of the villagers of Deir Yassin themselves. As explained by one local Arab villager, "there was no rape. He [Khalidi] said, 'We have to say this so the Arab armies will come to liberate Palestine from the Jews.'"[21] Another villager who fought against the attackers said that "There were no rapes. It's all lies. There were no pregnant women who were split open. It was propaganda that ... Arabs put out so Arab armies would invade."[22]

The spread of this type of atrocity propaganda had a powerful and unintended effect on the Palestinian population: it encouraged Palestinians to flee *en masse*. As noted by Nusseibeh: "This was our biggest mistake. We did not realize how our people would react. As soon as they heard that women had been raped at Deir Yassin, Palestinians fled in terror. They ran away from all our villages."[23]

---

[20] "Interview with Hazem Nusseibeh." *Fifty Years War*, BBC, 1998.
[21] Ibid.
[22] Paul Holmes, "Deir Yassin – A Casualty of Guns and Propaganda." *Reuters News*, April 6, 1998.
[23] See footnote 24.

In fact, the Deir Yassin massacre is often seen as a crucial incident – along with the events in Haifa and a handful of other places – that contributed to the tragic Palestinian exodus of 1948 (Morris 2005). It thus had a key effect on the 1948 Arab-Israeli War and the wider conflict to come. This illustrates the different elements of the model sketched out earlier: The event was perceived accurately by the local villagers, who saw it firsthand while in the line of fire, but it was grossly misperceived by those living elsewhere in the conflict zone – who saw it through the prism of their exposure to biased information, reinforced by their own predispositions – and it ultimately shaped their behavior in the conflict in profound and lasting ways.

Nazi Germany in WWII: Nazi Germany is probably one of the states most notorious for its gratuitous and effective use of propaganda and misinformation to seize and maintain social control in world history. With Hitler's charismatic rhetoric and the Nazi Ministry of Public Enlightenment and Propaganda led by the infamous Joseph Goebbels, Nazi propaganda efforts via print and radio played a notable role in the party's rise to power and establishment of a stranglehold over German society in the 1930s (e.g., Adena et al. 2015). During WWII, the Nazis pushed a number of different propaganda narratives at home and abroad, with central themes including German victimhood and oppression, Nazi power and the inevitability of victory, and the savagery and moral corruptness of the Allies, in addition to propaganda about Jews and other undesirable groups. While much of this propaganda appealed to people on subjective terms, factual misinformation was frequently used in service of these broader ideas. In fact, the Nazis' ostensible rationale for their invasion of Poland in 1939 was misinformation in the form of a false flag incident in which some of their operatives dressed up as Polish troops and attacked a German border town, killing one local and broadcasting that they had seized the town for Poland (Rossino 2003, Levin 2023). More broadly, once the war was in full swing, the Nazis relentlessly manipulated how they portrayed its progress in their favor, trumpeting ceaselessly the ideas that they were winning and that they were stronger than the Allies and suppressing or contesting any news of German losses and setbacks.

Yet even a state with as potent a propaganda apparatus as the Nazis found that these efforts had clear limits, especially as the war ground on and the tide of battle began to turn. Indeed, various studies of Nazi propaganda during WWII have concluded that it was at its most effective early on in the conflict (e.g., Kershaw 1987, Kallis 2005). But as the situation on the ground turned against the Nazis, and more German soldiers and civilians saw evidence of such shifts, the claims that they were stronger than the Allies and that they were winning the war began to ring increasingly hollow. One important breach in this narrative was the failure of the Russian campaign and the disaster at Stalingrad in February 1943, easily the most shocking and convincing defeat of the German army to that point in the war. As described in one historical analysis (Stout 2011: 3):

...nothing damaged the reputation of the propaganda ministry as greatly as the fall of Stalingrad and the terrible defeat for the Wehrmacht in February 1943. German propaganda had presented the campaign as though the Germans were winning, even as the German 6th Army was surrounded and slowly being destroyed. Not until a week before the actual surrender did Nazi propaganda change its tone, and when the fall of the city was reported by the [Propaganda Ministry], the German people were in a state of shock. All of a sudden Goebbels' propaganda lost a great deal of respect and credibility and was regarded more and more as a lie by the German people.

With large numbers of direct observers of these events on both sides of the war, and the inevitable deluge of news via letters from the front as well as foreign state propaganda and press reports that would follow, this defeat could not be totally kept from the German people. And indeed, it was not, ultimately being conveyed to them with various excuses and challenging quite seriously the Nazis' claims that they were winning the war.

Yet it was by many accounts the increasingly devastating Allied air campaign in Germany that most powerfully brought the war home to Germans and undermined Nazi propaganda efforts. As the Allied bombs began to rain down upon German cities and towns with growing consistency and ferocity from 1942 on, German civilians – especially those in affected areas – were able to see quite plainly their side's lack of air superiority and weakening position in the war more broadly. As it was put in the United States Strategic Bombing Survey (USSBS), a major US government study that was conducted in 1944–45 to examine the impact of Anglo-American strategic bombing during the war (USSBS 1947: 1): "'Black' radio listening and disbelief in official propaganda increased steadily during the last 2 years of the war ... Bombing had much to do with the final discrediting of propaganda and of the Nazis because it brought home to millions the tangible proof of almost unopposed Allied air power, indisputable proof completely at variance with the familiar Nazi propaganda."

These references to people being able to *see* the Nazis' weakness and vulnerability in the war and this exposure puncturing their wartime propaganda speak well to the central argument in the book. Indeed, these dynamics were evidently clear even to Goebbels himself. According to one historian, Goebbels "recognized that news could not disagree with people's direct experiences, ordering, for example, that reports of bombing damage should be accurate in the affected area: 'It is nonsense to distort facts which have taken place in front of everybody's eyes'" (Bytwerk 2004: 160). In this sense, one of history's most influential liars and ruthless propagandists – Joseph Goebbels – seems to have grasped the book's primary conclusion about the ability of direct exposure to constrain the impact of practices such as his quite well.

The 2022 Russian Invasion of Ukraine: The ongoing Russian invasion and occupation of Ukraine that began in February 2022 also presents a very salient and important case of factual manipulation in war. Russia, in particular, has promoted a veritable deluge of misinformation to shape Ukrainian, Russian, and international opinion, starting even before the war began.[24] Some of the major thrusts of this misinformation have included false flag incidents in Ukraine to

---

[24] Reflecting the fact that misinformation invariably appears in support of all "sides" in war, some suspect narratives have arisen on the Ukrainian side as well. These include heroic tales about Ukrainian soldiers like the Ghost of Kyiv – a single ace pilot who allegedly terrorized the entire Russian air force early in the war – or the story of a few brave Ukrainian troops who were reported to have self-sacrificially defied a major Russian warship at Snake Island but were later found to be alive. See, for example, Patrick Galey, "Ukraine Admits 'Ghost of Kyiv' Wasn't Real, But the Myth Was Potent for a Reason." *NBC News*, May 2, 2022. Available at www.nbcnews.com/news/world/ukraine-admits-ghost-kyiv-isnt-real-wartime-myth-russia-rcna26867. Of course, no equivalence should be drawn between the quantity and quality of misinformation pushed by Ukraine and Russia during the conflict.

justify intervention, claims about Ukrainian leaders fleeing and abandoning their country during the early fighting, propaganda about Ukraine being led by neo-Nazis with an intense amplification of the limited role of far-right extremists in the country's national defense efforts, and sweeping efforts to hide Russian setbacks and failures that have occurred in the conflict.[25]

Hard data on the influence of these narratives is limited so far, but there is significant reason to believe they have found little traction in Ukraine. Indeed, one journalistic investigation of these issues notes that Russian propaganda has been ineffectual in Ukraine, even in "areas that, before the war, were considered sympathetic to Russia: being forced to survive in cities reduced to ruins effects mindset change."[26] A Ukrainian analyst quoted in this investigation says that the Kremlin's misinformation "doesn't work for Ukrainians anymore because Ukrainians can see their physical action – they're being bombed by Russians."[27] These quotes speak nicely to both the informational (seeing the relevant events) and motivational (holding a survival mindset about them) mechanisms that combine to puncture wartime misinformation in this book.

In Russia, Kremlin propaganda about the war appears to have been more successful, which is unsurprising given the Kremlin's years of negative messaging about Ukraine and the West[28] and most Russians' lack of personal exposure to and removal from the fighting. Yet claims of universal Russian popular support for the war and belief in wartime propaganda should be seen skeptically given the harsh crackdown on anti-war dissent in the country and the vast potential for preference falsification in such contexts (Hale 2022). Moreover, there are intriguing signs that more accurate accounts

---

[25] For a nice overview of some of the most salient themes of Russian misinformation at the very start of the invasion, see "Russia's Lies in Four Directions: The Kremlin's Strategy to Misinform about Ukraine." *Miburo*, February 26. Available at https://miburo.substack.com/p/russias-lies-in-four-directions-the.

[26] Chris York, "How Ukraine Battles Russian Disinformation." *New Lines Magazine*, April 11, 2022. Available at https://newlinesmag.com/reportage/how-ukraine-battles-russian-disinformation/.

[27] Ibid.

[28] Oleksandr Pankeiev, "How Russia's Unanswered Propaganda Led to the War in Ukraine." *The Conversation*, March 30, 2022. Available at https://theconversation.com/how-russias-unanswered-propaganda-led-to-the-war-in-ukraine-180202.

of the conflict – borne of personal experience and exposure to the fighting – are seeping into the Russian body politic from several different channels, even as powerful forces from above work to block and suppress them.

One such source is in fact, Russian soldiers. Indeed, many Russian military units have faced significant morale issues and even levels of desertion during the war, fueled in part by the fact that soldiers' actual wartime experiences have often clashed sharply with the prewar propaganda given to them by political and military authorities. For example, one letter that was written by a platoon commander to his higher-ups and later leaked to the media stated:

...from the very beginning we were faced with [the command's] deception and concealment of the true goals and tasks of the military deployment. Incomprehensible "military exercise tasks" meant a dramatically different thing ... After our crossing the border into Ukraine, we completely discredited ourselves in the eyes of both the world and the Slavic community. From that moment on, our actions and nature were of an occupation army, which was clearly expressed by the reaction of the civilian population.[29]

Notably, the commander relates how his soldiers' actual experiences once they entered Ukraine – and in particular, their observation of the Ukrainian population's visible hostility to their presence – punctured the misinformation that was given to him before the war. And this case is far from the only one of Russian soldiers rejecting the propaganda fed to them before their deployments.[30]

In addition to Russian soldiers, another conduit for accurate information from the war in Russia is Russian-Ukrainian family ties. In one new study, Tymofii Brik, Aaron Erlich, and Jordan Gans-Morse conducted a survey of Ukrainians and found that those with family ties to individuals in Russia spoke with them regularly about the war and believed that, while their relatives embraced some of the

[29] Alya Shandra, "Russian Soldiers Refusing to Redeploy to Ukraine, Citing Unwillingness to Become 'Cannon Fodder.'" *Euromaidan Press*, March 16, 2022.
[30] For example, one source that vividly and harrowingly portrays these dynamics is a cache of intercepted phone calls from Russian troops in March 2022 to their families back home that were published that fall by the *New York Times*. See "'Putin is a Fool': Intercepted Calls Reveal Russian Army in Disarray." *New York Times*. Available at www.nytimes.com/interactive/2022/09/28/world/europe/russian-soldiers-phone-calls-ukraine.html.

Kremlin's propaganda, their own persuasion efforts were helping to chip away at it.[31] This pathway is somewhat indirect since it involves Russians obtaining accurate information from another population that is exposed to the fighting rather than experiencing it themselves. This may explain why its effects – as perceived by the Ukrainians involved – are at least somewhat limited. Still, it speaks to the power of personal experience in war that it inoculates the Ukrainians in these conversations firmly and even tends to erode misinformed beliefs among their Russian relatives.

Finally, some parts of Russia are faced with the realities of the war more directly. A recent investigation showed the stark gap between places like Moscow's shopping malls and river cruises, which feel totally removed from the war, and those like Russo-Ukrainian border towns where it is far more visible and palpable to people.[32] In the town of Belgorod on the Russo-Ukrainian border, for instance, military convoys leaving for the front, refugees fleeing from Eastern Ukraine, debris from intercepted missiles, and evacuation drills to prepare for Ukrainian attacks are frequent sights. The war is a popular and frightening topic for many in these communities, who feel consternation at the wildly different experiences of Russians insulated from its reach. In the words of one local, "[i]n Moscow, they are celebrating City Day, while here blood is being spilled … Here everyone is worried about our soldiers, while there everyone is partying and drinking!"[33] The difference in the war's salience for the two constituencies is thus clear. Proximity also means more accurate news about the war from fleeing East Ukrainian refugees and evacuees. Even while these civilians tend to have pro-Russian orientations, many have reportedly felt "shocked and effectively betrayed by a Russian army they saw as liberators, but that was on the run in the face of a sweeping Ukrainian offensive."[34] The complex and counter-attitudinal beliefs of these refugees can in turn be accessed and learned by Belgorod residents hosting and interacting with them,

---

[31] Tymofii Brik, Aaron Erlich, and Jordan Gans-Morse. "Is Russia's Wartime Propaganda More Powerful than Family Bonds?" *The Monkey Cage*, June 20, 2022. Available at www.washingtonpost.com/politics/2022/06/20/russia-ukraine-relatives-conversations-propaganda/.

[32] Valerie Hopkins, "War May Be Distant in Moscow, but in One Russian Border City, It's Real." *New York Times*, September 14, 2022.

[33] Ibid.   [34] Ibid.

illustrating how much harder it is to conceal Russian losses and set-backs from these more proximate audiences than from those who are more fully removed from the fighting.

In sum, the case of Russian misinformation about the war in Ukraine illustrates the theory and how it operates in practice in several ways. The power of personal exposure to counter wartime misinformation is clear both in the Russian misinformation's ineffectiveness among the Ukrainian civilian population (including even those who were previously sympathetic to the Kremlin) and its limitations among Russian soldiers and civilians who have direct or indirect channels of exposure to the actual fighting.

3 | Factual Misperceptions in the US Drone Campaign in Pakistan

US drone strikes in Pakistan are "killing nearly 100 percent innocent people."

  – Syed Munawar Hasan, head of Pakistan's Jamaat-e-Islami party[1]

This chapter examines factual misperceptions about the US drone campaign in the tribal areas of Pakistan. It is split into four sections. First, it provides a brief background on the campaign and shows that – despite the various controversies around it – the US drone campaign in Pakistan has empirically been quite targeted or discriminate in nature. Second, it shows that, in contrast to this, most Pakistanis think the campaign is highly indiscriminate in nature and routinely slaughters large numbers of civilians. Third, it demonstrates that this misperception has had some meaningful political consequences in Pakistan. And fourth, it shows that the local civilian population living in the tribal areas – where the overwhelming amount of US drone strikes in Pakistan *actually occur* – tends to have very different and more accurate beliefs about them, following the book's argument about exposure puncturing misbeliefs in war.

Before proceeding, it is worth briefly clarifying what is meant by the terms "discriminate" (or, alternatively, "selective") and "indiscriminate" in this context. This is an important distinction made in research on political violence and conflict, one that focuses on the nature of violence used by combatants. Notably, violence is generally thought to provoke less opposition and resistance – and thus to be more strategically effective – when it is discriminate and not indiscriminate in nature (Kalyvas 2006, Weinstein 2006, Kalyvas and Kocher 2007). This means that it targets individual

---

[1] See Sebastian Abbot, "New Light on Drone War's Death Toll." *Associated Press*, February 26, 2012. Available at www.usnews.com/news/world/articles/2012/02/25/ap-impact-new-light-on-drone-wars-death-toll.

enemy combatants – those who fight for the adversary – and avoids harming innocent civilians as much as possible. In other words, the violence "discriminates" between combatants and civilians. Yet this paradigm rests on the assumption that the noncombatant civilian population can accurately discern between selective vs. indiscriminate violence – if not, both will be equally futile and costly. In fact, one of the scholars who helped popularize these concepts in modern conflict studies, Stathis Kalyvas, recognizes that "in practice, the distinction between selective and indiscriminate violence hinges on public perceptions" (2006, 145). In reality, violence is not purely discriminate or purely indiscriminate but falls along a spectrum depending on how hard the perpetrator tries to target at an individual level and avoid harming civilian populations. This can range from carefully targeting individual enemy soldiers to, say, wiping out entire enemy cities.[2] This chapter looks at the extent to which people exposed to violence will perceive its "selectivity" in ways that are factually biased and at odds with how it is actually carried out on the ground.

In addition, a brief word is also helpful in situating this chapter within the broader empirical landscape of the book. In particular, it should be noted that most of the original empirical evidence in this chapter focuses on demonstrating that factual misperceptions about the US drone campaign in Pakistan are pervasive (Sections 3.1 and 3.2) and influential (Section 3.3) in Pakistani society. Meanwhile, the chapter marshals a wealth of compelling secondary evidence that strongly suggests that these misperceptions are not shared by the local population in the targeted areas (Section 3.4). However, more rigorous testing of this key part of the argument using original empirical evidence can be found in subsequent empirical chapters (Chapters 4 and 5).

---

[2] Some scholars treat the selectivity of violence as a dichotomous distinction. While sympathetic to their arguments, I conceptualize it more continuously as the degree to which the perpetrator strives to maintain individualized targeting and avoid collective harm more generally. As in classic formulations (Kalyvas 2006), the focus is on perpetrator intent – but in a way that allows both explicit desires to target collectives as well as indifference to collective harm in practice to count as deviations from selectivity. I thank Janina Dill for constructively engaging with me and helping me sharpen my thinking on this front.

3.1 Context and Conduct of the US Drone Campaign in Pakistan

While Islamist militancy has deep roots in Pakistan, its present struggle with the Pakistani state and international community can be traced back to the 2001 US-led invasion of neighboring Afghanistan, when scores of Al Qaeda and Afghan Taliban militants fled across the porous border between the two countries – the Durand line – to the Federally Administered Tribal Areas (FATA) of northwest Pakistan. Under intense US pressure, the Pakistani military entered FATA in 2002 to root them out, but its operation only enraged the fiercely independent local tribes (Qazi 2011). This enabled the militants to gain some tribal support, which they combined with killings of pro-government tribal elders to consolidate control of FATA in 2004. In 2007, various militant factions coalesced into the Tehrik-e-Taliban Pakistan (TTP), or Pakistani Taliban, under the leadership of Baitullah Mehsud. The TTP soon proved itself to be an existential threat to Islamabad (and serious one to Washington) when it rolled across the Swat Valley to within sixty miles of the capital in a full national insurgency. While this bold advance was blunted in 2009, the group continues to unleash deadly attacks from its stronghold in FATA, such as the 2014 Peshawar school massacre in which 132 children were slaughtered in an army public school. Nor is the country's struggle with Islamist militancy constrained to the northwest; the TTP and affiliated networks are active in the sprawling slums of Karachi, neglected areas of southern Punjab, and a number of other pockets countrywide. Additionally, before the US withdrawal from Afghanistan in 2021, the tribal areas also functioned as a key "launching pad" for the Afghan Taliban in Afghanistan, as well as a sanctuary for elements of Al Qaeda and various other groups outside the grasp of the Pakistani state (Fair 2004).

In order to confront these threats, the American and Pakistani governments have conducted a variety of military operations. The Pakistani military has at times engaged in quite pitched battles against these groups, including in its counterinsurgency operations to clear Khyber Pakhtunkhwa and FATA, which have often used heavy airpower to defeat the militants. It has also conducted a steady stream of arrests and raids against them in urban areas with significant militant activity like Karachi. Meanwhile, the USA has launched more

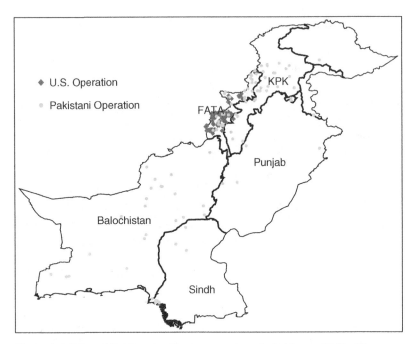

Figure 3.1 US and Pakistani military operations in Pakistan, 2003–13

than 400 strikes from Unmanned Aerial Vehicles, or "drones," against militants in the tribal areas since 2004.[3] These strikes were initially relatively infrequent, but their pace accelerated sharply in 2008 when the threats emanating from the tribal areas increased, peaking in 2010 with more than 100 operations. The attacks have scored a number of successes, including the elimination of dozens of Al Qaeda and Taliban leaders.[4] Yet there have also been some notable mistakes, such as the bombing of religious seminaries and tribal *jirgas* in FATA full of civilians. Moreover, the USA has also conducted a number of special forces raids and other covert actions in the country, including the 2011 Abbottabad raid that killed Osama Bin Laden. Figure 3.1

[3] See the New America Foundation (http://securitydata.newamerica.net/) and Bureau of Investigative Journalism (http://thebureauinvetigates.cmcategory/projects/drones/) strike-tracking databases.
[4] As of this writing, NAF data records eighty-four Al Qaeda and Taliban "senior leaders" killed in Pakistan. The elimination of high-value targets (HVT's) is not recorded by the BIJ.

shows the distribution of US and Pakistani military activities in the country, with their heavy concentration in the tribal regions.

3.1.1 The Surprisingly Discriminate Use of Drones in Pakistan

Despite its politically controversial nature, a careful look at the American drone campaign in Pakistan shows that, overall, it has been a very selective or discriminate application of force. As a starting point to understand this, consider the design of the technology itself. The drones used by the USA in Pakistan are designed to target individuals and minimize harm to civilians in two ways. First, they can gather more prestrike intelligence about their targets than conventional methods of aerial attack. With no onboard human pilot, armed drones can hover over their targets for hours at a time collecting signals intelligence from onboard sensors. This allows their operators to have better odds of positively identifying their target and waiting until they have a "clean shot" when that target is isolated and removed from civilians in the surrounding area. Second, US attack drones boast very precise weapons systems, including precision-guided missiles with "the capacity to target individuals, automobiles, or sections of structures such as rooms in a large house" (Walsh 2013: vii). This allows operators to pinpoint targets and limit collateral damage due to imprecision. Thus, from a technological perspective, US drone warfare is designed to be targeted and selective in nature in terms of its unique intelligence collection and precision strike capabilities.

Of course, such capabilities would mean nothing if the USA used them in an indiscriminate fashion or made so many serious targeting errors as to eliminate their value. Yet abundant evidence from Pakistan indicates that this is not the case. Indeed, despite the prevailing discourse in Pakistan and beyond, a plethora of evidence – both qualitative as well as quantitative in nature – shows that the US drone campaign has actually been quite targeted and discriminate in practice.

Qualitatively, a wealth of testimony has emerged from those best positioned to know what is happening in the tribal regions that clashes with prevailing perceptions of the strikes elsewhere. For example, an investigation by the Associated Press (AP) in 2011 in which a local news stringer was sent to interview FATA residents immediately after drone strikes occurred in North Waziristan – the tribal area most often targeted in the attacks – found that civilian casualties were much lower than is commonly reported.[5] The stringer found that about 70 percent of deaths in the strikes were militants, and this rose to 90 percent when an extreme outlier incident – one of the deadliest in the entire campaign – was excluded. These numbers diverge sharply from the widespread perception that most victims are civilians. Critically, many of the 80 villagers that were interviewed knew the people who had been killed in the strikes personally, and the overall casualty numbers (combining militants and civilians) obtained by the local stringer were similar to those provided by Pakistan's intelligence agencies at the time.

Similarly, candid admissions from senior Pakistani military officers and other top Pakistani government officials during the course of the campaign corroborate this picture. For example, in one unusually candid statement about the campaign, Pakistani Major General Ghayur Mehmood – a top commander in North Waziristan – explained to reporters in 2011 that: "Myths and rumors about US Predator strikes and the casualty figures are many, but it's a reality that many of those being killed in these strikes are hard-core elements, a sizable number of them foreigners. Yes, there are a few civilian casualties in such precision strikes, but a majority of those eliminated are terrorists, including foreign terrorist elements."[6]

Mehmood's words mirror revelations from WikiLeaks about top Pakistani officials' comments to their US counterparts in private. Notably, a US diplomat in a 2008 cable references a meeting with a top Pakistani official who says that he: "wanted to say in an unofficial capacity that he and many others could accept Predator strikes as they were surgical and clearly hitting high value targets. He mentioned the fear among the local populace in areas where the strikes have been occurring was lessening because 'everyone knew that they only hit the house or location of very bad people.'"[7] Likewise, a WikiLeaks cable from the US ambassador to Pakistan, Anne Patterson, states she

---

[5] Sebastian Abbot, "New Light on Drone War's Death Toll." *Associated Press*, February 26, 2012. Available at www.usnews.com/news/world/articles/2012/02/25/ap-impact-new-light-on-drone-wars-death-toll.

[6] Pir Zubair Shah, "My Drone War." *Foreign Policy*, February 27, 2012.

[7] Tim Lister, "WikiLeaks: Pakistan Quietly Approved Drone Attacks, U.S. Special Units." *CNN*, December 2, 2010. Available at www.cnn.com/2010/US/12/01/wikileaks.pakistan.drones/index.html.

was told by Yousaf Raza Gilani, the country's then-Prime Minister, in 2008: "I don't care if they do it as long as they get the right people. We'll protest in the National Assembly and then ignore it." In sum, statements from both Pakistani military and civilian officials in moments of candor reinforce the picture gleaned from the AP investigation and other credible local sources of information about the drone campaign, showing that many Pakistani officials knew the strikes were relatively precise – even though they were loath to say so publicly due to their political sensitivity.

Finally, ample testimony from local civilians in the tribal areas also reinforces these claims. Since this evidence dovetails with the issue of how local civilians *perceive* the strikes, however, it is saved for the appropriate section on local civilian perceptions later in the chapter. As elaborated there, local civilians' understandings of the strikes diverge sharply from those prevalent elsewhere in Pakistan and align far more closely with the other forms of qualitative evidence discussed here. This fact should further bolster confidence in the campaign's discriminate nature.

Meanwhile, quantitatively, a close look at the various datasets that systematically track the results of the drone campaign actually confirms this picture. There are three key publicly available databases on drone strikes in Pakistan. These databases are run by (1) the New America Foundation (NAF), a major American think tank, (2) the Bureau of Investigative Journalism (BIJ), a nonprofit news organization based in the UK, and (3) the UMass DRONE Project, an academic dataset based at the University of Massachusetts-Dartmouth. While these databases are created by very different types of organizations and rely on different methodological criteria, their data on drone casualties paint a surprisingly consistent picture. A more detailed discussion of the coding standards used by each database is presented in the Appendix, but the general picture of their broad convergence which is important for our purposes is shown here.

Table 3.1 shows the estimates from all three databases. As is clear, all three major publicly available databases tracking the results of US drone strikes in Pakistan show a militant-to-civilian casualty ratio around four militants to every one civilian killed. This convergence is striking when one considers their significant methodological variation. Critically, the 4:1 ratio they converge on is a highly discriminate figure. As noted by Plaw and Fricker (2012), who conducted a

Table 3.1 *Estimates of militants vs. civilians killed in US drone campaign in Pakistan*

	Militant casualties	Civilian casualties (incl. unknowns)	Ratio of militants to civilians killed
The New America Foundation (NAF)	2,490	544	4.6:1
Bureau of Investigative Journalism (BIJ)	2,574	697	3.7:1
DRONE Project at UMass-Dartmouth	2,585	665	3.9:1

Note: The means were used for all sources that provided casualty ranges (NAF, BIJ).

comparative review of the different datasets, it is much higher than a number of key benchmarks, such as Israeli targeted killings in the Palestinian territories from 2000 to 2008 (1.5:1), Pakistani military operations in the FATA region from 2002 to 2007 (2.2:1), and the global average for all armed conflict in the year 2000 (0.1:1) or the period 1989–2004 (2:1). The Pakistani army benchmark is particularly relevant, as it allows us to compare US drone strikes to operations conducted by the country's own armed forces against militant organizations in the tribal areas. Crucially, these figures also come from the Pakistani press, yet they show that US drone strikes are at least twice as discriminate as Pakistani military operations in the same places (Plaw and Fricker 2012).[8]

---

[8] One concern around these figures is whether there is any reason to believe that civilian casualties are systematically underreported in the Pakistani press (which serves as the foundation for most of these datasets). While there are almost certainly errors in both directions, in general, there is actually ample reason to believe the opposite. This is because, as noted earlier, drone strikes fall almost entirely in parts of FATA (notably North Waziristan) that are under the thumb of the Pakistani Taliban and other militant groups. This means the targets – not the perpetrators – of the strikes control the "scene of the crime," and thus the portrayal of events on the ground. As explained by Taj (2010: 530): "The reason why these estimates about civilian 'casualties' in the US and Pakistani media are wrong is that after every attack the terrorists cordon off the area and no one, including the local villagers, is allowed to come even near the targeted place. The militants themselves collect the bodies, bury the dead and then issue the statement that all of them were innocent civilians." With little access to these areas and the US government tight-lipped about the operations, these estimates often travel unchallenged in Pakistani

In sum, a careful look at the major quantitative strike-tracking databases actually buttresses the picture gleaned from our discussion of the various streams of qualitative evidence on the topic. Overall, there is a plethora of evidence – both qualitative and quantitative in nature – that the US drone campaign in the tribal regions of Northwest Pakistan has been highly discriminate in nature. In addition, my informal conversations with people from the tribal regions both within the country during an exploratory fieldwork trip conducted in Pakistan in the winter of 2014–15 and outside of it have consistently reinforced this picture of the local realities of the campaign.

3.2 Pakistani Perceptions of Drones Outside the Tribal Areas

Contrary to this empirical record, the US drone campaign in Pakistan is generally seen as anything but selective, targeted, or discriminate among Pakistanis living outside of the tribal areas. The main source of publicly available individual-level survey data about drone strikes in Pakistan is from the Pew Research Center's Global Attitudes Project (GAP). GAP is a continuous effort to track social and political attitudes globally since 2002, in which Pakistan has been included almost every year. GAP's surveys of Pakistan are broadly representative of the four primary provinces of Pakistan (i.e., Punjab, Sindh, Khyber Pakhtunkhwa or KPK, and Balochistan), and exclude the country's tribal areas.[9] This is suitable for our purposes because the surveys are being deliberately used to examine perceptions of drones among *the non-local civilian population* – that is, Pakistanis who live outside of FATA.

GAP began asking Pakistanis questions about their perceptions of the US drone campaign in 2009 and continued doing so (depending on the specific question) through 2012, 2013, or 2014. The surveys

and international media. The net effect is that, if anything, the civilian casualty figures in existing datasets are almost certainly *inflated*. Pakistan expert Christine Fair reaches a similar conclusion in her analysis of the issue, noting that extant databases include "exaggerated counts of innocents, including women and children" killed by strikes. See Christine Fair, "The Problems with Studying Civilian Casualties from Drone Usage in Pakistan: What We Can't Know." *The Monkey Cage*, August 17, 2011. Available at http://themonkeycage.org/2011/08/17/the-problems-with-studyingcivilian-casualties-from-drone-usage-in-pakistan-what-we-can%E2%80%99t-know/.

[9] GAP's surveys are also disproportionately urban in nature, though they are weighted to capture the actual urban vs. rural distribution of the country.

asked Pakistanis a number of questions about drones, including about their awareness of the American drone program, their overall attitudes toward it, and their perceptions of some of its most salient features. In order to gauge people's awareness of the strikes, the surveys asked the following question: *How much, if anything, have you heard about drone attacks that target leaders of extremist groups?* Of the people who responded to this question, only 35 percent said they knew about the strikes in 2009, but that figure increased to 49 percent in 2010, 71 percent in April 2011, 71 percent in May 2011, and 76 percent in 2012. Thus, while many Pakistanis had not heard about the drone campaign initially, awareness of it soon grew as it intensified during the late 2000s and eventually became widespread throughout Pakistani society.

To measure Pakistanis' general attitudes toward the drone strikes, the surveys asked those respondents who knew about them the following question: *Do you think these drone attacks are a very good thing, good thing, bad thing, or very bad thing?* Figure 3.2 presents the distribution of responses to the question from 2009 to 2012. As can be seen, US drone strikes were widely unpopular in Pakistan among

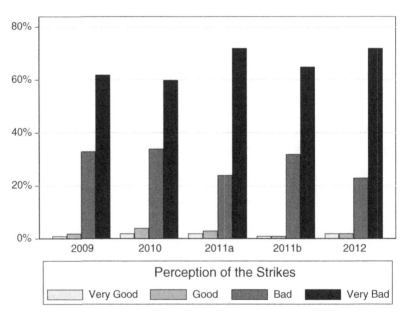

Figure 3.2 Pakistani overall perceptions of US drone strikes, 2009–12

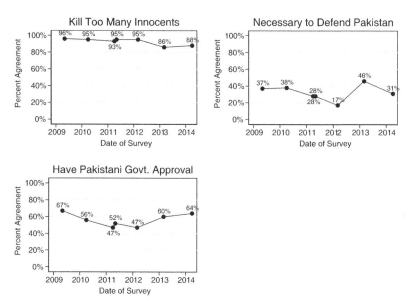

Figure 3.3 Pakistani agreement with statements about US drone strikes, 2009–14

those aware of their use. In fact, only around 3 percent of Pakistanis who were aware of the strikes reported a favorable view of them in 2009, a figure that shifted little over time – with 6 percent supporting the strikes in 2010, 5 percent in April 2011, 2 percent in May 2011, and 4 percent in 2012. In contrast, most of the respondents – between 60 percent and 72 percent, depending on the year – reported a very negative view of the operations. Similarly broad opposition to the campaign is evident in Gallup polls in Pakistan, though these are not analyzed in this chapter because individual-level data for Gallup's opinion polling in Pakistan are not publicly available.[10] In sum, the data show that the US drone campaign in Pakistan has been perceived very negatively in mainstream Pakistani society.

Turning now to more specific items, the surveys asked Pakistanis about their perceptions of three major issues surrounding the American drone campaign – its military necessity, its civilian death toll, and its violation of national sovereignty, or the extent to which it had approval from the Pakistani government. Figure 3.3 plots

---

[10] Specifically, Gallup found that 12 percent of Pakistanis who offered a response supported the strikes in 2009, with 18 percent in 2010, 21 percent in spring 2013, and 13 percent in fall 2013.

the distribution of answers to these three items, which were asked from 2009 to 2014. As can be seen, there was significant variation in Pakistani perceptions of the military utility and sovereignty violation issues, but more uniformity around the collateral damage issue. Notably, the drone strikes have been overwhelmingly perceived as killing too many innocent civilians in the country (though this perception did drop slightly in 2013). While the question posed by GAP was unfortunately worded in a subjective and suboptimal way for our purposes ("too many civilians" rather than something more explicitly factual like "mostly civilians"), it does indicate a widespread Pakistani concern with the civilian death toll around the campaign. In other words, the operations do not appear to be seen as very discriminate by the Pakistani population outside of the tribal regions where they occur based on extant national survey data.

This view of the US drone campaign in Pakistan as indiscriminate in nature is more clearly apparent in Pakistani political discourse, news coverage, and mass mobilization around the strikes. Indeed, prominent Pakistani politicians of all stripes have promoted misinformation that the attacks kill mostly or entirely civilians. Syed Munawar Hasan, the leader of the right wing Jamaat-e-Islami (JI) party in Pakistan, for example, declared on Pakistani television in 2012 that drones "are killing nearly 100 percent innocent people."[11] In a similar vein, the influential Pakistani populist political leader Imran Khan has oft appeared at broad anti-drone protests decrying the strikes' alleged high civilian death toll. At one such protest in 2012 Khan declared that "those who lie to the nation after every drone attack and say terrorists were killed should be ashamed."[12] One Pakistani scholar sums up the forces actively engaged in this misinformation as including "the Pakistani government, the military, and right wing politicians such as Imran Khan," and notes that these actors "have played a key role in inflaming public opinion, often by making wild claims about 'thousands' of civilian casualties resulting from the strikes" (Shah 2018: 72). In sum, Pakistani political discourse is rife with misleading information about the nature and the results of the campaign.

---

[11] Sebastian Abbot, "New Light on Drone War's Death Toll." *Associated Press*, February 26, 2012. Available at www.usnews.com/news/world/articles/2012/02/25/ap-impact-new-light-on-drone-wars-death-toll.

[12] Ibid.

So, too, is this misrepresentation of drones' civilian death toll clear in the Pakistani media. Scholars have noted that civilian deaths from drone attacks get "major play in the Pakistani media outlets," with scenes of their destruction splattered across the front pages of top newspapers such as *Dawn* and footage of the aftermath of the attacks and interviews with outraged villagers earning heavy airtime on Pakistani TV channels including *Pakistan TV* and *GEO TV* (Kaltenthaler, Miller, and Fair 2012: 2). Indeed, a comparative content analysis of news coverage of the drone campaign in four leading Pakistani newspapers – *Dawn, Daily Times, The Nation*, and *Daily Express* – found that "kill innocents" was the most prevalent theme in three of the four outlets, appearing in a total of 36 percent of the editorials analyzed (Fair and Hamza 2016). Flashy and yet false headlines with wildly inflated casualty numbers such as "60 drone hits kill 14 al-Qaeda men, 687 civilians"[13] (see Taj 2010: 531) appear with regularity in the Pakistani press. Thus, media coverage of the campaign has also disproportionately presented it as "a scourge targeting innocent civilians."[14]

A final indicator that points in the same direction is anti-drone protest activity in Pakistan. As the drone campaign crested in the late 2000s and early 2010s, a steady stream of public protests, rallies, and demonstrations materialized against the strikes in Pakistan, particularly in major cities such as Karachi, Rawalpindi, and Peshawar. Many of these demonstrations witnessed large crowds of thousands of protesters, often chanting slogans about the alleged civilian death toll in the strikes and brandishing posters like "Drones Fly Children Die," "Drones Kill Innocent Pakistanis," "Stop Killing the Muslims" and "Stop Killing Innocent Tribal Peoples [sic]."[15] In other words, there was a substantial groundswell of mobilization against US drone strikes in the country, one that painted the strikes as indiscriminate

---

[13] Note that this would imply an absurd militant-to-civilian casualty ratio of 1:49, orders of magnitude off from the various database estimates discussed earlier. Taj (2010) also notes how no sourcing is provided for this information and her requests for more information and justification of these numbers have gone unanswered. It is likely that all of those killed who were not high-value Al Qaeda or Taliban leadership targets here are treated as civilians.

[14] Pir Zubair Shah, "My Drone War." *Foreign Policy*, February 27, 2012.

[15] See, for example, "US Activists Join Drone Protest in Pakistan." *The National*, October 7, 2012.

and placed civilian deaths at the center of its messaging. Overall, then, even a cursory qualitative look confirms what can be seen via public opinion polling in the country: That the drone campaign is seen as not just deeply illegitimate but, more important for our purposes, as *empirically quite indiscriminate* throughout much of Pakistani society.

It is also worth comparing Pakistanis' outrage at civilian harm from American drone strikes to their indifference to the *greater* civilian harm from Pakistani army operations in the tribal areas. As discussed earlier, Pakistani army operations in FATA have been about twice as indiscriminate as the drone campaign, and testimony from locals shows that the former is recognized as far more destructive than the latter. During the major *Zarb-e-Azb* campaign in FATA which flattened whole villages and displaced hundreds of thousands in 2014–17, for example, one civilian in FATA noted that "America is our enemy, but they have never taken such cruel action against us which [sic] we had witnessed from the Pakistani government – our own country."[16] Yet outside FATA and those with links to it, there has been a striking lack of concern about this carnage in Pakistan. This reflects the divergent treatment of the two campaigns in the Pakistani press: A content analysis of Pakistani news coverage of Zarb found that about 67 percent of the stories examined were positive in tone (Khan and Akhtar 2016), whereas only 3 percent of stories in a similar analysis of US drone strike coverage were positive (Fair and Hamza 2016). Additionally, the analysis of Zarb coverage found that, while there was some attention to the issue of civilian displacement, "the main thing observed was lack of IDPs' narrative in the stories" (125). In other words, local narratives were not conveyed to the Pakistani public. It is thus unsurprising that Pakistanis' perceptions of the army's operations in FATA have been much softer than their views of US drone strikes as measured in opinion polls. For example, public support for the army's operations in FATA and adjacent Khyber Pakhtunkhwa province averaged 60 percent in the Pew polls from 2019 to 2015, yet those same polls showed only 4 percent support for drone strikes. Scrutinizing Pakistanis' reactions to their own army's operations in the tribal areas highlights the deeply distorted picture of events in FATA that permeates the rest of Pakistan, and how beliefs about the drone

---

[16] "Civilian Casualties Fuel Outrage Over Zarb-e-Azb." *AFP*, July 22, 2014.

campaign's consequences are not simply a function of its actual level of civilian harm but of the psychological, informational, and political context in which it occurs.

To summarize the chapter thus far, then, public opinion data in Pakistan indicates that US drone strikes are heavily linked to killing civilians in Pakistani society and that the operations are seen as far from selective and targeted in nature. A qualitative look at Pakistani political discourse, media coverage, and popular mobilization surrounding the strikes only reinforces this conclusion. Both deeply misleading media coverage of the strikes' as causing unprecedented collateral damage as well as outright misinformation about their targeting from prominent politicians and pundits – which aligns with preexisting attitudes and identities in much of Pakistani society – helps facilitate these beliefs. What all of this means is that there are widespread *factual misperceptions* about US drone strikes among Pakistanis living outside the tribal areas. The empirical record shows that the campaign has been quite selective in nature, yet it is overwhelmingly portrayed and perceived as anything but selective by most citizens of the country.

3.3 Why These Factual Misperceptions Matter

To explore the political consequences of the factual misperception that the drone campaign in Pakistan is indiscriminate in nature, this section conducts several analyses. First, examining the GAP survey data, it shows that the inflated concern about collateral damage appears to be a critical source of Pakistani opposition to the strikes. Second, it shows that Pakistani backlash to the strikes is important with two analyses. In one, it uses an "event study" approach to investigate the strikes' impact on Pakistani attitudes more broadly, showing that they fuel anti-American, anti-incumbent, and pro-militant sentiment regularly in the country. On the other, it analyzes event data to show that the strikes facilitated violent protests and attacks on NATO shipping routes in Pakistan, two natural outgrowths of the public alienation that they engender. Separately, each of these analyses has its limitations, tracing just one link in a possible causal chain. But together they are quite suggestive in showing how the misperceptions about US drone strikes that have emerged in Pakistani society have contributed to important and incendiary political dynamics in the country.

3.3.1 Importance for Pakistani Opposition to Drone Strikes

Using the Pew data, this section now turns to investigate the extent to which concerns about collateral damage are an important component of Pakistani opposition to drone strikes in general. Specifically, it presents the results from a number of regressions predicting Pakistani views of the strikes. The dependent variable in these regressions is the aforementioned question about whether Pakistanis see US drone strikes as a very good, good, bad, or very bad thing. As noted earlier, this question was asked in five different Pew surveys, which were fielded respectively in 2009, 2010, April 2011, May 2011, and 2012. Meanwhile, the main independent variables in the model are the three aforementioned questions about specific features of the drone campaign – that is, its military necessity, collateral damage, and violation of sovereignty. The model also includes items asking Pakistanis about their opinions of the US government, their own government, and the Taliban, as well as several standard demographic covariates along with province and wave-level fixed effects. The models are estimated with linear regression for the sake of simplicity and ease of interpretation of the variables' substantive influence, although the results are not sensitive to the use of alternative modeling choices.[17]

Table 3.2 shows the results. Model 1 includes only the items about Pakistanis' perceptions of the three different aspects of the drone campaign, Model 2 adds their perceptions of the different actors involved in the campaign, and Models 3–4 add demographic factors. The dependent variable in all models is coded such that higher values indicate greater support for the attacks. As is evident, concern about collateral damage is associated with significantly lower support for drone strikes in each of the four models – that is, the association holds even when accounting for Pakistanis' beliefs about other aspects of the drone program, their views of the key actors involved (such as the USA), and their demographic backgrounds. Moreover, the impact of this collateral damage issue is among the strongest predictors in the model, reducing support for the campaign by roughly 10 percent points (or 0.39 on a 4-point scale). This effect

---

[17] For example, the results are substantively unchanged with an ordered logistic regression model used to account for the ordinal nature of the outcome variable more precisely. See Table A3.1 for the results and accompanying discussion in the Appendix for further details.

Table 3.2 *Predictors of Pakistani support for US drone strikes, 2009–12*

	M1	M2	M3	M4
Attitudes				
Military necessity	0.20***	0.14***	0.13***	0.13***
	(0.02)	(0.03)	(0.03)	(0.03)
Collateral damage	−0.39***	−0.39***	−0.39***	−0.39***
	(0.04)	(0.05)	(0.05)	(0.05)
Sovereignty violation	−0.05*	−0.05*	−0.04	−0.04
	(0.02)	(0.02)	(0.02)	(0.02)
Pro-American		0.06***	0.05***	0.05***
		(0.01)	(0.01)	(0.01)
Pro-government		0.05***	0.05***	0.05***
		(0.01)	(0.01)	(0.01)
Taliban is threat		0.01	0.01	0.01
		(0.01)	(0.01)	(0.01)
Demographics				
Age			−0.00	−0.00
			(0.00)	(0.00)
Gender			0.08**	0.08***
			(0.02)	(0.02)
Education			−0.00	−0.00
			(0.01)	(0.01)
Religiosity				−0.18***
				(0.04)
Muslim				−0.25***
				(0.08)
Pashtun				−0.03
				(0.04)
Fixed effects				
Province fixed effects	Yes	Yes	Yes	Yes
Wave fixed effects	Yes	Yes	Yes	Yes
Constant	1.63***	1.42***	1.43***	1.49***
	(0.06)	(0.07)	(0.10)	(0.14)
Observations	2976	2693	2678	2675
R^2	0.098	0.099	0.103	0.116

Note: Results from linear regressions. Standard errors in parentheses.
*$p < 0.05$, **$p < 0.01$, ***$p < 0.001$.

is comparable to the size of other key predictors like whether the respondent is Muslim or whether he or she is religiously observant, and stronger than the influence of the other negative drone-specific questions that were asked by Pew.

Ultimately, what this indicates is that concerns about collateral damage and civilian death are among the most important ingredients in Pakistani opposition to the American drone campaign. Of course, care must be taken to note that these results should not be interpreted in a unidirectional causal manner. As argued in this book, factual beliefs about conflict are themselves influenced by prior attitudes among people beyond the "line of fire." In other words, high animosity toward the USA would make someone much more likely to think that American drone strikes are killing large numbers of civilians. But such beliefs are not *only* the product of preexisting attitudes but also of other factors such as the information that one absorbs; the relationship between political attitudes and factual beliefs in this sense is bidirectional. Specifically, the fact that these models control for Pakistani attitudes toward the relevant actors (including their perpetrator, the USA) as well as other negative perceptions of the US drone campaign, and *still* find that collateral damage grievances are among the strongest predictors of anti-drone views suggests that anger over the civilian death toll is indeed a key ingredient in Pakistani hostility toward the strikes in its own right.

3.3.2 Impact on Broader Political Attitudes in Pakistan

Is this opposition to US drone strikes – fueled in important ways by factual misperceptions – politically consequential in Pakistan? In fact, there has been a fierce debate among scholars and policymakers about whether – and, if so, how – drone strikes have affected political attitudes and behaviors in their target countries. On the one hand, many scholars contend that US drone warfare in countries like Pakistan has fostered substantial alienation and even radicalization – often termed "blowback" – throughout the targeted societies (Boyle 2013, Cronin 2013). Yet other analysts have challenged this "blowback narrative," pointing toward the unpopularity of the perpetrator in these countries before the strikes and questioning the salience of the violence relative to other concerns (Byman 2013, Fair, Kaltenthaler, and Miller 2014, Shah 2018). This foreign policy-oriented debate speaks to broader theoretically-oriented questions about how counterinsurgent and counterterrorist violence shapes the attitudes and loyalties – or "hearts and minds" – of civilian populations (Bueno de Mesquita 2005, Kalyvas 2006, Lyall 2009).

To gain some leverage over this question, one useful approach is to examine the influence of US drone strikes that happened to occur *during the implementation of public opinion surveys in Pakistan.* Because Pakistani political attitudes can then be compared immediately before and after the strikes, this offers a very clean window into understanding the impact of the strikes on Pakistani opinion, at least in the short term.[18] This type of "event study" in which violent events that occur *during* the fielding of mass public opinion surveys or other behavioral data collection efforts are analyzed has been used effectively in other contexts, such as to examine the impact of violence on trust in Africa (Garcia-Ponce and Pasquale 2015, Young 2015) and the link between violent crime and academic performance in Chicago (Sharkey 2010). In order to provide ample periods of time to observe any effects, fourteen-day windows on either side of the events are used.

In terms of data, the violent event data come from the BIJ database of US drone strikes in Pakistan, while the attitudinal data are the Pew GAP polls. The dependent variables in our analysis are simply four-point favorability scales (*"Please tell me if you have a very favorable, somewhat favorable, somewhat unfavorable, or very unfavorable opinion…"*) of a number of relevant actors in the conflict, including the United States, American people, Pakistani incumbent and opposition leaders at the time of the strike, and Al Qaeda and the Taliban. The key comparison in the study is whether each interview was completed up to fourteen days before (*control group*) vs. up to fourteen days after (*treatment group*) one of the

---

[18] As noted by Garcia-Ponce and Pasquale (2015), the ideal strategy to judge the impacts of violence on opinion – at least methodologically – would be to *randomize exposure to violence* and compare the attitudes of exposed (*treated*) and unexposed (*control*) populations. However, as this ideal experiment is "neither possible nor desirable in real-life settings" (16), the best feasible strategy is to compare public opinion before (*control*) vs. after (*treated*) the relevant events. The critical assumption is that the timing of those events is unrelated to the timing of the surveys, providing a clean "natural experiment" with which to analyze their effects.

strikes. The models include a number of key demographic covariates to control for potential imbalances between the prestrike vs. poststrike respondents, though the results are substantively similar with or without their inclusion.

To construct the sample, all GAP Pakistan survey waves during which one – and only one – US drone strike was conducted were identified. This yielded four waves (2005, 2007, 2012, and 2013) jointly containing 5,640 responses. While one cannot expect the four pertinent strikes to be fully representative of over 400, it is notable (1) that the four strikes in question were all conducted in North Waziristan, in which a significant majority of the drone strikes in Pakistan have occurred, (2) that they resulted in a 2.3:1 militant-to-civilian casualty ratio, not terribly far from the broader casualty ratio given the very small sample of events used, and (3) that they only killed one militant leader according to the NAF database (Al Qaeda bomb-maker Haitham Al-Yemeni in May 2005), which broadly corresponds to the rate of killing such "high-value targets" in the overall campaign (roughly 16 percent of the time according to the NAF data). Moreover, the sample includes a wide range of time points from throughout the campaign's history, from the second US drone strike ever launched in Pakistan in early 2005 through a strike in 2013 when the campaign was winding down in frequency and intensity.[19] Thus, these four drone strikes do not appear to provide a particularly unrepresentative selection of US drone strikes in Pakistan.

For this to be a credible comparison, the mean values that respondents exhibit on a variety of demographic control variables should look similar before vs. after the drone strikes in question. This demographic balance before vs. after the relevant strikes can be gauged by regressing a simple binary measure of treatment status ("0" if the interview was prestrike, "1" if it was poststrike) on a number of key demographic variables. Figure A3.1 in the Appendix shows the results of this test, which reveals that the sample is well-balanced on most demographics, with the sole exception of respondents' level of educational attainment. However, all of the substantive results remain robust to the inclusion of education (or any of the other demographics in question) in our models.

---

[19] Specifically, the strikes used in the analysis were those on (1) May 8, 2005, (2) April 27, 2007, (3) March 30, 2012, and (4) March 21, 2013. All four were researched extensively to ensure that there were no inconsistencies in BIJ dates, locations, and casualties across their reporting in different news sources.

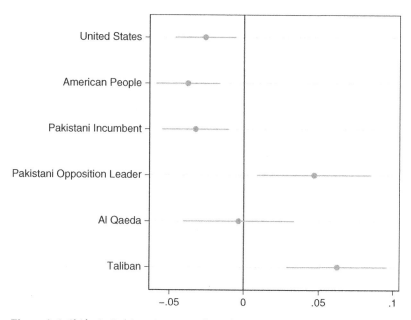

Figure 3.4 Shifts in Pakistani support for relevant actors after US drone strike

Figure 3.4 presents the main results of the analysis. It shows the effects of the drone strike "treatment" on Pakistani public opinion toward six different actors: The USA, the American people, Pakistan's incumbent leader, Pakistan's opposition leader, the Taliban, and Al Qaeda. The models used are linear regressions with demographic covariates as well as province and wave fixed effects. As can be seen, US drone strikes significantly diminish the perceived favorability of the USA, the American people, and the Pakistani incumbent office-holder, who is likely seen as either complicit in the drone campaign or too weak to stop it. In contrast, they increase sympathies for the Pakistani opposition leader and for the Taliban, representing attitudinal shifts broadly speaking toward actors who might challenge American influence more following a strike.[20] Meanwhile, the drone

---

[20] Indeed, Pakistan was governed by secular-nationalist forces (the dictatorship of Pervez Musharraf from 1999 to 2008, and the Pakistan People's Party or PPP from 2008 to 2013) during this period that cooperated quite closely with the USA on security issues. In contrast, the leading opposition parties during this period such as the Pakistani Muslim League Nawaz (PMLN) and later

strikes have no effect on public sentiments toward Al Qaeda, which has little popular support in Pakistan and is even perceived in some segments of Pakistani society as an American conspiracy or proxy designed to undermine the country (e.g., Yusuf 2011).

Additionally, the effects are meaningful in substantive terms: The perceived unfavorability of the USA, for example, increases by around 2–3 percent points after a drone strike. Moreover, this is only the intention-to-treat (ITT), and not the average treatment effect (ATE), as news of the incident undoubtedly does not reach all respondents within the fourteen-day response window (or at all). To "back out" the ATE, we can divide the ITT by the share of people that received the "treatment" (the share exposed to news about the event). While this quantity is unknown for our specific strikes, the 2010 survey did ask people if they had heard about a particularly notable strike that killed TTP leader Baitullah Mehsud several months before the survey. This offers a conservative benchmark both because it was a very high-profile strike and because respondents had several months in which to hear about it. Almost exactly 25 percent of the respondents reported knowledge of this incident, so we can divide the ITT estimates by 25 percent. This fairly conservative approach suggests that US drone strikes increase Pakistani animosity toward the USA by roughly 10 percent points in their aftermath. One should also note that this is only the effect of one single "dose" of treatment. In sum, this suggests that American drone strikes *do* lead to a meaningful hardening of Pakistani political attitudes toward their perpetrator.

This "event study" analysis shows that US drone strikes regularly stoke anti-American, anti-incumbent, and pro-militant attitudes throughout mainstream Pakistani society. Their impact is substantial as well: For instance, anti-USA sentiment increases by an estimated 10 percent after a strike, with similar or even larger spikes in anti-incumbent and pro-Taliban attitudes as well. The nature of the analysis here does not allow us to look at the strikes' attitudinal consequences beyond a two-week window (and indeed logically we would not expect them to last much longer than that, given the frequency with which drone strikes take place and the "ceilings" against

Pakistan Tehreek-e-Insaf (PTI) tended to appeal to a more conservative and Islamist-oriented set of constituencies that was less comfortable with a cozy US relationship.

which some of these attitudes would run up). Yet, regularly *inflaming* the attitudes examined here is a meaningful downstream consequence of the American drone campaign in Pakistan in and of itself. So far, then, our analysis thus suggests that misperceptions about US drone strikes as highly indiscriminate in nature contribute to their deep unpopularity in Pakistan and that this unpopularity in turn triggers surges of attitudinal backlash when drone strikes are carried out in the country.

3.3.3 Impact on Broader Political Behavior in Pakistan

The preceding two analyses have shown that false perceptions about collateral damage are an important source of opposition to US drone strikes in Pakistan, which in turn sparks alienation throughout the country (in particular, triggering anti-American, anti-government, and pro-militant sentiment). Following the links of this chain one step further leads to the question: do these shifts in attitudes facilitate any changes in Pakistani political behavior? Indeed, while the extant literature has shown that American drone strikes diminish terrorism *in the tribal areas of Pakistan* (Johnston and Sarbahi 2016, though see Gartzke and Walsh 2022 on it simply being displaced to other areas), there has been little work examining their impacts on other kinds of political behaviors throughout Pakistani society more broadly.

Specifically, one might think that American drone strikes could fuel two types of political behaviors in Pakistan at large. First, they might spark *political protest* in the country. Indeed, there has been substantial political protest in Pakistani society in recent years, including pro-democracy protests like the "Lawyers' Movement" (Rincker, Aslam, and Isani 2016), Islamist protests about cultural wedge issues like the country's controversial "Blasphemy law," protests over government services and other more pocketbook issues, and protests against US activities in Pakistan. In this context, the main targets of public ire have often been the sitting civilian government in Islamabad and its American patron in Washington. US drone strikes might trigger protests against either or both of these targets due to the public anger and alienation they provoke.

Second, drone strikes might facilitate *political violence* against US and US-linked targets in the country. While there are few easily targetable US assets in Pakistan for this precise reason, one way this could occur during the peak years of the campaign was the targeting of the country's NATO supply lines to Afghanistan. Due to its Arabian Sea coast and its proximity to Afghanistan, Pakistan was for years the main country through which NATO forces in Afghanistan were supplied – intelligence sources estimate that about 80–90 percent of NATO supplies went through Pakistan as late as 2009 (before they shifted increasingly toward Central Asia). There were two key NATO supply routes in the country, both of which started in Karachi: A "Northern Route" through Sindh, Punjab, KPK, and the Khyber Pass in FATA, and a "Southern Route" that went through Sindh and Balochistan (Stratfor 2009). These routes together crossed through all four major provinces of the country (as well as FATA) and thousands of miles of highways, offering substantial opportunities for ambush and attack. And, indeed, there were hundreds of attacks on NATO convoys in Pakistan in the 2000s and 2010s (PIPS N.D.), leading to the loss of a considerable amount of NATO supplies including fuel, technology, uniforms, weapons, and vehicles for NATO in Afghanistan. While the perpetrators of these attacks were often either militant organizations such as the Pakistani Taliban or criminal gangs, the US drone strikes – and the widespread popular backlash that was associated with them – likely gave these organizations greater political cover for their operations and made it politically costlier for the Pakistani authorities to intervene and stop them. Moreover, in some cases the convoys appear to have been ransacked in a more bottom-up fashion by large crowds of angry rioters in places like Peshawar rather than by militant or criminal organizations, suggesting a more direct pathway from mass public alienation to the disruption of NATO logistics.[21]

To test these expectations, several sources of violent event data in Pakistan are combined. The main source of data used in the analysis is the BFRS database of political violence in Pakistan, created by Ethan Bueno de Mesquita, C. Christine Fair, Rasul Bakhsh Rais, and Jacob N. Shapiro. The BFRS database includes data on 28,731 political violence events in Pakistan from 1988 to 2011. The events included in

---

[21] Islamist protesters, for example, blocked and harassed trucks along the Northern Route in 2013. See, for example, "Pakistan Protesters Block NATO Supply Route." *BBC*, November 26, 2013. Available at www.bbc.com/news/world-asia-25099473.

the database were coded from media reports in *Dawn*, the country's most widely-read and reputable English-language newspaper. Two types of events are utilized from this database. One is *violent political demonstrations* (VPDs). These are defined as "mobilization(s) of crowds in response to a political event that at some point becomes violent" – essentially political protests that turned violent. This is used as the main measure of Pakistani political protest activity. The other is *Pakistani military operations* against militant organizations. This allows us to look at both US and Pakistani military operations and their consequences in the analysis.

The BFRS data are combined with violent event data from two other sources. First, for data on *US drone strikes*, the aforementioned BIJ dataset is used. The BIJ is the most comprehensive, reliable, and transparent publicly available database on US drone warfare in the country. Second, for information on *NATO convoy attacks*, data are drawn from the Pak Institute for Peace Studies (PIPS), a Pakistani NGO and think tank that collects data on security issues in the country from Pakistani media reporting in outlets such as *Dawn* as well. PIPS contains extensive information on a variety of different types of events in Pakistan, including data on 481 attacks on NATO convoys in the country. While these data are only available since 2007, this is not particularly problematic since there were very few US drone strikes in Pakistan before then.

To explore the relationship between these different types of events, the analysis uses a type of model called a vector autoregression (VAR). A VAR model is a system of equations often used to explore how different actors, actions, or events react to one another over time. Each equation in the system has p lags of itself and of all the other variables. Unlike a conventional regression setup, the model thus allows us to account for the interdependencies between all of the different actions in the system. Additionally, it does not exclude explanatory variables based on the analyst's prior beliefs like the Structural Equation Model from which it emerged (Box-Steffensmeier et al. 2014). Instead, the VAR takes a more inclusive and agnostic approach to gauging empirical relationships. The VAR model estimated here predicts the levels of *each* of the four different types of violence – US drone strikes, Pakistani military operations, violent political demonstrations, and attacks on NATO shipping containers – at a given moment in time based on the previous levels of *all* of these types of violence, as well as a series of covariates. The control variables used are dummy variables for each year included in the analysis, as well as the weekly Islamic day of prayer (*Friday*) and the most significant holiday in the Islamic calendar (*Ramadan*).[22] The unit of observation is the day, and the analysis spans 2007 through 2011.

VAR modelers generally employ a couple of main empirical tools to evaluate their results. Chief among these is the Granger causality test (1969), which evaluates the "joint significance" of all of the lagged values of one explanatory variable on the dependent variable in a given equation. In this case, for example, one might want to test: Does the present level of political demonstrations depend on past levels of US drone strikes?

To estimate the model, tests for an appropriate lag length are conducted, with a maximum period of three weeks as a realistic window within which the types of violence should react to each other. Testing indicates that we should use twelve lags in our model to maximize the model's predictive power. Table 3.3 shows the Granger causality results for the twelve-lag model. The results reveal that the number of violent political demonstrations ($p = 0.03$) and attacks on NATO convoys ($p = 0.00$) both depend significantly on prior US drone strikes. Thus, there is a significantly higher chance of violent political protest and retaliatory anti-American violence in Pakistan after US drone attacks. Meanwhile, it is worth noting that neither of these forms of violence is significantly more likely in the wake of a *Pakistani* military operation ($p = 0.63$ and $p = 0.67$), which suggests that these findings are indeed picking up responses to distinctly *American* military behaviors.

Can these results be given a causal interpretation? One issue in the interpretation of VAR results as causal is the potential for forward-looking behavior. Is it possible, for example, that US drone attacks are launched *in anticipation of* more violent protests or NATO ambushes in Pakistan? This is extremely implausible for a couple of reasons. Recall that the drone campaign is conducted in FATA, while the violent protests and NATO shipping attacks are overwhelmingly occurring in the four primary Pakistani provinces of Punjab, Sindh, Khyber

---

[22] Existing research suggests that Muslim political actors might conceivably exercise more restraint during these times in their use of political violence (see, e.g., Reese, Ruby, and Pape 2017).

Table 3.3 *Granger causality tests for drone strikes and other violent events in Pakistan*

Outcome variable	Excluded variable	χ^2 value	p-value
US drone strikes	Pakistani operations	20.96	0.05
US drone strikes	Violent protests	11.14	0.52
US drone strikes	NATO shipping attacks	25.25	0.01
Pakistani operations	US drone strikes	6.46	0.89
Pakistani operations	Violent protests	11.85	0.46
Pakistani operations	NATO shipping attacks	12.14	0.43
Violent protests	US drone strikes	22.44	**0.03**
Violent protests	Pakistani operations	9.90	0.63
Violent protests	NATO shipping attacks	24.42	0.02
NATO shipping attacks	US drone strikes	50.71	**0.00**
NATO shipping attacks	Pakistani operations	9.36	0.67
NATO shipping attacks	NATO shipping attacks	10.74	0.55

Notes: The table shows the results of Granger causality tests on the extent to which each type of violence predicts one of the others. Statistically significant p-values mean that a given type of violence (the "excluded variable" in the table, labeled as such since it is excluded from the equation in the test) is useful in predicting one of the outcome variables. The two main p-values of interest are bolded.

Pakhtunkhwa, and Balochistan. As illuminated in this book, these areas are worlds apart. Launching drone attacks in FATA would do little to suppress protests and NATO shipping attacks throughout the rest of the country. Moreover, given that the strikes prompt public alienation, as evidenced in the "event study" conducted earlier, doing so would in fact be counterproductive on this front. In other words, the idea that US drone strikes in Pakistan are launched in expectation of protests or attacks against NATO shipping across the country simply does not make a lot of sense.[23]

Ultimately, these results suggest that the alienation triggered by US drone strikes has had some real behavioral consequences in Pakistan. Notably, there is evidence that drone strikes have triggered violent protest behavior and attacks on NATO supply lines in the country.

[23] It is also notable that protest is largely unrelated to terrorism in the BFRS dataset, either in FATA ($r = -0.03$) or more broadly ($r = 0.06$), suggesting that this is not a story of anticipation of terror attacks either.

In the case of the NATO supply lines, this is a clear strategic cost that weakened US-led forces in Afghanistan, cost the USA and its allies billions of dollars,[24] and enriched and empowered militant organizations like the TTP in Pakistan who either kept the goods for themselves or sold them on the black market. In the case of the protest, this may be a double-edged sword: While protest has had democratizing impacts in Pakistan in recent years, it can also have a destabilizing one – particularly if it is violent. Additionally, it is unclear whether the kinds of "nationalist protest" that react to US drone attacks are merely used as diversionary tools or bargaining chips by the Pakistani state (e.g., Weiss 2013) or if they actually fuel public demands for improved governance or accountability. Either way, the findings suggest that US drone attacks and their attendant backlash have had some important and potentially troubling effects on political behavior within Pakistani society.

3.4 Local Pakistani Perceptions of the Drone Campaign

Do the perceptions of local Pakistani civilians – the people actually living in the tribal areas – about the drone campaign follow those of their more distant counterparts? In a word, no. While the idea that drones were targeting and terrorizing civilians gained widespread currency in most of Pakistan, it did not find fertile ground in FATA itself. As explained by Farhat Taj, a leading scholar who hails from the tribal areas and has studied the issue deeply (2010):

> There is a deep abyss between the perceptions of the people of Waziristan, the most drone-hit area and the wider Pakistani society on the other side of the River Indus. For the latter, US drone attacks on Waziristan are a violation of Pakistani's [sic] sovereignty. Politicians, religious leaders, media analysts and anchorpersons express sensational clamour over the supposed "civilian casualties" in the drone attacks. I have been discussing the issue of drone attacks with hundreds of people of Waziristan. They see the US drone attacks as their liberators from the clutches of the terrorists into which, they say, their state has willfully thrown them.

---

[24] In addition to the cost of replacing the lost material, the Central Asian supply route was reportedly more expensive, costing an additional $100 million per month. See, for example, "Pakistanis March against NATO Supply Line." *Al Jazeera*, July 8, 2012. Available at www.aljazeera.com/news/2012/7/8/pakistanis-march-against-nato-supply-line.

Indeed, Taj wrote a spate of articles for media outlets and even scholarly journals along these lines, ultimately branding 2010 "The Year of the Drone Misinformation" in response to the proliferation of false and misleading claims about the strikes. Meanwhile, another scholar from the tribal regions named Muhammad Zubair published op-eds with a similar thrust based on his personal experiences and discussions with other locals. In one piece published in 2012,[25] Zubair for example stated that tribal residents know well that US drone strikes tend to be accurate and precise, contrasting them sharply with the heavy bombardment of their villages by the Pakistani army:

Quite contrary to the media's unverifiable reports, the IDPs of South Waziristan and people of North Waziristan tell a different story about such attacks, albeit in whispers due to fear. The IDPs claim that drones did not disrupt their social life or cause infrastructural damage or killed [sic] innocent civilians because of the precise and targeted nature of their attacks. An old woman in the IDPs camp in D I Khan told me last year, "Son, bang-bangane (local name for drones) go after the gunehgar (sinner) and not the innocent." They recalled the dreaded, heavy and indiscriminate bombing of civilian populations and infrastructure by the heavy artillery of the Pakistani army and PAF jets and compared it with the targeted and precise attacks on individual militants by drones.

While such claims by writers like Taj and Zubair initially gained fairly limited attention in the narrative wars about drones, subsequent developments have only added more evidence to them. For one thing, credible journalistic investigations like the one by the AP that was mentioned earlier in the chapter have shown that tribal residents recognize that most drone casualties are militants; other journalists with ties or access to FATA such as Pir Zubair Shah and Irfan Hussein have also found similar dynamics. More importantly, however, is the fact that multiple systematic academic research studies on people's perceptions of drones in the tribal areas have emerged in recent years. In particular, two Pakistani political scientists have gained access to tribal residents and separately conducted large-scale interview-based scholarly research studies on these issues. These represent the only two systematic, scholarly research

[25] Muhammad Zubair, "View: Drone Attacks – Myth and Reality." *The Daily Times*, June 4, 2012.

studies in which sizable samples of people from the tribal areas were interviewed about drones to date – and both provide clear confirmation that locals tend to perceive drones as discriminate.

One such study was conducted by the political scientist Aqil Shah. Shah (2018) interviewed a diverse convenience sample of 167 tribal residents who were displaced from Waziristan during a Pakistani army operation about their perceptions of the US drone campaign, publishing his results in the prominent political science journal *International Security*. Shah found that most of his sample said that drones did not meaningfully radicalize FATA residents and that they dreaded the Pakistani army's brutal and heavy-handed military attacks much more than the American drone strikes. He also found that these views cut across people of different ideological and political persuasions. One local business owner summed up the prevailing view rather poignantly by exclaiming (58): "Drones did not destroy our property. Drones did not displace us. Drones did not humiliate us. The Pakistani Army did. If anything, our youth should be motivated to pick up arms against them Punjabi soldiers."

The other major academic study to interview large numbers of civilians from FATA about drones was conducted even more recently by a political scientist named Neha Ansari, reaching remarkably similar conclusions. Ansari interviewed a diverse convenience sample of 116 tribal residents. She found that US drone strikes were generally perceived as "precise and popular" in the tribal areas, contrary to her expectations when she began the project. Her interviewees were mostly of the belief that "drones had done what local militias and even Pakistani military operations could not do: Kill the bad guys, with little-to-no collateral damage" (Ansari 2022). And she too found that these perceptions cut across individuals of very different political and ideological orientations within the tribal areas. Ansari's work on this issue is part of a wider dissertation project, though some of her findings have already been published in the leading national security blog *War on the Rocks*.

In sum, the evidence is clear that local civilians in the tribal areas by and large do not share the factual misperceptions about the nature of the US drone campaign that are prevalent elsewhere in Pakistan. Rather, in line with the book's thesis that seeing is disbelieving in war, those who live with drone strikes as a regular feature of life in their villages and communities hold quite accurate beliefs about their conduct and shun falsehoods about their targeting or results.[26] Circling back to the competing perspectives on civilian populations and their behavior in conflict that we discussed in Chapters 1 and 2 (e.g., Kalyvas 2006, Lyall, Blair and Imai 2013), this suggests that Pakistanis outside of FATA fit more of an "identitarian" model in their thinking about the drone campaign – embracing misinformation about the strikes that aligns with their preexisting political orientations – while those within the tribal regions are thinking about them in ways much more consistent with a "rationalist" model of civilian populations in war.

3.5 Conclusion

This chapter examined factual misperceptions about the nature of the US drone campaign in Pakistan. The first two parts of the chapter showed that there is a pervasive misperception about the drone campaign throughout much of Pakistani society, one driven by mis and disinformation: While the strikes are in actuality very targeted and selective, they are widely seen as indiscriminate among nonlocal Pakistanis. The third part of the chapter investigated the political impacts of these misperceptions. Specifically, it first demonstrated that civilian casualty concerns are one of if not the most important ingredients in the strikes' broad unpopularity across Pakistan. Then, it showed that this unpopularity is consequential – as American drone strikes regularly stoke anti-American, anti-incumbent, and pro-militant sentiment in Pakistani society, and foster violent demonstrations and attacks against NATO shipping that are encouraged by this backlash. The final section of the chapter showed that the local population that lives in the tribal areas generally does not share these misperceptions and holds much more accurate beliefs about the campaign, supporting the book's central argument that exposure and proximity constrain factual beliefs in war.

---

[26] Additionally, it is telling that, while the American drones are referred to as *bangana* (a term for an annoying insect) in the tribal regions, they are also often called *ababil* (the holy swallows that defended the Ka'ba) and *spinay farishtay* (white angels) by tribal residents as well. See, for example, Mohammad Taqi, "Shooting Down Drones with Academic Guns?" *The Daily Times*, 4 October 2012.

4 | *Proximity to the Fighting and the Puncturing of Factual Bias in Iraq*

I was in Chechnya once, in a time of peace, and an old man looked at me and said, have you ever been where they are bombing from planes? And I said, yes. He said, then you know. That was all we said; it was everything.
– War Reporter Megan K. Stack (2010: 224)

This chapter investigates the dynamics of factual misinformation and misperception in Iraq during the US-led international Coalition's air campaign against ISIL beginning in the summer of 2014. As discussed later, false claims were widespread about the Coalition's behavior during the campaign, including its targeting of local militias and its alleged collusion with ISIL. These narratives had the potential to strain the already uneasy coexistence of Iraqi society with the anti-ISIL Coalition, which played a critical part in rolling back ISIL's insurgency.

To explore these issues, this chapter examines a unique nationwide opinion survey of 3,500 Iraqis conducted in 2016. Importantly, the survey contains questions on Iraqis' factual perceptions of the campaign and their exposure to the fighting. Moreover, the survey is paired with geo-located data on Coalition airstrikes from the NGO *Airwars* in order to measure people's distance from the strikes, allowing for analysis of how people's factual beliefs shift with their observed proximity to events. Overall, the results support the book's key claims about the impact of exposure on people's beliefs in conflict: Both self-reported experience in the targeted areas and observed proximity to Coalition airstrikes significantly *diminish* factual misperceptions about the nature of the anti-ISIL campaign, including false beliefs about its targeting and effects.[1]

---

[1] This chapter draws significantly on research by Silverman, Kaltenthaler, and Dagher (2021). Immense thanks are due to my collaborators Karl Kaltenthaler and Munqith Dagher who have graciously encouraged me to use it in this book.

4.1 The Context of Coalition Airstrikes in Contemporary Iraq

In August 2014, the USA began carrying out an aerial campaign against ISIL in order to impede the organization's impressive territorial advance across northern Iraq that summer and protect besieged communities in the area. Soon, leaders in Washington were assembling a growing Coalition of Western and Arab states to take offensive military action against the group. This was the start of a substantial international bombing campaign against ISIL in Iraq – as of October 31, 2016 (about the time of our survey), the US-led Coalition had conducted 10,291 airstrikes against ISIL targets in Iraq, with 6,979 by the USA and 3,312 by allied nations (Airwars 2017). In addition to conducting thousands of airstrikes against ISIL, the Coalition also collected a significant amount of aerial intelligence and surveillance data, trained many thousands of Iraqi soldiers, and supported Iraqi military operations against the organization both strategically and tactically, with US special operations forces embedded with Iraqi units. This support from the Coalition was vitally important in turning the tide of battle in Iraq against ISIL.

Critically, while there were a number of mistakes, overall the Coalition's air campaign was highly discriminate in nature – especially during the period under analysis. Indeed, it is crucial to clarify that the violence of interest is the air war during the second term of US President Barack Obama up through the fall of 2016, as the survey used was conducted in September and October 2016 and the focus is on Iraqi beliefs about the campaign up through that point in time. Thus, while there was a significant spike in the degree of collateral damage in 2017 as President Donald Trump relaxed Obama-era targeting rules,[2] the timing of the survey enables us to avoid the complications that would arise in characterizing any later conduct. On the contrary, the Obama-era campaign was criticized by some in US and Iraqi military circles at the time for its high degree of restraint and strict rules to minimize civilian casualties. According to disgruntled US pilots, well-known ISIL structures were left standing due to concerns about harming human shields, drones were forced to hover over targets for hours until they had "clean shots," and about three-quarters

---

[2] See, for example, Samuel Oakford, "Coalition Civilian Casualty Claims Double under Donald Trump." *Airwars*, July 17, 2017. Available at https://airwars .org/news/trumps-air-war-kills-12-civilians-per-day/.

of aerial missions saw no weapons released at all due to collateral damage concerns.[3] In brief, some wished that the USA were *less* committed to such exceptional caution and precision pre-2016.

This picture is corroborated by the available quantitative evidence. Data from *Airwars* – a UK-based NGO that compiles the most comprehensive and transparent database of the airstrikes – shows that even when including contested events, the 10,291 strikes to this point had killed an estimated 1,396 Iraqi civilians. This means that, when the survey was fielded, there was a ratio of around one civilian casualty for every 7.4 Coalition airstrikes. Given that the campaign has killed tens of thousands of ISIL fighters in Iraq and Syria, this implies a very high combatant-to-civilian casualty ratio.[4] For the sake of comparison, consider that in the US drone campaign in Pakistan – which, despite its controversial nature, is recognized by scholars as a very discriminate campaign (Taj 2010, Plaw and Fricker 2012, Fair, Kaltenthaler, and Miller 2016, Silverman 2019) – there is roughly one civilian killed for every 1.6 strikes according to data from the Bureau of Investigative Journalism (BIJ 2017). Meanwhile, the same source shows that there has been one civilian death for every 1.4 US drone strikes in Yemen and every 2.5 US airstrikes in Somalia – in other words, other targeted killing programs have killed civilians much more frequently than the campaign in question. In sum, a close look shows that the pre-Trump Coalition airstrikes against ISIL in Iraq were not only effective in helping to defeat it on the battlefield in Iraq but also quite targeted and discriminate in nature.

Yet, unsurprisingly given our discussion of information as a "weapon" in war, there were considerable efforts to spread rumors

---

[3] See Eric Schmitt, "U.S. Caution in Strikes Gives ISIS an Edge, Many Iraqis Say." *New York Times*, May 26, 2015.

[4] Reliable estimates of the number of ISIS militants killed during the campaign are scarce, as militant casualties are not tracked by monitoring organizations like *Airwars*. Yet, top Coalition officials estimated that they had eliminated 45,000 ISIS militants in Iraq and Syria by August 2016, shortly before the survey. Even if we conservatively assume that just one-third of these were in Iraq (with two-thirds in Syria), and that this figure is twice as high as it should be, it would still imply a very high militant-to-civilian casualty ratio of over 5:1 using the Airwars civilian casualty data. See Terry Moon Cronk. "OIR Campaign Reached Turning Point in Ramadi, Commander Says." *DOD News*, August 10, 2016. Available at www.defense.gov/Explore/News/Article/Article/910747/oir-campaign-reached-turning-point-in-ramadicommander-says/.

and misinformation about the campaign. To begin with, ISIL itself was one of the key sources of such propaganda. ISIL's narrative about the campaign largely focused on claiming that it was (1) ineffective, with ISIL continuing to advance despite the strikes and (2) indiscriminate, with the Coalition targeting or at least harming primarily innocent civilians. This information was disseminated both virtually through ISIL's *Amaq* news agency, *Dabiq* online magazine, and affiliated Twitter accounts, and in more traditional forms in its own territory in Iraq (and Syria) through the group's radio channel, dedicated propaganda centers, and other brick-and-mortar tactics.[5] To select just one example, the fourth issue of *Dabiq* magazine – released on October 11, 2014 – was titled "The Failed Crusade" and dedicated largely to the "Crusader airstrikes" and their ineffective and indiscriminate results, emphasizing their inability to prevent ISIL's advances and their slaughter of innocent Muslims in both Iraq and Syria (ISIL 2014). Claims like these were often amplified via ISIL's legions of affiliated Twitter accounts and seeped into traditional media in Iraq and beyond.

Another key source of propaganda about the Coalition campaign was the *Hashd al-Sha'abi* or Popular Mobilization Forces (PMF). The PMF is a group of mostly Shi'a Arab militias in Iraq that coalesced in 2014 to fight ISIL with Iranian support (though it has now been at least nominally incorporated into the Iraqi government). While the PMF played a key role in the fight against ISIL in Iraq, it always existed in an uneasy alliance with the Coalition due to concerns about its abuse of Sunni Arab civilians and its anti-American orientation, and close ties to Iran. For these reasons, despite its official cooperation with the Coalition in the Obama era, the PMF emerged as a major source of misinformation about the campaign. This misinformation centered around several major themes. First, it stressed how the Coalition's airstrikes were weak and ineffectual, positioning itself as the real force liberating Iraqi society from ISIL's grasp (Garrison 2017). Second, it questioned the Coalition's goals and increasingly suggested that it was actively helping ISIL on the battlefield, even posting photos of Western helicopters which it alleged

---

[5] See, for example, "Inside the Propaganda War for Mosul." *Journal of Middle Eastern Politics and Policy*, February 5, 2017. Available at http://jmepp .hkspublications.org/2017/02/05/mosul-propaganda-war/.

were transporting ISIL leaders from site to site.[6] Third, it painted the
Coalition as actively targeting the Shiʻa Arab militias themselves, seiz-
ing on rare "friendly fire" incidents from erroneous airstrikes (and
fabricating others) in order to push this theme (Garrison 2017). Like
ISIL, the PMF used a variety of methods to advance this misinformation, most notably its official *al-hashed.net* site and *Team Media
War* Twitter account (which had one million followers by the end of
2016). In addition, its voice is often amplified by Iranian state news
as well as other pro-Iranian outlets within Iraq.

Overall, there was thus a wealth of propaganda and misinformation
from various sources in Iraq about the Coalition's campaign against
ISIL, suggesting that it was both (1) ineffective and even counterproductive against the organization and (2) inaccurate and indiscriminate
in nature. While these claims often originated from combatants in the
conflict such as ISIL and the PMF (as well as Iran and Russia), they frequently influenced and infiltrated more traditional forms of media coverage in the country. For instance, analysts have noted that infographics
created by combatants such as ISIL or the PMF showing information
from the battlefield "can prove particularly effective in shaping traditional media coverage: Because accurate casualty figures are notoriously
difficult to obtain, the government faces continual pressure to refute
[such] claims."[7] This is critical for the analysis because traditional
media outlets such as *Al-Iraqiyya* state television continue to be among
the most significant in the Iraqi media landscape (Amos 2010). In sum,
then, the Iraqi population was exposed to a considerable amount of
propaganda, misinformation, and fake news surrounding the dynamics
and consequences of the Coalition's behavior in the dispute.

4.2 Hypotheses on Factual Bias and Its Mitigation

The critical question then becomes: who believed this misinformation
and who did not? As discussed in Chapter 2 and elsewhere throughout the book, there are a couple of traditional factors that we should

[6] Ahmad Majidyar, "Iran-Supported Militia Groups Intensify Anti-U.S.
Propaganda." *Middle East Institute*, May 16, 2017. Available at www.mei.edu/
publications/iran-supported-militia-groups-intensify-anti-us-propaganda-iraq.
[7] "Inside the Propaganda War for Mosul." *Journal of Middle Eastern Politics
and Policy*, February 5, 2017. Available at http://jmepp.hkspublications
.org/2017/02/05/mosulpropaganda-war/.

expect to fuel factual biases and openness to misinformation in war. One of these is civilians' prior orientations toward the combatants – especially the perpetrator of violence. This is the idea of directional reasoning discussed earlier: Iraqis who hold more unfavorable views of the Coalition will be more likely to embrace negative stories about its performance or behavior, as these "fit" more with their preexisting worldviews. Another is people's "information diets" and exposure to different information channels about the fighting. Civilians relying on sources that are more critical of the Coalition – and thus more likely to emphasize its excesses and setbacks instead of its restraint and its successes – should be more likely to believe (negative) misinformation about the campaign as well.

Yet the main hypotheses of interest here center around the *mitigation of bias*. In particular, the book's central argument is that motivational and informational biases should be disciplined by people's exposure and proximity to relevant events. Thus, one should see that local Iraqis who live under or near the airstrikes are less likely to accept misinformation about them than their nonlocal counterparts. As elaborated in the theory chapter (Chapter 2), this is both because such people can actually see the campaign's dynamics (*informational advantage*) and because they have a powerful motive to understand them (*accuracy motive*). To illustrate this point, consider the experiences of civilians living in a place like Tikrit, which is a key Iraqi town that was conquered by ISIL in June 2014 and then liberated in March 2015 prior to the survey. Tikritis could see which buildings and neighborhoods were targeted by anti-ISIL airstrikes and which ones were not during the campaign. They also had a clear motive to pay attention to this information because they needed to know how exactly to stay safe and which areas to avoid most during the fighting. Likewise, they were likely to know whether the Coalition attacks made ISIL run and hide, change its routines, or retreat. This information, too, was critical for their survival and their decision-making about whether to stay in place, flee, or even resist ISIL as the Coalition and its allies approached in 2015.

In addition, another empirical implication of the argument is that one should see people's exposure and proximity to the strikes shape the impact of other kinds of factors. In particular, Iraqis who have more direct exposure to the violence should be less influenced by their prior orientations and information sources in the conflict. Rather, such civilians should not only hold more accurate beliefs but also be willing to *update* them accurately regardless of their prior views or information diets in the dispute. In other words, the impact of these factors will be diminished or even disappear among more proximate civilians. In both the accuracy of people's beliefs and the extent to which they are anchoring on their broader preexisting worldviews, then, the thinking of people closer to the strikes should thus better fit a rationalist model of civilian populations in war, while the thinking of people further from the fighting should follow more of an identitarian framework (e.g., Kalyvas 2006, Lyall, Blair, and Imai 2013).

4.3 Data and Methods

In order to examine these hypotheses, data are used from a unique nationally representative survey of Iraq administered by the Iraqi research firm Independent Institute and Administration Civil Society Studies (IIACSS) in September and October 2016. The survey was conducted with multistage stratified probability sampling of the entire adult (18+) population of the country, excluding territory under direct ISIL control (chiefly Mosul). The survey included urban and rural areas throughout the country; the ultimate sampling units were blocks in the urban areas and villages in rural ones. The interviews were carried out face-to-face by a mixed-gender team of experienced Iraqi survey enumerators, with women interviewing women and men interviewing men. Overall, the survey includes 3,500 Iraqi respondents from the covered territory. Figure A4.1 in the Appendix presents a map of the survey responses as well as Coalition airstrikes and ISIL terrorist attacks across the country.

The survey included extensive safeguards to maintain the safety of all respondents as well as enumerators. No interviews from areas under ISIL control or active contestation were collected. After the interviews were done, the survey was weighted using demographic information from 1997 to 2010 enumeration of all households in Iraq supplemented with 2015 projections from the Iraqi Central Organization of Statistics (COSIT). To probe for falsification of survey responses, the program "Percentmatch" was used, revealing no evidence that any fabrication of data occurred. Analysis of these data was done with IRB approval.[8]

---

[8] Specifically, the survey was initially developed and fielded by Munqith Dagher of the Iraqi polling firm IIACSS in 2016 for use by the US government. Data

Demographically, the sample is 54.2 percent male, with about half of the respondents under the age of 35 and over half never reaching secondary school. The ethnic and sectarian distribution of the sample is 12.9 percent Kurd, 39.0 percent Sunni Arab, and 45.4 percent Shi'a Arab. Overall, these demographics are similar to other high-quality surveys in Iraq, including the Arab Barometer. The key demographic characteristics of the sample are compared with the second and third waves of the Arab Barometer – conducted in Iraq in 2011 and 2013 respectively – as well as recent Iraqi COSIT projections in more detail in Table A4.1 in the Appendix.

Substantively, the survey contained a number of different batteries of questions, with major modules about citizens' perceptions of the primary challenges that face Iraq, their levels of support for the political actors in the country, their means of acquiring political information, their views of sectarian and ethnic tensions among Iraqis, and their attitudes and beliefs about the ongoing violent conflict with ISIL. A wealth of demographic information was also collected about each individual, including their socioeconomic profile, experiences in the war, and ethnic and sectarian affiliation. In this sense, the survey provides a rich source of information about Iraqi wartime attitudes, beliefs, and experiences with which to explore our hypotheses.

For the dependent variables, two items are used that measure Iraqis' factual misperceptions about the Coalition campaign. In particular, Iraqis were asked about their degree of agreement with the following claims on a Likert scale: (1) *Coalition airstrikes mainly target PMF forces* and (2) *Coalition airstrikes mainly help ISIL.* The scales for both questions ran from "disagree strongly" to "disagree somewhat" to "neither agree nor disagree" to "agree somewhat" to "agree strongly."[9] Overall, an average of 55.6 percent of respondents agreed

collection followed ethical best practices for international survey research and was done with the same standards and respondent protections as other IIACSS projects such as the Arab Barometer and the World Values Survey waves in Iraq. Subsequent to the data collection, Munqith Dagher asked for permission to use the data for academic research purposes from the US government and that permission was granted. The authors of this study then requested and obtained university IRB approval to analyze the data (which are fully non-identifiable) in 2017 in order to investigate Iraqi beliefs and attitudes about the conflict.

[9] The neutral response was not explicitly offered but marked if respondents expressed ambivalence about the claim.

to some extent (somewhat or strongly) with these claims, providing substantial variation in the outcomes to be explained.

As alluded to earlier, both of these claims are empirically false. In the first case, the US-led Coalition's anti-ISIL airstrikes under President Obama did not "mainly target" the PMF; they targeted ISIL. While the Coalition did on (extremely rare) occasion hit PMF troops, there was no secret American policy of bombing the Shiʿa Arab-led militias in the country at that time. In fact, data from the strike-tracking NGO Airwars help corroborate this point, given that they contained only fifty-five "friendly fire" claims out of more than 10,000 airstrikes at the time of the survey. Setting aside the fact that these were undoubtedly almost all unintentional incidents, and many did not even hit the PMF but other groups, claiming that the international anti-ISIL campaign in 2016 "mainly targeted" the PMF and not ISIL was thus clearly untrue.[10]

Turning to the second claim, the strikes did not "mainly help" ISIL. In contrast, they were profoundly and clearly damaging to the organization, destroying much of its financial and resource base, severely disrupting its operational activities, killing thousands of its fighters, and ultimately helping "roll back" almost all of its territorial gains in the country since 2014 (Jones et al. 2017).[11] Despite this, a skeptical reader might wonder if – although it was effective against ISIL on the battlefield – the Coalition campaign could still be counterproductive if it generated extensive resentment among Iraqis and boosted support for the group. This idea, however, clashes sharply with observed reality on the ground. In fact, ISIL has been highly unpopular in Iraq since the start of the campaign, with no discernible rise in support since then. The level of Iraqi sympathy for the group was around 2.0 percent in fall 2014, 0.5 percent in fall 2015, and 1.5 percent in the

---

[10] Despite its outlandish nature, this idea builds on loud allegations by the PMF and other pro-Iranian elements in the country that these rare friendly fire events were intentional, as well as the strong undercurrents of anti-Americanism within Iraqi society, making it appealing to many Iraqis. See, for example, Arraf (2016).

[11] This idea actually taps into conspiracy theories promoted by some in the country that the Coalition is "in cahoots" with ISIL and is operationally assisting it on the battlefield; claims that have included photos of US helicopters flying over Iraq on Twitter with red circles showing them allegedly "caught" transporting ISIL leaders and allowing them to escape the country's grasp.

survey in fall 2016.[12] In sum, the idea that the international anti-ISIL campaign was making the group popular or sympathetic in Iraq is belied by the available evidence.

For the primary independent variables in the analysis, a variety of different items are used. Two distinct measures capture people's exposure and proximity to the strikes. The first is a pair of questions about the degree to which they have lived in ISIL-ruled territory, which is where almost all the Coalition's anti-ISIL airstrikes actually occurred. Two related items were asked about this. First, respondents were simply asked whether they lived in an area while it was under the control of ISIL. 21.3 percent of the sample ($N = 746$) reports living under ISIL's territorial control at some point. Reassuringly, this is very similar to the 19 percent of Iraq's population that ISIL is estimated to have ruled over in Iraq when it was at its territorial peak in mid-2014 (Jones et al. 2017). Those who said yes to the first question were then asked how long they had lived under ISIL's rule, with a five-point scale ranging from "less than one month" to "more than a year." In the base models, these two items are combined into a single ordinal measure of experience in targeted areas. Second, results are also presented using another, observational measure of exposure – explained more fully later in the chapter – based on respondents' distance from the nearest anti-ISIL airstrike as recorded by Airwars' airstrike-tracking database.

Motivated biases surrounding the Coalition and its campaign are measured in two ways. The first is by using questions about respondents' attitudes toward some of the main combatants in the conflict, in particular the USA and the PMF. The question about the USA is a four-point measure of Iraqis' confidence in the United States' ability to responsibly deal with problems in the region. Given that the USA was the primary force behind the Coalition's campaign, the expectation is that people with little confidence in the USA will want to believe the negative factual misperceptions about the strikes. Meanwhile, the question about the PMF is a three-point measure of Iraqi support for its goals and activities. Given that the PMF is a key rival of the

---

[12] Moreover, more indirect items in the survey such as questions asking Iraqis to estimate the amount of sympathy for ISIL countrywide provide roughly similar results, with a median estimate of 3 percent. Results from IIACSS surveys in Iraq from 2014 to 2016. Approval for 2014 and 2015 surveys obtained along with 2016 survey, via process described in footnote 13.

US-led Coalition in Iraq and a key source of opposition and suspicion toward it, the expectation is that Iraqis who support the PMF will be motivated to accept these misperceptions. Second, Iraqis' subnational group identities – in particular whether they are Shiʿa Arab, Sunni Arab, or Kurd – are used as another way to tap into motivated biases toward the campaign. In today's Iraq, broadly speaking, Shiʿa Arabs tend to hold more negative orientations toward the USA because it has served as a check on Shiʿa and Iranian influence in the country, while Sunni Arabs and Kurds tend to harbor less hostile orientations toward the USA for the same reason (Kose, Ozcan, and Karakoc 2016). Given these realities, one would expect Shiʿa Arabs to generally be more likely to embrace the misperceptions of interest, and Sunni Arabs and Kurds to generally be less likely to do so.[13]

To tap into informational biases around the campaign, several questions are used on Iraqis' "information diets" and how heavily they rely on different Iraqi media sources in the dispute. The Iraqi media environment is sharply polarized along sectarian and other political lines (Amos 2010), with different Iraqi media channels varying widely in their representation of the counterinsurgency against ISIL among other issues.[14] The analysis focuses on individuals' degree of exposure to three key outlets with different sectarian leanings: *Al-Iraqiyya TV*, which is the country's state television channel and is quite influential but viewed as largely pro-government and pro-Shiʿa in orientation, *Al-Sharqiyya TV*, a private satellite channel that is more Sunni-friendly and often quite critical of the government, and *Rudaw TV*, a Kurdish outlet that is closely linked to the ruling Barzani family in Iraqi Kurdistan. Due to these outlets' respective political alignments, one can expect reliance on *Al-Iraqiyya* to be linked with greater Iraqi belief in the misperceptions and reliance on *al-Sharqiyya* and *Rudaw* to be associated with the opposite.

---

[13] The models omit the Kurdish variable so that our sectarian dummies can be easily interpreted against a clear baseline category (otherwise the baseline would be Iraqis not affiliated with any of the main sects, a small segment of the data). Kurds and other small minorities can thus be thought of as the primary baseline group.

[14] For instance, pro-Sunni sources like *Al-Baghdadiyya TV* have branded ISIL as "tribal revolutionaries," while pro-Shiʿa sources like *Al-Iraqiyya TV* have employed terms like "terrorists" or "terrorist gangs." See Salih, Mohammed. "Iraqi Media Divided in Coverage of IS Conflict." *Al-Monitor*, September 4, 2014.

Finally, several covariates are added to the models to account for their potential influence on the misperceptions. To begin with, the models include Iraqis' age, gender, education, income, and urban vs. rural status. These represent important socioeconomic factors that have been linked to conspiracist beliefs and misperceptions in the region and beyond (Gentzkow and Shapiro 2004). They also include a binary indicator of internally displaced person (IDP) status, as being displaced can strongly impact how people think about armed conflicts (e.g., Bohnet, Cottier, and Hug 2018), and yet it is conceptually distinct from actual proximity and exposure to the fighting.[15] The models here are estimated with linear regression,[16] with the dependent variables coded from 0 to 4 so that higher values indicate greater support for each false claim.

It is worth pausing here to underscore that the primary goal of this chapter is to investigate the relationship between people's actual exposure and proximity to events and their susceptibility to lies and misinformation about them. Any observed association between either the informational (reliance on different news channels) or the motivational (attitudes toward different combatants or sub-national group identities) bias measures and the factual misperceptions in question should not be interpreted in a unidirectional causal manner. It is likely that just as the relevant misperceptions are attractive to people with these biases, they may reinforce the biases as well. Observed linkages between these variables should therefore just be viewed as suggestive, reinforcing qualitative and quantitative evidence from elsewhere in the book as well as from the literature – which has already indicated that people's preexisting worldviews and information channels in conflict settings shape their beliefs about what is happening within them (e.g., Driscoll and Maliniak 2016, Greenhill

---

[15] While one might initially think IDP status is a good indicator of local violence exposure, in fact, IDPs in war zones often flee for social, economic, or psychological reasons rather than actual violence exposure (Engel and Ibañez 2007). Moreover, even if they are fleeing violence here, it may be other types of violence besides Coalition's airstrikes. Thus, IDP status is actually a poor measure of exposure to the strikes. Yet because IDPs often have especially strong grievances in disputes, it is an important covariate to account for in the models.

[16] I also include descriptive statistics for all variables used in the analysis as well as the full wording for all attitudinal items used from the survey in the Appendix (Tables A4.2–4.3).

and Oppenheim 2017, Lucas in press). The key question of interest here is the extent to which there is evidence of the mitigation of bias due to being in or near the "action."

4.4 Empirical Results: The Impact of Proximity and Exposure in Iraq

Table 4.1 shows the base results. Since the main interest here is the influence of exposure and proximity to the campaign, the first two columns present naïve models that include this alone, while the subsequent columns add the additional sets of independent variables described earlier in order to control for other key factors linked to the misperceptions.

As can be seen, the models show that exposure has the expected effect – that is, Iraqis who have lived in the areas actually targeted by the Coalition's airstrikes are significantly less likely to believe disinformation that they are attacking their allies or assisting their enemies than those who have not. These findings hold in the naïve exposure-only models (Columns 1–2), and after adding a richer set of motivational (Columns 3–4) and informational (Columns 5–6) factors. While many of these other variables are strongly linked with the misperceptions as well, the significant impact of exposure persists across the board. In other words, even after accounting for these key predictors of factual bias, there is evidence that those who have faced the most risk of harm from the airstrikes are less likely to hold false beliefs about them. This provides support for the book's main argument and the idea that seeing is disbelieving in conflict.

Meanwhile, most of the other factors in the model behave as expected. Being a Shi'a Arab is associated with significantly more belief in both misperceptions about the campaign, as is being a Sunni Arab – although more modestly and inconsistently.[17] This reflects the growing animosity toward the USA among Shi'a Arabs in recent years, while Sunni Arab views toward the USA have softened

---

[17] Specifically, Sunni Arab identification only robustly boosts belief in the misperception about the Coalition aiding ISIL and not the one about it targeting the PMF. This makes sense given that the Iranian-supported PMF principally appeals to Shi'a Arabs; most Sunnis have little need for a narrative with the PMF as the central victim.

Table 4.1 *Impact of exposure on Iraqi misperceptions about coalition airstrikes*

	Airstrikes Target PMF	Airstrikes Help ISIL	Airstrikes Target PMF	Airstrikes Help ISIL	Airstrikes Target PMF	Airstrikes Help ISIL
Exposure						
Time in	-0.27***	-0.24***	-0.13***	-0.13***	-0.12***	-0.13***
targeted areas	(0.02)	(0.02)	(0.02)	(0.02)	(0.03)	(0.03)
Orientations						
Shi'a Arab			0.81***	0.93***	0.65***	0.77***
			(0.10)	(0.10)	(0.12)	(0.12)
Sunni Arab			0.20*	0.43***	0.09	0.25*
			(0.09)	(0.09)	(0.11)	(0.11)
Confidence in USA			-0.40***	-0.33***	-0.31***	-0.24***
			(0.02)	(0.02)	(0.03)	(0.03)
Support for PMF			0.29***	0.30***	0.18***	0.24***
			(0.04)	(0.04)	(0.05)	(0.05)
Information						
Iraqiyya TV					0.12***	0.05
					(0.03)	(0.03)
Sharqiyya TV					-0.19***	-0.12***
					(0.03)	(0.03)
Rudaw TV					-0.28***	-0.29***
					(0.04)	(0.04)
Constant	2.62***	2.43***	1.78***	1.36***	2.21***	1.85***
	(0.12)	(0.12)	(0.14)	(0.13)	(0.16)	(0.16)
Observations	2,990	2,992	2,934	2,934	2,262	2,262
R-squared	0.05	0.04	0.28	0.26	0.33	0.31

Notes: Results from linear regressions. Demographics (age, gender, education, income, urbanity, IDP status) are not shown. Standard errors in parentheses.
***$p < 0.001$, **$p < 0.01$, *$p < 0.05$.

substantially (though not to the level of Kurds and smaller minority groups in Iraq, which is the omitted baseline category for the variable). In addition, confidence in the USA is associated with significantly lower levels of belief in both misperceptions, while support for the PMF is linked with significantly higher levels. These effects support expectations about civilians' beliefs aligning with their broader identities and loyalties in the dispute.

The informational factors largely move in expected directions as well. Indeed, reliance on the generally pro-Shi'a *al-Iraqiyya TV* predicts greater belief in the "Targets PMF" misperception, which makes sense given the PMF's Shi'a appeal and Iranian backing. In contrast, reliance on the Sunni-friendly *al-Sharqiyya TV* and especially the Kurdish-oriented *Rudaw TV* predicts less belief in both misperceptions. These effects align with the general orientations of the different channels, yielding evidence that is consistent with our informational expectations. While one should exercise caution in ascribing causality to associations between people's media habits and factual beliefs, they are suggestive of the role of divergent sources of information in the dispute.

Finally, some of the effects of the demographic variables are also noteworthy. In particular, men and IDPs are significantly more likely to believe both misperceptions, while wealthier Iraqis are significantly less likely to do so. I did not have clear directional expectations about the effects of these variables a priori, although it is worth noting that the income effect aligns with some other existing studies on factual misperceptions and conspiratorial beliefs that highlight the role of social class in driving false beliefs (Hogg et al. 2017), while the IDP effect suggests that grievances due to conflict-induced displacement may fuel false perceptions in war. Future research may wish to follow up on these results, though they may well be somewhat contextual in nature.

To gauge the substantive significance of the main finding more clearly, the misperceptions are transformed into binary variables so that they represent simply the percentage of respondents who believe in each claim. The models from Table 4.1 (Columns 5–6) are then reestimated with these new dichotomized variables as the outcomes.[18] Figure 4.1 shows the results of this exercise, with predicted levels of belief in each misperception plotted across the amount of time respondents lived in the targeted areas. The figure reveals that exposure to the relevant events has considerable influence on the misperceptions in substantive terms. Specifically, it shows that roughly

---

[18] I use logistic rather than linear regression here given the dichotomous nature of the recorded dependent variable.

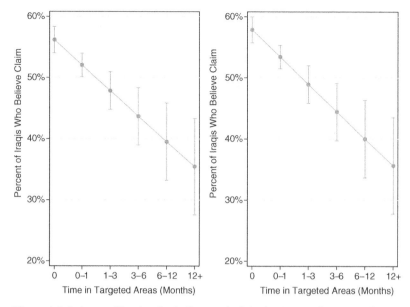

Figure 4.1 Percent of Iraqis who believe each claim by time in the targeted areas

55 percent of respondents with no personal experience living in the targeted areas believe each of the factual misperceptions, while the percentage of those who spent more than a year in the targeted areas that embrace the falsehoods is only about 35. People's exposure to the relevant events thus tracks with a substantial decline in their susceptibility to false perceptions of them.

To investigate the expectations laid out in the chapter even more thoroughly, however, one can look at several different slices or "cuts" of the data. As noted earlier, if the theory is correct, it should be observed not only that (1) Iraqis who are more exposed to the strikes hold more accurate factual beliefs about them, but also (2) that their beliefs are less shaped by their broader political orientations and information channels in the conflict, since they are more likely to accurately update their understandings of what is going on regardless of these other major influences.

One way to evaluate this is to use interaction terms that test whether some of the principal sources of directional bias are moderated by personal exposure. In this vein, Figure 4.2 shows how the effects of (1) confidence in the USA and (2) support for the PMF vary with

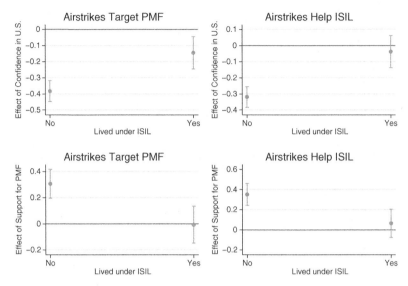

Figure 4.2 Impact of Pro-USA and Pro-PMF views on Iraqi misperceptions by exposure

experience under ISIL rule. Starting with pro-American attitudes (the top two panels), it is apparent that confidence in the USA significantly reduces both misperceptions among the unexposed population, but among more proximate respondents this effect disappears or is at least sharply diminished. Turning toward pro-PMF views (the bottom two panels), the same pattern emerges: support for the PMF markedly increases both misperceptions about the airstrikes among unexposed Iraqis, but these effects fade away among those who have lived in the targeted areas. This helps drive home the claim about the power of personal exposure, showing that, while factual beliefs in war are generally biased in the direction of civilians' preexisting orientations and worldviews in the conflict, such biases can be "disciplined" and diminished by exposure to the events in question.[19]

Despite the evidence presented so far, a skeptical reader might still be concerned that the measure of the primary independent

[19] All four effects are statistically significant for unexposed Iraqis (shown on the left side of each plot), yet three of the four lose their significance among exposed Iraqis (shown on the right side of each plot) while the magnitude of the fourth is greatly diminished. The difference in difference between them is significant in all four cases.

variable – exposure to the fighting – is self-reported in nature. This could leave it vulnerable to potential reporting or recall biases, among other issues. To address such concerns, I use data obtained from the strike-tracking NGO *Airwars* on the observed locations of all 10,000-plus Coalition airstrikes in Iraq. Premised on the model of the Bureau of Investigative Journalism's Drones Project – the most comprehensive, transparent, and reliable publicly available database of US drone warfare in countries like Pakistan (Bauer, Reese, and Ruby 2021) – *Airwars* tracks the frequency, results (civilian casualties), and locations of all reported foreign airstrikes in Iraq and Syria. In its effort to do so, the organization relies on a wide variety of sources, including international and local media, NGO reporting, social media sites (e.g., so-called "martyrs' pages"), and official statements by the combatants themselves. It then attempts to triangulate between these sources and investigate wherever possible, producing a five-point scale of reporting quality for the alleged civilian casualties in each event, which runs from Discounted to Confirmed. Because the survey's respondents are geolocated, they were able to be matched with the *Airwars* data to create a measure of distance from the closest observed strike for each individual.

To gauge the impact of this measure, it is added to the base models for both misperceptions (i.e., the variables included are the same as those in the final two columns of Table 4.1). To assess how the predicted levels of each factual misperception change with proximity clearly, the distance measure is binned by increments of 100 kilometers. This allows us to see how the two outcomes' values change at each additional 100 kilometers away from the closest airstrike. As in Figure 4.1, the outcomes are dichotomized so that the percentage of belief in each claim as one moves closer to or further away from the violence can be visualized. These coding choices do not substantively change the results but are done to help convey them in a simple and intuitive way.

The results show that proximity significantly reduces both misperceptions. Notably, Figure 4.3 plots the predicted percentage of people that endorse each misperception by their proximity to the nearest airstrike, along with the associated 95 percent confidence intervals. This figure shows how both factual misperceptions – that the strikes target the PMF, and that they help ISIL – decline substantially as one moves from areas that are far away from a strike to those that are much closer to (and ultimately underneath) one. Moreover, the figure also shows effects that are substantively significant: about two-thirds

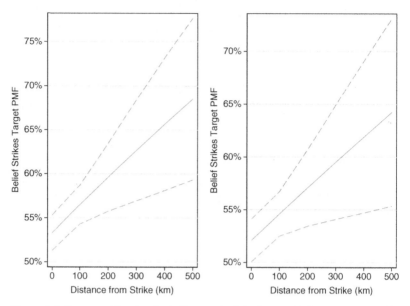

Figure 4.3 Percent of Iraqis who believe each claim by proximity to nearest strike

of the respondents furthest away from the strikes are likely to believe each of the misperceptions, while that figure declines to close to half among those in areas that have experienced or are very close to the campaign. This offers further evidence, based on a more direct and behavioral measure of exposure, which is consistent with the book's central thesis: that seeing is in fact disbelieving when it comes to factual misinformation in war.

Several other tests are also conducted to raise confidence in the results. Perhaps the primary confounder concern is that local civilians might be distinctive in other ways besides proximity that threaten our findings. In particular, a key alternative story could be that proximate civilians might be motivated not by accuracy but by anti-ISIL bias. Locals might be more vehemently opposed to ISIL due to its brutalization of adjacent communities or the more immediate threat that it represents to them ("we could be next"). That could make them more supportive of any attempt to eliminate it, Coalition airstrikes included (and thus skeptical of negative claims toward them). This concern is addressed in two ways. First, the base models are rerun with several measures of attitudes toward ISIL. Second, a "placebo test" is conducted in which support for valid claims about human rights abuses by the PMF in its anti-ISIL operations is examined. If locals were genuinely motivated by a desire to expunge ISIL, they would be more likely to discount not just negative claims about the Coalition but those about the PMF too, as the PMF has been among its most effective adversaries.[20] Yet, the results of these tests show the opposite (Tables A4.4–4.5 in the Appendix); controlling for attitudes toward ISIL has no substantive influence on the findings, and personal exposure does not make Iraqis more skeptical of the *valid* claims about the PMF's anti-ISIL activities (as it does with the false claims about the Coalition's actions). This offers additional evidence consistent with the argument and against the idea that the results are due to anti-ISIL bias.

4.5 Discussion and Conclusion

In sum, this chapter examined Iraqis' belief in factual misinformation about the Coalition air campaign against ISIL in their country. In order to do so, it used a combination of a rich national public opinion survey as well as geo-located event data on thousands of airstrikes. The results were broadly consistent with the book's overarching argument – Iraqis' factual beliefs about the efficacy and targeting of the strikes were generally biased in ways consistent with their broader worldviews and their sources of information in the conflict, but these biases were significantly ameliorated by exposure and proximity to the events in question. This was clear when looking at exposure's direct effects on people's beliefs and its influence on the relationship between people's beliefs and their broader political attitudes, and when using both observed and self-reported measures of proximity to the Coalition's campaign. In this sense, the results yielded substantial evidence in support of the idea that proximity to the fighting helps limit people's scope for factual biases in war.

While the downstream effects of these dynamics in Iraq are hard to quantify, anti-USA and anti-Coalition sentiment was undoubtedly an important part of the Iraqi political landscape during the fight against ISIL – and it has remained so since. In the most concrete sense, the

---

[20] By showing that exposure does *not* diminish willingness to embrace valid and well-substantiated claims about the conflict, this check also helps address concerns about misinformation studies looking exclusively at fictitious claims rather than at discernment ability which should be the primary outcome of interest (Guay et al. 2022).

anti-Coalition propaganda that spread during the campaign against ISIL was highlighted as "posing security risks to US military advisers that [were] helping Iraqi security forces in the country."[21] More broadly, such misinformation fed into the wider geopolitical struggle over the direction of Iraqi politics. Indeed, Iraq has been caught in the midst of a competition between American and Iranian influence since at least 2003, and more backlash to one outside power or another – such as the pervasive opposition toward the USA during the 2003–11 Iraq War, or the surge of anti-Iranian sentiment that occurred around the 2019 Tishreen Uprising – can tilt its politics in different directions (Silverman, Kaltenthaler, and Dagher 2021).

During the campaign against ISIL, Iraqi suspicions of the US-led Coalition limited its role and encouraged the Shi'a-Arab dominated PMF militias – many loyal to Iran – to lead the fight. This, in turn, meant a greater dose of these militias' heavy-handed tactics during the fighting, while facilitating their outsized role in Iraqi politics after ISIL's defeat (Mansour and Jabar 2017, Smith and Knights 2023). While the public opposition toward the USA and its allies that facilitated these developments has deep and diverse roots, incendiary propaganda about American behavior during the battle against ISIL no doubt helped provide useful "focal points" for the militias to keep such sentiments fresh and use them to their strategic advantage. Indeed, in the wake of the 2019 Tishreen popular uprising, when pro-Iranian factions in the country came under tremendous pressure in Iraq, they used strikingly similar misinformation to distract from their domestic challenges and to rally hard-line support against the West.[22] It is thus not difficult to see how the kinds of misinformation examined in this chapter have figured into Iraqi politics, and why their mass uptake (or lack thereof) has important political and security implications.

---

[21] Ahmad Majidyar, "Iran-Supported Militia Groups Intensify Anti-U.S. Propaganda." *Middle East Institute*. May 16, 2017. Available at www.mei.edu/publications/iran-supported-militia-groups-intensify-anti-us-propaganda-iraq.

[22] See, for example, Hamdi Malik, "Militia Disinformation and the Zainab Isam al-Khazali Shooting." *Washington Institute for Near East Policy, Policy Analysis*, October 5, 2022. Available at www.washingtoninstitute.org/policy-analysis/militia-disinformation-and-zainab-isam-al-khazali-shooting; Mohammed A. Salih. "Much Ado About Nothing: Disinformation Campaigns and Foreign Policy in Iraq." *Carnegie Endowment for International Peace*, October 3, 2023. Available at https://carnegieendowment.org/sada/90681.

5 | Truth Discernment and Personal Exposure in the Syrian Civil War

"I did not believe what I could not see."

– Syrian refugee from Damascus

This chapter looks at the dynamics of people's factual beliefs during the Syrian civil war. Specifically, it investigates people's belief in things they heard during the war and their confidence in their ability to discern true and false information. To do so, it uses data from a significant sample of semi-structured interviews with Syrian refugees (N = 179) in Turkey that was collected by Schon (2020) and generously shared with me for this research. While these interviews focused chiefly on people's survival strategies during the war, they also elicited rich data on their factual beliefs, truth discernment abilities, information diets, and wartime experiences while in Syria that enable them to shed light on the key ideas in this book. Additionally, since most interviewees gave detailed narrative answers, I was able to dig into their stories qualitatively and code parts of them up for quantitative analysis in new ways. Overall, the analysis suggests that it was hard for civilians to tell what was true and false in Syria, but that those with more exposure to the war and personal experience with the fighting were better positioned to do so. It also uncovers suggestive evidence that it was indirect exposure ("seeing") and not direct exposure ("suffering") to the fighting that is most responsible for these learning processes.

5.1 The Syrian Civil War and Its Informational Landscape

Syria was thrust into civil war in 2011 when the "Arab Spring" – the series of revolutionary uprisings that swept across the Middle East and North Africa region in 2010–11 – hit the country. After long-standing dictators in Tunisia and Egypt were ousted by protesters in early 2011, publics facing even some of the region's most repressive regimes hoped for meaningful change. In Syria, a country that had been tightly controlled by the personalist dictatorships of Bashar al-Assad and his father since 1970 (Wedeen 2015), protests finally broke out in mid-March 2011 in the southern city of Deraa and soon spread to other key cities in the country like Damascus, Aleppo, and Homs. The Assad regime responded to this mobilization ruthlessly, shooting into the crowds of protesters and arresting and torturing countless demonstrators in the early weeks and months of the uprising. As this vicious crackdown continued, the protests hardened into armed rebellion and began to seize territory from the regime. This only further escalated the government's tactics, as it turned toward indiscriminate shelling and airstrikes as well as the unleashing of brutal militias from the dominant Alawite sect to "cleanse" rebel-held population centers.

The intensifying war drew in a variety of different actors. On the rebel side, the ostensibly more "moderate" rebel groups like the Free Syrian Army (FSA) that led the fight were soon joined by domestic and foreign jihadis, some released from prison by Assad specifically to discredit and undermine the rebels (Lister 2016). Different rebel factions answered to different sponsors as well, with Turkey, some of the Gulf states, and the USA backing their own proxies. This fueled corruption and infighting in the rebel ranks. The emergence of ISIL also complicated the picture, as it seized large swaths of territory in both eastern Syria and northern and western Iraq in 2014 and fought against both the Syrian regime and other opposition factions. Kurdish armed groups such as the People's Defense Units also emerged to defend Kurdish communities in northern and eastern Syria, though they faced some international criticism too as they displaced Arab residents living in mixed Arab-Kurdish areas.[1]

Meanwhile, allied as it was with the region's so-called "Shi'a crescent," the Syrian regime received considerable support from Iran as well as the powerful Lebanese Shi'a militia Hezbollah as it attempted to crush the rebellion. The government was also aided by Russia,

[1] For example, allegations of ethnic cleansing have been made against the Kurdish-dominated administration in the country's north and east by Amnesty International. "Syria: US Ally's Razing of Villages Amounts to War Crimes." *Amnesty International*, October 13, 2015. Available at www.amnesty.org/en/ latest/news/2015/10/syria-us-allys-razing-of-villages-amounts-to-war-crimes/.

with which it had a longstanding relationship dating to the Cold War. Russia's assistance to the regime was initially more limited in nature, but in 2015 – with various rebel factions surging and the government facing its most serious risk of collapse – it began a large-scale bombing campaign against the rebellion. This combination of robust Iranian and Russian support has proved decisive in propping up the government and allowing it to steadily reassert control over most of the country since 2015. As of this writing, Assad controls most (some 70 percent) of Syria's territory,[2] with only a few relatively limited slices outside the regime's grasp, including a Kurdish zone of control underwritten by US support in the country's northeast, a Turkish "buffer zone" that is dominated by Islamist groups in the northwest, and the Israeli-ruled Golan Heights in the southeast. While the regime has been able to reestablish control over most of the territory, it has come at a terrible price: The Syrian civil war has been one of the deadliest conflicts of the post-Cold War era, with about 300,000 civilian deaths during the dispute and nearly twelve million people – over half the country's prewar population – fleeing their homes since it began.[3]

The information environment in Syria reflects many of these dynamics. Before the war, the media channels in Syria were tightly controlled by the regime, with state-run television, radio, and newspapers – along with a handful of private outlets owned by regime-linked elites – dominating the landscape. The war has significantly changed this picture, bringing to prominence a wide range of other information sources. One trend has been the rise of scores of "citizen journalists" in Syria, who have used social media to document the war – particularly the regime's brutal role in it – and broadcast it to the wider world. Major pro-opposition news websites, radio stations, and television channels have also emerged, often operating from nearby countries

---

[2] See Philip Loft. "Syria's Civil War in 2023: Assad Back in the Arab League." *UK Parliament, House of Commons Library*, June 9, 2023. Available at https://commonslibrary.parliament.uk/research-briefings/cbp-9378/.

[3] On the civilian death toll, see "Behind the Data: Recording Civilian Casualties in Syria." *United Nations Office of the High Commissioner for Human Rights (OHCHR)*. Available at www.ohchr.org/en/stories/2023/05/behind-data-recording-civilian-casualties-syria. On the status of Syrian refugees, see "Syria Situation: Global Report 2022." *UN High Commissioner for Refugees (UNHCR)*. Available at https://reporting.unhcr.org/operational/situations/syria-situation#:~:text=Over%2012%20million%20Syrians%20remained,from%205.7%20million%20in%202021.

like Turkey due to government repression of their efforts in Syria. These new citizen journalists and opposition outlets have faced very difficult working conditions, with repression not only from the regime but from other parties in the conflict as well. Indeed, Islamist factions like Jaysh al-Islam and ISIL have spread their own propaganda and targeted local journalists who have been critical of their repressive behavior. And, while it has been less brutal, the Kurdish autonomous administration in the country's northeast has pressured and censored critical media as well. Understandably, in this context, many Syrians have turned to local Facebook pages affiliated with their communities for news about the war. Overall, the conflict has thus yielded a less state-dominated information landscape, but one in which various powerful combatants – the government, the Islamist rebels, and the Kurdish groups – aim to project favorable narratives and control information within their areas of control and influence.

Given these realities, it is not surprising that there has been ample misinformation pushed within Syria about the conflict. Perhaps the most internationally infamous case of misinformation in the conflict is the regime's denial of its use of chemical weapons on civilians in rebel-held areas like Khan Shaykhun, Ghouta, and elsewhere. More broadly, the government's narrative portrays the conflict as a battle against hard-core religious terrorists that are seeking to destroy the country and wreck the order and security it positions itself as bringing to ordinary Syrians (Wedeen 2019). Within this context, it has denied the many harms inflicted on civilian populations in its "counterterrorism operations" and falsely attributed some of its worst violence to the opposition. It has also sought to scare the country's various minority groups – including the Alawites, the government's nominal core supporters, as well as the Christians and Druze – into remaining loyal to the regime by ginning up false claims about imminent attacks on their communities. For example, the war correspondent Janine di Giovanni recounted a conversation with an aspiring pro-regime politician, Maria Saadeh, who exhibited such thinking (2016: 58):

She also refused to believe that the government had tortured, maimed, and killed civilians. When I listed the atrocities one by one she stopped me, putting down her cup of tea. There was an angelic smile on her face. "Do you think our president could put down his own people?" she asked me incredulously. "Gas his own people? Kill his own people? This is the work of foreign fighters. They want to change our culture."

Meanwhile, while the opposition and its biases are diverse, pro-opposition outlets have also pushed misinformation denying atrocities against government supporters, as well as overstating the rebels' performance and territorial gains in the conflict. False pro-opposition rumors have also repeatedly swirled about the death of Bashar al-Assad and other top government officials in the war. In sum, a wealth of misleading information has been promoted by different combatants and their supporters in Syria. As one analysis of the informational dimension of the war stated, "the procurement and publication of information is inseparable from the strategies and tactics of those pursuing interests within the conflict. It is a matter of managing perceptions of hope and glory, injustice and pain" (Powers and O'Laughlin 2015: 175).

5.2 The Interview Data and Questions

To explore people's factual beliefs in Syria, this chapter examines a set of semi-structured interviews ($N = 179$) with Syrian refugees in Turkey. The data are from Schon's (2020) compelling book *Surviving the War in Syria: Survival Strategies in a Time of Conflict* and were generously shared with me for the purposes of this research. While much of the substance of these interviews focuses on civilians' migration experiences and other types of survival strategies during the war, they also include rich data on how people navigated new information that they encountered during the conflict – as well as their wartime experiences and attitudes – that serve as excellent fodder for examining some of the main ideas in this book.

This section first offers more information on how the interviews were carried out and the attributes of the sample before turning to the major questions used in the analysis. Overall, the data are a large and diverse convenience sample of Syrian refugees in Turkey, with ample variation in key characteristics. To collect the data, Schon first conducted test interviews with Syrian refugees living outside of the region and in Jordan (total $N = 39$). This allowed him to substantially develop his questionnaire and methodology. He then completed 179 semi-structured interviews in Turkey, using an Arabic translator where necessary. Since his major fieldwork trip occurred amid the 2016 Turkish coup attempt and sharp tensions between the Turkish government and Kurdistan Workers Party, Schon decided to avoid visiting the Syrian border areas and focus on collecting data from selected major cities in the country. Specifically, he conducted his fieldwork in Istanbul and Izmir, which offered "large Syrian refugee populations and relative safety" at the time (48). Schon used snowball sampling with multiple points of insertion in the target community in order to reach a variety of individuals, forging many of his connections by visiting Syrian schools and language academies as well as major Turkish universities with large numbers of Syrian students.

Descriptive statistics from Schon show that he achieved substantial diversity in his sample, Geographically, Schon reached civilians from various parts of Syria, including Damascus, Homs, Hama, Latakia, Idlib, Aleppo, Hasakah, and Deir ez-Zor. His participants fled at a wide range of times during the war, ranging from 2011 to 2016 when he conducted fieldwork. He also obtained meaningful variation in income, education, and other demographics among those he interviewed. That said, Schon's sample reflects the dynamics of the population of Syrian refugees that went to Turkey instead of other countries when they left the conflict. In particular, those sampled by Schon tended to be Sunni Arab, anti-government, and come from the northern half of Syria – all of which make sense given the types of Syrians who migrated to Turkey (Pearlman 2016).[4] Additionally, his sample tended to skew toward younger, male, and more educated respondents, which may have been a function of his use of universities as a major conduit for sampling. In sum, these interviews are not a random sample of Syrian refugees but do offer functional diversity with which to explore relationships of interest in this chapter. Moreover, like other batches of semi-structured interviews, they also provide a rich stock of narrative material to

---

[4] Differences among the types of Syrian refugees who fled to different neighboring states are clear. For example, the refugee population that fled to Lebanon tends to be *relatively* well-off and pro-government in its political orientation compared to the Syrian population more broadly (see, e.g., Corstange 2019). While the interviews provide a rich store of information on factual beliefs in a contemporary war zone, it is possible that some of the characteristics described above influenced the patterns uncovered in this chapter. In particular, a more widely representative sample of Syrians including more southerners and westerners might have revealed more exposure to pro-government rumors and might have yielded more variation in political orientations between individuals – potentially making the anti-Assad/pro-Assad variable more relevant and predictive in the analysis.

mine for insights about people's thinking in war in ways that complement the survey-based analyses used elsewhere in this book.

One final feature of the interviews that should be noted is that not all respondents provided narrative responses. In particular, 129 respondents completed full in-person interviews with either the researcher, his interpreter, or both asking questions. The narrative answers of these individuals were recorded in full. However, fifty respondents preferred to complete the questionnaire privately and return their responses by email. These individuals only answered the close-ended questions in the survey and did not provide narrative material. This means that the quantitative elements of this chapter can take advantage of the full sample of 179 respondents, whereas the qualitative elements have slightly fewer respondents available (N = 129).

There were several parts of these interviews that were particularly relevant to our analysis. First, people were asked a set of questions about their engagement with new information in Syria, including whether they had confidence in their ability to differentiate true from false information. The specific question wording was "Do you think that you were able to tell the difference between rumors, or false information, and accurate information while you were in Syria?" This measure of *truth discernment* is the primary dependent variable in our analysis. Indeed, this builds on a recent argument that research on misinformation should focus on people's truth discernment ability rather than their belief in false information per se, as the latter could be conflated with general skepticism as opposed to resistance to misinformation specifically (e.g., Batailler et al. 2022, Guay et al. 2022). In the sample of interest, 73.7 percent of those interviewed were confident in their ability to distinguish between true and false information while they were in Syria. Of course, it should be noted that the measure used here captures people's self-reported confidence in their truth discernment ability – they may be over or underconfident about their ability to discern true and false information. This limitation must be acknowledged. Still, the data offer rare insights into people's engagement with false information in war on a large scale. And the semi-structured nature of the interviews allows us to delve into the narratives of those who express high (or low) confidence in their discernment ability, helping corroborate any observed patterns with ample qualitative material.

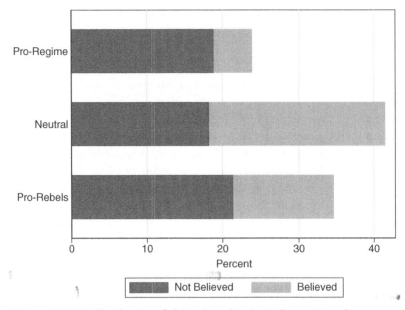

Figure 5.1 The distribution of claims heard in Syria, by partisan thrust

Interviewees were also asked to generate examples of things they heard in Syria that they believed and that they did not believe. The question wording was: "Do you specifically remember any of these things that you heard? If yes, please share some examples of things that you heard that you did believe, as well as some examples of things that you did not believe." This question was a useful way both of generating relevant data about people's beliefs and of "priming the pump" and encouraging them to recall the major rumors and claims they encountered in the war. Overall, ninety-six people answered this question, providing a total of 182 claims they heard. I coded each of these claims for (1) their partisan thrust, which I categorized as broadly pro-regime, neutral, or pro-rebels in nature and (2) their primary topic, using an inductive approach to identify eight frequent topics based on a systematic and iterative effort to code the transcripts.

Figure 5.1 plots the distribution of things that respondents mentioned they heard during the war by their partisan thrust. There is ample variation on this score, with 24 percent of the claims mentioned classifiable as broadly pro-regime, 35 percent as broadly pro-rebels, and 42 percent as not clearly benefiting either side. This shows that

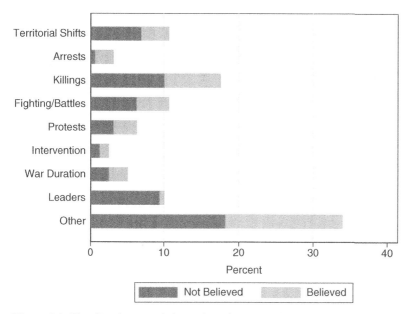

Figure 5.2 The distribution of claims heard in Syria, by primary topic

respondents in the sample were exposed to new information that aligned with multiple different perspectives on the war. Meanwhile, roughly half the claims in the neutral category were believed, with lower shares of belief in the claims within the pro-rebels and especially the pro-regime categories. This suggests some disinclination to accept propaganda with a clear partisan thrust in the conflict, especially if it was pro-regime.

Figure 5.2 shows the distribution of claims by their main topic. The categories inductively generated by identifying the themes and topics that repeatedly emerged in the data were: territorial shifts, arrests, killings (individuals killed by a combatant or by parties unknown), fighting/battles (military engagements or activity between combatants), protests, intervention by external powers, the duration of the war, and information about leaders. As is clear, the claims that were mentioned focused on a wide variety of topics, with killings, fighting/battles, and territorial shifts being some of the most common themes among those that were identified. That said, roughly one-third of the claims did not focus on any of the identified topics, again speaking to their diversity – as it was difficult to place them into a relatively small number of buckets. There was variation in the extent to which claims within each of the different categories were believed as well. The main outlier here was the leadership category, which mainly consisted of rumors about Bashar al-Assad and other top regime officials being killed. Respondents said these rumors popped up persistently in Syria, but that they almost invariably knew they were false.

In order to explain variation in people's perceived ability to tell true from false information in Syria, several explanatory variables are used. Recall that the central argument made in the book is that "seeing is disbelieving" – in other words, that civilians with greater exposure and proximity to the relevant events in war will tend to form more accurate perceptions of and be less vulnerable to false information about them. This analysis gets at the logic of the argument in multiple ways. First, the rich information on people's conflict experiences collected in the interviews allows us to capture their degree of exposure to wartime violence in Syria. In particular, respondents were asked whether they had witnessed each of three different types of violent events while they were in Syria. These included witnessing a battle between armed groups, witnessing beatings or torture of other people, and witnessing a killing. These items were aggregated into an additive index of the number of different types of violent events that were witnessed by respondents in the sample. This measure reveals substantial variation, with roughly 24 percent of respondents having witnessed none of the events, 32 percent having witnessed one, 22 percent having witnessed two, and 22 percent having witnessed all three.

Another key proxy for exposure to the fighting is how long people actually spent in wartime Syria. Helpfully, the interviews contain extensive information on respondents' migration decisions and trajectories out of Syria, including the timing of when they left their homes and left the country. This information is recorded at the daily level. Since the start of the conflict is often dated to March 15, 2011 (e.g., Schon 2020), the number of days from this date until respondents exited Syria was used as the primary measure of temporal exposure.[5] There is considerable variation on this score, with

---

[5] As an alternate measure of temporal experience, I calculated the number of days from the start of the war to when respondents first fled from their homes – rather than when they left the country – as people might conceivably be able to learn more effectively from experiences while in their original

respondents spending between 30 and 1,944 days in wartime Syria before leaving the country. Looking at this measure annually highlights the variation nicely as well: Approximately 4 percent of the people who were interviewed left Syria in 2011, 14 percent in 2012, 21 percent in 2013, 18 percent in 2014, 34 percent in 2015, and 8 percent in 2016.[6]

As far as controlling for other factors, the relatively limited sample size from a quantitative perspective ($N = 129$, with fewer observations on some variables) argues against pushing the data too hard and including a large number of control variables. That said, the models do contain some key control variables. First, they include the binary variable *wasta*, which is an Arabic term for the degree of social connections or "juice" one has in society. This is one of the two primary pieces of the argument made by Schon (2020) to explain civilians' decision-making and behavior in conflict. Here, the idea would be that those with more *wasta* will have greater confidence in their ability to tell true from false information in Syria. Second, they include an ordinal measure of respondents' educational attainment, as this is a common predictor of belief in misinformation and conspiratorial thinking in the literature, and has in particular been linked to conspiracism in the Middle East and North Africa region (Gentzkow and Shapiro 2004). Third, the models contain a binary measure of whether respondents describe themselves as anti-Assad in their political orientation. Scholars have highlighted people's political orientations and worldviews as an important predictor of their belief in misinformation in general (e.g., Miller, Saunders, and Farhart 2016), as well as war and conflict in particular (e.g., Greenhill and Oppenheim 2017). Holding an anti-Assad ideology or worldview might make people more confident in their truth discernment ability if they firmly believed claims pushed by one side but not the other.

---

communities rather than under the unusual conditions of actively migrating through a war zone. Table A5.1 and Figure A5.1 in the Appendix report the results of this check, which shows that the core findings are substantively unchanged with the alternate measure.

[6] Moreover, the correlation between the temporal measure and the event-based "witnessing" measure discussed above is positive but relatively weak at $r = 0.26$. This implies that, while both speak to the overarching argument, they are meaningfully different measures and thus represent unique "cuts" at the question.

5.3 The Drivers of Discernment during the War

Table 5.1 displays the results of the analysis. Since the outcome – people's confidence in their truth discernment ability – is binary, the models used are logistic regressions. As is apparent, both measures of individuals' personal exposure to the fighting positively and significantly predict greater confidence in their truth discernment ability. Specifically, more days spent in wartime Syria and more types of violent events witnessed in Syria are both associated with a significantly greater probability of being confident in one's truth discernment skills. Meanwhile, there is little evidence that people's social connections (*wasta*), educational attainment, or political orientations explains variation in their discernment confidence.

To understand the substantive impacts of these two variables, the predicted probability of a respondent being confident in her truth

Table 5.1 *Predictors of Syrian refugees' confidence in their ability to discern between true and false information during the war*

	Discernment confidence	Discernment confidence
War exposure		
No. days in wartime Syria	0.00***	
	(0.00)	
No. event types witnessed		0.48**
		(0.22)
Other factors		
Wasta	0.04	−0.51
	(0.52)	(0.47)
Education	−0.04	−0.09
	(0.19)	(0.18)
Anti-Assad	−0.64	−0.44
	(0.59)	(0.55)
Constant	−0.29	1.12*
	(0.90)	(0.67)
Observations	112	108

Note: Results from logistic regression models. Standard errors in parentheses.
***$p < 0.01$, **$p < 0.05$, *$p < 0.1$.

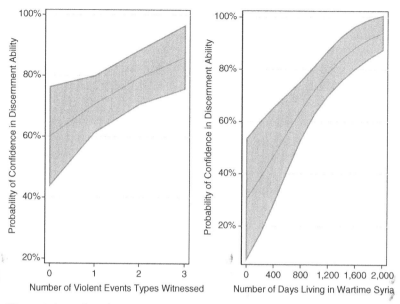

Figure 5.3 Predicted probability of confidence in discernment ability by war exposure

discernment ability is plotted across each of their values. Figure 5.3 shows that their substantive influence on the outcome is quite large in real-world terms. In particular, the panel on the left shows that as the number of violent events witnessed by a civilian while they were in Syria grows from zero to three, the predicted probability that they are confident in their truth discernment goes up from about 60 percent to about 90 percent. Similarly, the panel on the right shows that as the number of days spent living in wartime Syria increases from about zero to about 2,000, the predicted probability of discernment confidence rises from about 30 percent up to about 90 percent. These are weighty shifts in people's beliefs that they can discern truth and falsehood in the war, underscoring the power that exposure to the fighting can have.

In addition, further analysis was done to boost confidence in the mechanisms at work here. Indeed, while the agreement and strength of the results around time in Syria and events witnessed are encouraging, these variables do not directly test the causal mechanisms in the book's argument. To probe the underlying process further, I coded the narratives in all of the interviews for whether there was evidence that people actually relied on personal experience to vet information while they were in Syria or not.[7] Such evidence appeared in two forms. First, some refugees explicitly stated that this strategy was used to verify things in Syria. For example, one respondent from Damascus (T020) said about how he discerned truth from lies during the war, "you can base this on your own observations and experience." Second, other interviewees implicitly demonstrated that they relied on their personal experience to figure out what was going on in Syria. For instance, a civilian from Aleppo (T075) related that "the Syrian regime forces used to say that the demonstrations were full of weapons. I didn't believe that because I witnessed many of these demonstrations in my area and there were not weapons." If either explicit or implicit evidence of personal experience reliance was found, a one was coded for this measure – if not, it was coded as a zero.[8] Ultimately, this coding revealed that 44 percent of the respondents relied on personal experience to navigate information while they were in Syria.

With this as the main independent variable of interest, the model above was rerun. Figure 5.4 shows the resulting predicted probability plot, which reveals that there is a significantly greater chance that an individual will be confident in their truth discernment ability if they rely on personal experience to vet information. Specifically, the probability goes up from around 71 percent that they will have confidence in their truth discernment ability if they do not use personal experience to 92 percent if they do. This suggests that reliance on personal experience to judge the veracity of new information – which gets at the heart of the book's argument about what buffets people against misinformation in violent conflicts – is indeed promoting people's (perceived) ability to tell apart truth and lies in situations like the war in Syria.

---

[7] Thanks are due to Yousef Khanfar at Carnegie Mellon University-Qatar (CMU-Q) for excellent research assistance on this reanalysis of the Syrian interview data. Yousef undertook a very useful preliminary coding effort that I built upon for the analysis in this chapter. The data were fully de-identified before we received them.

[8] This use of both explicit statements about people's reliance on personal experience and implicit demonstrations that they did so when responding to relevant questions roughly fits the distinction between "manifest" and "latent" coding items discussed in Aberbach and Rockman (2002).

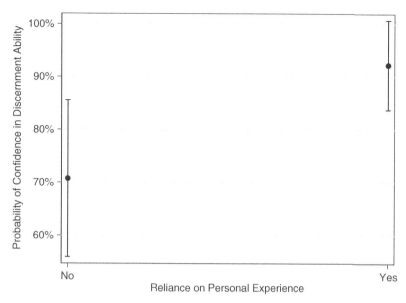

Figure 5.4 Predicted probability of confidence in discernment ability by evidence of reliance on personal experience

5.3.1 Qualitative Evidence from the Interviews

Of course, the interviews also contain a rich store of qualitative material, and a careful look at this material helps complement the quantitative findings. To begin with, there were a number of interviewees who explicitly emphasized the amount of time spent in Syria as essential for people's ability to adjudicate information during the war. As stated by one civilian who hailed from Homs (T012), "I didn't know how to check the information at first, but I learned as I had experience from the conflict." Similarly, another individual from Damascus (T019) said "after five years of conflict, anyone has to have the experience to know. At the beginning of the conflict, you cannot distinguish fact from fiction." Meanwhile, a third individual who came from Homs (T033) echoed these ideas, declaring that "after a duration, things get clearer. Even the children discover that the media often says false things." Another from Damascus (T049) related his observation that people's gullibility was highest at the beginning of the dispute, saying "at the beginning of the conflict, people believed everything they heard. Later, I went back and found that the people had changed." In sum, temporal experience was often explicitly discussed by the respondents in the sample as a key ingredient in people's ability to know what was happening in the fighting.

Moreover, a number of individuals underscored the significance of personally witnessing different kinds of events in the conflict for developing a clear understanding of what was going on. The Aleppo refugee mentioned above (T075) who did not believe the regime's propaganda about the protests after seeing them was one such example. Likewise, another individual who left Aleppo (T100) evinced this type of thinking when discussing his factual beliefs clearly. When asked about examples of things he believed while in Syria, he recounted "When the FSA said that we will enter Aleppo to free it I believed that because I witnessed them." In contrast, when asked about examples of things that he did not believe while in Syria, he answered "When I heard that the Syrian regime will close the zone which was the only exit between western Aleppo and eastern Aleppo. I didn't believe that, but I discovered [it was] true because they closed it." In other words, this individual relied on personal observation to check things that he heard in the war, either confirming his preexisting beliefs or updating them when necessary. In sum, these quotations demonstrate how civilians were able to evaluate new information about things like shifts in territorial control and the dynamics of protests based on their personal observations and experiences.

The interviews indicate that personal experience was similarly crucial in learning the truth about wartime atrocities and massacres. For instance, one Aleppo refugee (T028) related learning about a pair of harrowing atrocities that were perpetrated by the regime after personally witnessing their aftermath. He explained that:

I heard that in the park close to where I lived, people were saying that there were a bunch of dead bodies. I went there to check because I didn't believe it. I witnessed the bodies. They had to burn the bodies in the park ... I heard that a school full of children was targeted by an air strike. I went there and saw the dead bodies.

Similarly, a civilian from Homs (T033) recalled learning about a bloody massacre that occurred in the city's central square and that the regime tried to conceal after he personally saw the carnage:

There is a big square in Homs called The Watch. There were many civilians holding a demonstration there. They were only sitting. The Syrian regime brought weapons and killed many people. At first, I didn't believe this. The next morning, I learned that it was true. The regime sent trucks for the bodies ... On the next day, the people burned the bodies. The regime killed them with weapons. Later, we discovered that many dead people were in the trees.

Terrible atrocities and cover-up efforts by their perpetrators in the war were thus often discoverable by local civilians who could ascertain what had happened either by seeing them or observing some signs that they occurred in the immediate area.

Meanwhile, still other interviewees simply conveyed the crucial role of personal witnessing in how they navigated new information in the conflict more broadly. For instance, another civilian who was displaced from Aleppo (T171) stated about his information habits: "I only depended on what I witnessed. I was not interested in this other information. I witnessed many events. At the beginning of the demonstrations, I [watched] many TV channels. This news was reported before I witnessed the event. They are all propaganda ... for any event, I am curious. I follow it to the end."

This quotation speaks to the civilian's ability – as well as their motivation – to verify events locally in the war by relying on personal observation and investigation. Or as one refugee from Damascus (T007) put it – in perhaps the simplest and most pointed articulation of the dynamics described in this section – "I did not believe what I could not see." In sum, there is an abundance of qualitative evidence in the interviews – across a variety of different issues, from protest dynamics to territorial shifts to atrocities and more – of civilians either implicitly using their personal experience to check things they heard in the war or explicitly recognizing its value for figuring out what was going on. This detailed qualitative material helps flesh out and substantially buttress the quantitative findings highlighted in this chapter.

5.4 Dissecting Experience: Observation or Victimization?

One secondary question these data can help speak to is what kinds of personal experiences are most beneficial for effectively navigating wartime information. In particular, the detailed data on people's conflict exposure allows us to compare the impacts of personal observation vs. personal victimization on discernment. The quantitative analyses above used a scale that contained several items about the extent to which people personally observed or witnessed different types of violence during the war. However, in that section of the interviews there were also a number of items about whether people were victimized – that is, whether they themselves or their loved ones were harmed by combatants – in a variety of different ways in the war. Does resistance to misinformation in war come more from witnessing things, being harmed by them, or both equally?

To examine this question, one can compare the model with the scale of personal witnessing to an additive scale made from different items about people's personal victimization in the dispute. In particular, there are eight different items that asked about personal victimization. These capture whether an individual: (1) had their personal property taken or destroyed, (2) had someone shoot at them or their home, (3) received a severe beating to the body by someone, (4) was attacked with a knife or blunt object, (5) was kidnapped or detained as a prisoner, (6) received a serious physical injury during a battle, (7) received a serious physical injury during a bombing, and (8) was betrayed and put at risk of death or injury. On average, the individuals in the sample had experienced 2.5 of these eight victimization events, with a significant amount of variation among them.[9]

The results of the analysis are shown in Table 5.2. As is clear, personally witnessing more types of violent events has a positive and significant association with people's confidence in their discernment ability during the conflict ($p = 0.03$). In contrast, being personally victimized in more ways during the conflict has a positive association with people's confidence in their discernment ability, but the effect is not close to statistical significance ($p = 0.2$). In other words, while both of these measures push in the "right" direction, we can only confidently say that personal observation helps buttress individuals' (perceived) discernment ability. Definitively answering this question is difficult with these data, but they point toward the idea that it is seeing rather than suffering from wartime violence that is the surest path to resilience toward misinformation in conflict.

---

[9] In particular, 19 percent of the respondents experienced one such event, 33 percent experienced two, and 31 percent experienced three, with fewer respondents toward the tails of the distribution.

Table 5.2 *The influence of observation vs.*
victimization on Syrian refugees' confidence
in their discernment ability

	Discernment confidence	Discernment confidence
War exposure		
Observation scale	0.48**	
	(0.22)	
Victimization scale		0.25
		(0.19)
Other factors		
Wasta	−0.51	−0.49
	(0.47)	(0.46)
Education	−0.09	−0.02
	(0.18)	(0.18)
Anti-Assad	−0.44	−0.35
	(0.55)	(0.56)
Constant	1.12*	0.94
	(0.67)	(0.75)
Observations	108	108

Note: Results from logistic regression models. Standard errors
in parentheses.
***$p < 0.01$, **$p < 0.05$, *$p < 0.1$.

5.5 Discussion and Conclusion

This chapter investigated people's susceptibility to misinformation
in the Syrian civil war. In order to do so, it examined a sizable sample of semi-structured interviews with Syrian refugees in Turkey.
These interviews were originally conducted by Schon (2020), but
they were mined for new insights quantitatively and qualitatively
in this chapter. After first providing a brief overview of the conflict
and the various informational biases that characterize it, I described
these interviews and the items used from them in detail. I then ran a
series of models predicting people's confidence in their ability to tell
true from false information during the war, while also digging for
qualitative insights about how they judged new information in Syria.
The results of this analysis showed that individuals' actual exposure

to the conflict – conceptualized both in terms of how much time they spent in wartime Syria, and the range of violent events they witnessed there – is strongly associated with having higher confidence in their truth discernment ability. Moreover, a careful coding of the narratives in the interviews showed that actively using personal experience to vet new information is an important part of this story, speaking to some of the key mechanisms in the book's argument. Finally, the quantitative findings were supplemented by ample qualitative material which showed that people indeed highlighted things like the amount they spent in the country, the witnessing of different types of events, and the use of direct and indirect experiential knowledge as important safeguards against the allure of misinformation.

These results build on and complement those from Chapter 3 (on the US drone campaign in Pakistan) and Chapter 4 (on the anti-ISIL air campaign in Iraq), driving toward the same overall point but from different angles. Several differences between the analyses are worth appreciating. First, the Pakistan and Iraq chapters (Chapters 3 and 4) focus on people's belief in specific prominent misinformation claims or narratives in conflict – such as the idea that the US drone campaign in Pakistan is killing mostly civilians, or that the anti-ISIL airstrikes from 2014 to 2016 targeted allied militias – while this chapter analyzes people's general ability to distinguish between truthful and fictitious information. Second, the type of conflict and violence in the cases is quite different: Examining people's belief in misinformation about both the US drone campaign in Pakistan and the anti-ISIL Coalition air campaign in Iraq entails a focus on external interventions and aerial bombardment, while focusing on truth discernment in the Syrian civil war means claims about a wider range of combatants and types of violence. Third, different methods were employed in these cases, with a quantitative large-n analysis of survey and violent event data in Iraq, a case study approach with quantitative elements in Pakistan, and an analysis of detailed semi-structured interview data in Syria. Given these myriad differences, the fact that the findings of Chapters 3–5 converge and agree so strongly should seriously bolster our confidence in the central argument that exposure and proximity to the fighting are powerful antidotes to misinformation in war.

Finally, this chapter offers a prime opportunity to touch on the issue of wartime migration and displacement. Indeed, the book recognizes that people often flee from the front lines of war or from war-affected countries entirely, and leaves ample room for this process to occur. Of course, this could pose a problem if people with better information habits were less likely to do the fleeing, leaving those closer to the "action" with more accurate beliefs – but via a process of selection and not learning. While this would indeed be troubling, two key points militate against this concern. First, the bias it implies should run *against* the results in this book. Indeed, people with better prior information habits should be able to more accurately identify risks and thus be *less exposed* to violence in war. This would mean that the relationship between exposure and accuracy found in this book would be underestimated. Second, this book's findings are borne out regardless of displacement. Indeed, this chapter demonstrated evidence of experiential learning among Syrian refugees, while Chapter 4 showed it among Iraqis who remained in Iraq during the ISIL conflict. And Chapter 3 showcased the accurate conflict perceptions of people from the tribal areas of Pakistan whether they remained in or fled from their communities. All of this suggests that the central story here is about the extent to which people are personally exposed or proximate to the fighting rather than whether they are displaced or not in a conflict per se.

6 | *Understanding and Mitigating the Appeal of Falsehood in Wartime*

"You can't cover up the sun with a finger."

– Pashtun saying

In the fifth Harry Potter novel, *Harry Potter and the Order of the Phoenix*, the story centers around misinformation in a society teetering toward war. The villainous Lord Voldemort is back, having successfully restored himself to a body at the end of the fourth novel. Harry Potter and his mentor Professor Albus Dumbledore attempt to alert the world about this and rally support to fight Voldemort. But the Ministry of Magic, the magical world's governing body, and *the Daily Prophet*, its leading newspaper, push a deluge of misinformation about the growing threat and brewing war. This misinformation alleges that Voldemort and his supporters have *not* returned, and either denies the increasing attacks and disturbances in the magical world or else blames them on other sources. With many predisposed to be skeptical toward the controversial Harry and Dumbledore and their terrifying claims, and with the overwhelming control over information maintained by the Ministry, this misinformation is very effective: Most of the magical world initially refuses to accept the truth of Voldemort's return. As noted by one of Harry's teachers, Professor Lupin (Rowling 2003, 94): "While the Ministry insists there is nothing to fear from Voldemort, it's hard to convince people he's back, especially as they really don't want to believe it in the first place."[1]

---

[1] People also divide based on prior political and informational factors early on in the book. For example, one student who stands by Harry's and Dumbledore's versions of events explains that his grandmother said "if Dumbledore says he's back, he's back" (219), while another declares that his "family have always stood firm behind Dumbledore, and so [does he]" (262). Meanwhile, students who are skeptical of Harry tend to have parents who work for the Ministry or are loyal *Daily Prophet* readers. This further speaks to how political leanings and information diets shape people's factual beliefs when they are not directly exposed to the events at issue.

Yet once Voldemort and his supporters' acts of sabotage and violence become so bold and ambitious as to make denial or blame on other forces implausible, this wall of misbelief begins to crack. After a mass breakout of Voldemort's worst supporters from the magical world's highest-security prison, one of Harry's initially skeptical peers approaches him and says "I just wanted to say … I believe you" (583). And the bubble finally bursts when Voldemort himself is seen during an attack on the Ministry of Magic by the Minister and his aides, who must then accept the painful reality. "He's back!" the Minister splutters upon seeing Voldemort in the popular film adaptation of the book.

While the story is of course fictional, it speaks nicely to the primary findings in this project. Indeed, I have shown in this book that people in war are often quite susceptible to lies and delusions about what is going on. Like most of the magical world immersed in denialism about Voldemort's return, people often believe a mixture of what they want to (*motivated bias*) and what they are told to (*informational bias*) about conflict, regardless of whether their beliefs are false or true. And yet, the book also examined the limits of wartime misinformation, showing how people who are more directly exposed to a given feature of conflict tend to have better information about it and a stronger motivation to understand it accurately. As in the case of the Minister of Magic when he ultimately encounters Voldemort in the Ministry atrium, proximity and exposure can puncture even powerful misinformation in war. Chapters 1–5 advanced this argument by first laying out a theory of how people form factual beliefs in conflict (Chapters 1–2), and then examining its key implications with empirical evidence about people's susceptibility to factual misperception and misinformation in the context of the American drone campaign in the tribal areas of Pakistan (Chapter 3), the US-led Coalition's air campaign against ISIL in Iraq (Chapter 4), and the Syrian civil war (Chapter 5). These analyses are summarized in the outline of the book at the end of Chapter 1 as well as within the introductions of each chapter.

This concluding chapter steps back to think through the wider implications of the findings. What can they teach us about war and peace, as well as misinformation and political psychology? What practical solutions do they suggest about how to navigate armed conflicts and how to counter the dangerous misinformation that so often thrives within them? How are the dynamics examined in the book evolving over time, and what might the phenomenon of wartime misinformation look like moving forward? And what are the most fruitful avenues for future research and investigation in this area? Chapter 6 of the book engages with each of these questions in turn.

6.1 Implications of the Book for Theory and Scholarship

This section discusses the key scholarly implications of the book's findings. It first focuses on what they can teach us about the dynamics of modern war and peace. Then, it turns its attention to the insights that they suggest for our understanding of factual misinformation, misperceptions, and political psychology.

6.1.1 Implications for Our Understanding of War and Peace

The book has four major implications for how we think about contemporary war and peace. First, and most directly, it highlights factual distortion in war as a key phenomenon that demands the attention of scholars and practitioners who focus on security, peace, and conflict, and reveals where it is most and least likely to thrive in conflict situations. Notably, we saw how communities that have strong partisan biases toward one side or another in a conflict but who are *removed* from the relevant aspects of the fighting are the most vulnerable to manipulation about what is actually taking place. In these communities, lies have the potential to initiate, exacerbate, or extend violent disputes, even when people with similar worldviews who are more directly exposed to the fighting might think differently. In this sense, the book helps us understand where we should expect to see dangerous lies and false beliefs spread their tentacles most in conflicts, and thus where we should attempt to allocate our scarce resources to best thwart and counter them.

Second, these findings contribute in important ways to our understanding of why wars last and why peaceful resolution of them is often elusive. They do so by building on bargaining models of war, which have become an important part of conflict studies and International Relations (IR) (Fearon 1995, Blattman 2022a). Bargaining models of war highlight how war is ex-post inefficient because there should always be a "deal" or bargain that matches the postwar outcome but avoids the (potentially very steep) costs of fighting. This raises the puzzle of why war occurs and persists, or alternatively why groups fail to reach these deals. One of the main answers to this puzzle is that persistent "information asymmetries" about actors' relative capabilities and resolve get in the way. In one classic formulation, Blainey (1973) argued that "mutual optimism" is at the heart of all war. Yet since one of the key functions of war is to reveal information about relative strength, this only raises the question of why such issues do not disappear as a conflict unfolds. In the words of two IR scholars in this tradition (Filson and Werner 2002: 820), "war itself provides the information necessary for disputants to reach a settlement and to end the war." Or, as the question was put by a top civil conflict scholar (Blattman 2022b: 19): "Why doesn't the overconfidence correct itself after the first battles?"[2]

Paying appropriate attention to lies and misperceptions in war gives us one key answer to this puzzle. Moreover, doing so actually extends bargaining models of war to illuminate more fully the conditions under which wars persist. In particular, while the battlefield may reveal information in war, this book shows that it only does so reliably *to those who are actually exposed to it*. Thus, this book suggests that the greater the relative size and power of the constituencies in war that are removed from the front lines of the fighting, the more likely conflict is to last even if it is extremely costly or futile – as these realities can be concealed from them. This helps illuminate one possible reason why large diasporas are often connected to persistent rebellions, why foreign misadventures by great powers such as the USA or the Soviet Union can take decades to end, and why salient but highly geographically concentrated disputes such as the conflict in Kashmir seem to be among the toughest to resolve. In all of these cases, most individuals in the relevant countries or communities are far removed from the front lines of the fighting, which leaves them highly vulnerable to factual manipulations and distortions about what is going on. Investigating these macro-level relationships and

---

[2] This question comes from the teaching slides accompanying Chris Blattman's recent book *Why We Fight* (2022a). Blattman goes on to state that questions like these "elevate problems of belief formation" (21), calling attention to the need for additional research on how people develop different factual perceptions in war.

their connections with persistent wartime misperceptions represents a promising if challenging domain for future research.[3]

Third, the book has some key implications for our understanding of civilian populations in conflict and how they think and act more broadly. As discussed in Chapter 2 and elsewhere throughout the book, scholarship on civilian populations in war has largely been split between two competing views. In the rationalist view, civilians are seen as highly pragmatic agents who respond to material rewards and punishments carefully and strategically to maximize their odds of survival (Popkin 1979, Kalyvas 2006). In the identitarian view, they are seen as entrenched partisans whose attitudes and behaviors are powerfully shaped by their group identities and heavily biased against outgroup actors in conflict (Lyall 2010, Lyall, Blair, and Imai 2013). The results of this research suggest that both views are partly right and partly wrong. Specifically, they demonstrate that there are two layers of civilian populations in conflict settings: Locals on or near the front lines who tend to view the conflict in a quite strategic and pragmatic fashion, and non-locals removed from it who tend to think about it in a much more partisan and identity-driven way. The book thus has strongly integrative implications for our knowledge of civilian populations in conflict, showing how both rationalist and intergroup bias-oriented models can apply to civilians at different levels of removal from the front lines of the fighting.

Fourth, and relatedly, these insights about civilian psychology in conflict in turn have some crucial implications for how we think about counterinsurgency. Notably, much of the conventional wisdom around counterinsurgency embraces the ideas that (1) civilian

---

[3] Indeed, it should be noted that – while the findings in this book are consistent with these macro-level patterns and provide one possible explanation for why they occur – it would be difficult to disentangle the extent to which macro-level variation in the longevity of wars was due to their relative space for factual misperceptions as opposed to other differences between them. For example, one could look at the duration of ethnic rebellions and measure the overlap between the front lines of the fighting and the settlement patterns of the central identity groups behind them to get at the extent to which those groups are directly exposed to conflict. But more overlap could explain shorter conflicts in multiple ways, including via a simple rationalist mechanism in which the relevant groups are more effectively repressed as opposed to the idea that they are less free to believe they are winning the war even when they are not. Attempting to solve this represents a very intriguing but also deeply challenging prospect for future research.

support is crucial to victory, as insurgents can hide among and draw support from civilian populations and (2) civilian support is winnable if combatants simply protect civilians and treat them well, or take the "right" actions within their communities. This "population-centric" idea of counterinsurgency has been influential in many military circles (e.g., Petraeus and Amos 2009), and is undergirded by a number of careful econometric studies showing that how combatants act toward civilians in war produces predictable consequences from civilian populations. For example, studies by Kalyvas (2006) and Kalyvas and Kocher (2007) show that indiscriminate violence by states in cases as diverse as the Vietnam War and 1940s Greece boosts violent resistance from the targeted areas. Similarly, work by Condra and Shapiro (2012) shows that collateral damage inflicted by US-led Coalition forces in the Iraq War only incited more insurgent attacks from the affected districts. Meanwhile, studies by Lyall (2019) and Silverman (2020) show that when states compensate civilians they harm in counterinsurgent wars, it reduces insurgent attacks in their areas.

While these findings are undoubtedly important, it is worth noting that most of them are focused on a *highly localized scale*: They reveal that combatants can "win the village" with a careful application of force and generous dose of aid to its inhabitants. This book provides some important context around these findings – notably, that they depend on processes of factual belief formation, and the fact that local civilians tend to "get it right" and accurately discern the signals around them in war. But the book has also shown how people far from conflict dynamics often "get it wrong" and develop dangerous misbeliefs about them. They may not accurately recognize a combatant as taking benign actions toward their community (if it is), or think it is victimizing them (if it is not). This suggests we should exercise great caution when considering the likely impacts of influential counterinsurgency models beyond a localized level. In particular, external interveners facing broad hostility in target countries may find that population-centric approaches are popular and effective in communities directly exposed to their actions, but deeply alienating and even counterproductive in the broader society or transnational conflict environment in question. This argues for a cautious understanding of the *scalability* of prevailing counterinsurgency approaches and the microlevel conflict studies that underlie them, especially when they are executed by external actors or forces that are likely to be viewed as deeply illegitimate in a society.

6.1.2 *Implications for Our Understanding of Misinformation and Misperceptions*

In addition, the book's findings also have some key implications for our understanding of misinformation, misperceptions, and political psychology more broadly. In recent years, there has been a surge of behavioral research on rumors, conspiracy theories, misperceptions, and fake news in social life (e.g., Taber and Lodge 2006, Nyhan and Reifler 2010, Oliver and Wood 2014, Miller, Saunders, and Farhart 2016). This research corresponds to a general idea among many pundits and members of the public that we are mired in a "post-truth era," in which facts exert an increasingly limited impact on how people form beliefs about the world. The literature on misinformation paints a much more nuanced picture, as it shows that interventions like factual corrections, digital literacy training, and accuracy nudges can help mitigate misperceptions (e.g., De Vries, Hobolt, and Tilley 2018, Wood and Porter 2019, Porter, Velez, and Wood 2022) and that the spread of misperceptions varies along with many different individual-level factors. And yet it leaves little room for the role of the *situation* in which people find themselves and its structural features to systematically shape and constrain people's susceptibility to lies and misinformation about what is going on.

In contrast to the prevailing zeitgeist, this book reveals that, while lies are common in war, there are some sharp situational boundaries to their appeal. In particular, it suggests that exposure can be an effective antidote to misperceptions: People who directly observe high-stakes events and who need to make good decisions in order to survive will tend to seek out the facts and see through the lies. In this sense, the book offers a note of qualified optimism to the gloom and doom notions popular among commentators that whether we are beyond truth – when people have enough "skin in the game" and can directly observe the risks they face, there will be strong pressures on them to resist delusions and get it right. And to scholars, it suggests that top-down efforts to inform, train, or nudge people are not the only pathways out of fantasy and delusion; individuals that are on the front lines of high-stakes phenomena like war may just have the means and motives to know better. This raises the question of what other types of issues or situations – from climate change to global pandemics to natural disasters – make people think like local civilians on the front lines of conflict when they are proximate or exposed to the relevant phenomenon? This is a critical area for future research and a potentially promising way to learn more about the limits of biased perceptions more broadly in contemporary social, economic, and political life.

In particular, one might create something like Figure 6.1 as an attempt to think through the framework's broader generalizability. The two dimensions of the figure are an effort to outline the *generalized* conditions that make the mechanisms behind the book's core argument possible. The y-axis is labeled "survival motivation," and it captures the degree to which accepting false beliefs about a specific issue can kill you. For example, holding false beliefs about fake COVID-19 cures could indeed kill you if it leads you to avoid effective treatments or consume dangerous "snake oil" cures once you have the disease. In contrast, holding false beliefs about evolution or the Earth being flat will not lead you into any physical danger or harm. Thus, only issues in the lower half of the figure have the potential to trigger a powerful, survival-oriented accuracy motive of the kind explored in this book on the front lines of violent conflict. Meanwhile, the x-axis can be labeled "experiential falsifiability," and it connotes the extent to which people can learn about what is true and false on an issue using their own five senses in their immediate surroundings. For example, climate change can be deadly to those in low-lying, shrinking, or otherwise vulnerable areas, but while individuals in these areas can personally observe the change in their communities due to flooding or sea level rise, their ability to "see" its underlying causal drivers is much more constrained. In this way, only issues on the right side of this figure yield the local informational advantage we examined in this book among frontline communities in war.

		Experiential Falsifiability (Can you see what's right?)	
Survival Motivation (Can being wrong kill you?)		*No*	*Yes*
	No	• Theory of evolution • Earth flatness/roundness • Most conspiracy theories	• State of your local economy • Level of everyday "street level" corruption in your community
	Yes	• Covid cures/treatments • Climate change (causal) • Pollution (diffuse)	• *Nature of fighting in war* • Climate change (descriptive) • Pollution (point source)

Figure 6.1 Generalization of the book's argument across issue areas

Consider the case of people living on Tangier Island, a small island in the Chesapeake Bay that is fast disappearing due in large part to climate change-driven sea level rise. Though residents of this roughly 700-person island are united in their knowledge of the shrinking and flooding issues that they face and the overwhelming urgency of this problem, a significant number insist that it is due to simple erosion (driven by the wind and waves) and has nothing to do with climate change.[4] This is because the increasing disappearance of their land is a *descriptive* trend that they can directly see, but its underlying source is a complex, macro-level *causal* process that can only be demonstrated convincingly with considerable scientific evidence. While misperceptions in both of these domains can have serious consequences for people, only the former can be checked by personal experience. This sharp distinction between descriptive and causal perceptions of the climate – and the idea that only the former should be strongly and reliably updated with exposure to relevant events because it focuses on something that is directly and experientially observable – resonates with studies that show a limited impact for local weather on concerns about manmade climate change (e.g., Fownes and Allred 2019, Gartner and Schoen 2021, Blair and Arias 2023).

This framework may also undergird some key results about people's economic perceptions. For example, studies show that people's perceptions of the state of the economy strongly converge when economic conditions are clear, such as during a major downturn (e.g., Parker-Stephen 2013). And yet, while sharp economic downturns such as the 2008 Great Recession may make perceptions of the state of the economy converge, research also shows that people's judgments of *responsibility* or blame for those realities can diverge just as sharply based on partisanship and other differences (Bisgaard 2015). This makes sense given the ideas sketched out earlier, because people can directly observe trends in the state of the economy – by observing changes in salaries and prices, as well as things like closures and layoffs – to a considerable degree within their local communities. Yet those changes are caused by structural market

---

[4] See, for example, Simon Worrall. "Tiny U.S. Island is Drowning. Residents Deny the Reason." *National Geographic*, September 10, 2018. Available at www.nationalgeographic.co.uk/animals/2018/09/tiny-us-island-is-drowning-residents-deny-the-reason.

forces that are *not* directly observable to people, and so exposure to powerful changes or swings in the economy does not necessarily create convergent beliefs about *why* they are taking place. This directly pertains to misinformation since economic conditions are often the subject of intense propaganda by governments around the world. Indeed, one intriguing study reveals that Russian state television channels generally acknowledge poor economic realities in the country rather than seeking to deny their existence, but often blame them on the West and other external forces outside the regime's control (Rozenas and Stukal 2019). The extent to which different kinds of economic beliefs are constrained by personal experience – and can be distorted and manipulated by political actors – is thus another issue further illuminated by this framework.

One other issue on which this framework sheds some light is conspiracy theories. Indeed, conspiracy theories and their appeal in political life have become issues of immense scholarly and public interest in recent years (Oliver and Wood 2014, Uscinski and Parent 2014, Miller, Saunders, and Farhart 2016, Radnitz 2021). What is key to notice about conspiracy theories here is that most if not all of the conspiracy theories that exist would fall on the left side of Figure 6.1, since being closer to the events on which they focus would give you little ability to discern what happened in them. This is because conspiracy theories by definition allege some malevolent actions perpetrated by a *secret* cabal (i.e., a "conspiracy") to undermine public welfare, rather than something that takes place in full public view. This definitional feature has key implications from our perspective, as it implies that conspiracy theories may be especially resistant – vs. other types of misinformation or unsubstantiated claims – to being punctured when people are exposed to relevant events because there is nothing that they can see to clearly debunk them. This may be a crucial idea as scholars move toward theorizing the nature of conspiracy theories more thoroughly and situating them vs. other related phenomena, as well as thinking through their influence and correctability.

In sum, this table provides a preliminary way of thinking about the extent to which – *across different types of issues and situations in the world* – proximity and exposure to the phenomenon of interest will puncture factual misperceptions about it. The nature of fighting in war falls into the lower-right quadrant of the figure, where both the means and motives to see through lies exist with more proximity and exposure to the relevant events. This is because wartime violence is generally both high-stakes and highly visible or verifiable to those around it. The key question is where other types of issues and phenomena fall. Future research in the behavioral social sciences more broadly could benefit from investigating this question and evaluating the ideas about the situational limits of misperceptions that are suggested by this framework.

6.2 Implications of the Book for Policy and Practice

The book also suggests some practical implications about fighting misinformation in war. In particular, if proximate civilians tend to form more accurate beliefs and see through lies in war, the most promising remedy to the issues highlighted in this book may be to *amplify* their voices. This approach would exploit the fact that the gap between local and non-local populations may be *not only a problem, but also a solution* to the issues of factual distortion and manipulation in war. The question then becomes: how might we do this? This requires an understanding of the pathways through which accurate local information "gets out" in conflict.

Figure 6.2 visualizes the most important pathways through which accurate information can typically be transmitted from the front lines of conflict: Through social media platforms, journalists, open-source intelligence (OSINT) organizations, refugees and displaced persons, and soldiers and combatants more broadly. It is worth thinking briefly through the roles that each of these "actors" can play in the truth-trafficking process and how their transmission of accurate information in war can be supported and amplified.

Perhaps the most important pathway through which accurate local information can get out today in war is via social media platforms like

Figure 6.2 Potential pathways for the spread of accurate local information in war zones

Twitter, YouTube, and Facebook. To be sure, social media now plays a massive role in conveying news, images, and information of all sorts from war, both for good and ill (Zeitzoff 2017, Brooking and Singer 2018). With this in mind, one intriguing way to amplify the volume of frontline voices in war would be for major social media companies to promote their activity. Indeed, while laypeople do not have fine-grained geospatial information on most social media users, that information is generally available within the platforms themselves. This means that social media employees could boost the reach of posts emanating from sources at or near the front lines in conflict relative to other kinds of information, or flag frontline information from conflict situations so that it could be easily identified by users.

It appears that Twitter (now rebranded as "X") may have experimented with moves in this direction in 2022 – prior to its takeover and transformation by Elon Musk – based on the introduction of recommended lists in users' news feeds such as the "Ukraine: Latest News" list, which stated that it helps its followers "stay informed about the latest updates from Ukraine through experts and on-the-ground sources."[5] A sufficiently willing leadership at Twitter could do much more on this front though, for instance by bringing scholars with detailed knowledge about armed conflict and conflict event datasets into the platforms' operations so that posts near episodes of violence could be algorithmically amplified in close to real time. Working closely with scholars, platforms such as Twitter could even create a designated label for posts that were spatially verified as emanating from areas of wartime violence. Figure 6.3 shows a mock-up of just such a label placed on a tweet from Aleppo while it was under bombardment by the Syrian government. While the spread of dangerous misinformation in war-torn societies like Myanmar, Syria, and Ethiopia on social media has long been lamented by observers, this represents an innovative and actionable solution that social media platforms could implement to help curtail its distribution.[6]

---

[5] See "Ukraine: Latest News" Twitter list. Available at https://twitter.com/i/lists/1498457571216134144.

[6] The platforms would need effective virtual private network (VPN) detection tools that ensured users could not easily fake their locations in order to obtain the "local source" designation. While the prospect of fraud and deception would undoubtedly be an issue, tools to at least reliably identify whether someone is using a VPN – if not their true location – are widely available.

Lina shamy
@Linashamy

To everyone who can hear me!
#SaveAleppo
#SaveHumanity

0:25 / 0:39

4:23 PM · Dec 12, 2016   LOCAL SOURCE

499   22K   11K   1

Figure 6.3 Example of potential "local source" label on tweet in war

Besides social media, there are several other forces that can amplify accurate on-the-ground information from conflict zones. One is traditional journalism. On the one hand, this project offers a gentle reminder for journalists that accurate conflict reporting requires being "on the ground" in directly affected areas and talking to local civilians, rather than reporting from the safety of capital cities or nearby nations. This was a key critique of the reporting in disputes like the Soviet-Afghan War in the 1980s, which were frequently "reported from across the border in Pakistan, from brief visits to Kabul, or from furtive interviews with guerrilla fighters who soon developed a reputation for being willing to tell the correspondent whatever he wanted to hear" (Knightley 2004: 476). Yet on the other hand, independent and high-quality war reporters perform a great public service, and their work is still one of the best ways of amplifying local voices in war to the outside world. This book, for example, is deeply indebted to the efforts of intrepid war reporters like Megan K. Stack, Janine di Giovanni, Joe Sacco, and many others, who assumed great personal risk to visit the front lines of numerous modern war zones and relate what they heard and saw from victims, witnesses, and perpetrators in conflicts. With the number of journalists killed in conflicts rising significantly in recent decades, from just two in WWI to 66 in Vietnam to 127 during the Iraq War (Liosky and Henrichsen 2009), finding ways to protect the ability of high-quality war reporters to do their work and convey what is actually taking place in war zones remains an important part of the fight against factual distortion in war. Potential policy solutions include making sure media outlets only employ those with the requisite local social capital to safely undertake such difficult work and redoubling global efforts to sanction combatants that intentionally harm reporters.

Another important actor that can amplify accurate local information from conflict settings is OSINT organizations. The model for this is a group called Bellingcat based in the Netherlands. The organization's name comes from the phrase "belling the cat," which is based on a fable about a group of mice who are individually vulnerable to being eaten by a stealthy cat, but work together to place a bell around its neck so that it is rendered audible and harmless. In this fashion, Bellingcat brings together a far-flung network of individuals to debunk misinformation and fact-check events in conflicts using a combination of satellite imagery, social media posts, citizen photos and videos, and other sources of information. While the group uses a variety of different information sources, its challenging of top-down propaganda and its reliance on videos, photos, and other information from people who actually witness or experience relevant conflict events means that it frequently helps bolster the voices of local civilian communities in conflict. Supporting and empowering organizations like Bellingcat with sufficient resources, promotion of their activities, and protection from combatants' retaliation attempts is thus another important way to foster local and bottom-up information in war relative to top-down distortion and propaganda.

Two other actors can serve as potential conduits for accurate local information from wars, even without intending to. One of these is refugees and other displaced persons. While the role of refugees in telling the story of any violent conflict is a crucial one, a cautionary note is warranted here since not all refugees are created equal in terms of their actual degree of wartime experience. Sometimes people in war flee *preemptively* – before the fighting or much of it reaches them – due to their fear of being victimized or simply because others are doing so (Laughlin 2018). Not having witnessed the fighting, these refugees are as vulnerable to misinformation about what is happening as those in areas untouched by the war (if not more, due to their grievances and partisan loyalties). This idea fits well with the evidence in Chapter 5, which showed that there was *wide variation* in the wartime experience of Syrian refugees, variation that was connected to their confidence in their truth discernment ability. This is unsurprising given that some of these people left as early as 2011 whereas others only escaped Syria years later. In a similar vein, much of the civilian population of Belgium that fled the advance of the German army in WWI did so before it arrived, and seems to have been as vulnerable to false stories of German atrocities like the infamous "Belgian baby" as their British counterparts (Knightley 2004, Chapter 5). With all of that said, refugees and displaced persons who do have deep frontline experience have traditionally been a crucial source of accurate information about events on the ground in wars. These individuals have even helped tell the story of this book, from the displaced FATA residents interviewed by Shah (2018) that were discussed in Chapter 3 to the Syrian refugees interviewed by Schon (2020) which were analyzed in Chapter 5. In sum, while we must be careful and discerning about the types of refugees and displaced people in question, protecting *frontline* refugee and displaced communities and helping them tell their stories is an important way to amplify truthful accounts in war.

Finally, another potential conduit for local accurate information from war zones is soldiers. Soldiers deployed in active war zones for any prolonged stretch of time often have much the same means of and motives for learning about what is going on as frontline civilians. What is happening around them in the war is frequently directly visible to those who are deployed as well as important for their survival. This is one reason why soldiers often become disillusioned with war, as they see that the propaganda to which they were exposed clashes sharply with their experiences in conflict. And soldiers returning to or communicating with their communities back home have traditionally been an important challenge to wartime misinformation. For example, mail back to the home front in WWI in many Western countries often painted the war candidly as a brutal and senseless meat grinder in ways that were sharply at odds with nationalistic propaganda narratives (Hanna 2014). Likewise, examples were explored in Chapter 2 of how Russian soldiers in their country's ongoing invasion of Ukraine have offered scathing rebukes of their superiors' efforts to mislead them about the nature of the war. The Kremlin's attempts to suppress the Union of the Committee of Soldiers' Mothers of Russia – a prominent network of soldiers' families that might have amplified these types of personal accounts of the conflict – and to limit the use of regular Russian soldiers in favor of proxies and mercenaries in the conflict likely reflect in part an understanding of these dynamics and the extent to which soldiers and their loved ones back home can puncture Kremlin propaganda. Overall, then, soldiers and other combatants also provide a pathway through which accurate local information can spread from war zones. While one should think through their roles and experiences in war in a careful and case-specific fashion, they can be a meaningful piece of the solution to the problems of factual distortion and misperception in war.

In sum, there are several key channels through which truth can spread in war, from civilian social media activity to open-source investigative organizations to returning soldiers. Yet as noted earlier, many of these conduits can also push false information to broader audiences, as in the case of refugees who flee preemptively from war or soldiers who are never deployed to the front lines. Thus, the extent to which each of these pathways actually taps into sustained frontline experience in a particular conflict should be evaluated when considering its potential to amplify accurate local wartime information. Figure 6.2 can offer a useful template for thinking through these issues and some of the key ways in which the truth can spread effectively in war.

Of course, accurate portrayals of war from the front lines must not only be spread but also *believed* by relevant audiences in order to make a significant impact. And a skeptical reader might point out that a greater flow of accurate information from the front lines could still run up against the distorting effects of motivated bias among constituencies removed from the fighting. However, people's factual beliefs about conflict are not *only* a product of their motivated biases, but also of a myriad of other factors such as their exposure to different channels of information and what those channels tell them, the beliefs of their families and broader social networks, the cues they receive from relevant elites in their communities, and other psychological processes like cognitive biases. While motivated bias is a key problem in driving false beliefs about war among non-local civilians, it is variable and part of a rich tapestry of factors that shape people's wartime thinking. Moreover, recent research on misinformation and its correctability points toward the primacy of "information effects" in shaping people's factual beliefs, showing that what people believe on a variety of factual issues is highly sensitive to the information to which they are exposed – rather than intransigently rooted in their overarching political worldviews or identities (e.g., Pennycook, Cannon, and Rand 2018, Pennycook and Rand 2019, Wood and Porter 2019, Porter, Velez, and Wood 2022, Porter and Wood 2022). These points both provide compelling reasons to expect that a greater supply of accurate frontline information in war would have at least *some* positive influence on the landscape of factual beliefs in wartime.

6.3 Wartime Misinformation and Its Limits Moving Forward

This section looks to the horizon, focusing on how the problem of wartime misinformation is evolving over time and what it might look like moving forward – as well as the most promising future research avenues to understand and counter it. Indeed, it begins by considering the trajectory of misinformation in war over time and the extent to which, broadly speaking, it represents a story of continuity or one of change. Then, it briefly explores the primary lessons from the ongoing war in Gaza, which – as the most recent major conflict to erupt and an intense arena for misinformation – is worth engaging with when thinking about the phenomenon's trajectory into the future. Finally, it lays out the most promising research avenues to build on the insights in this book and gain more analytical leverage over wartime misinformation moving forward.

6.3.1 Continuity and Change Over Time

In order to understand where the problem of wartime misinformation may be heading, one has to think carefully about its historical trajectory. This raises the question: is the story in the book chiefly one of continuity or change over time? In one sense, it is important to note the fundamental continuity in the dynamics outlined in this book. Indeed, the book's core claim – that misinformation often proliferates widely in war, fed by informational and motivational biases, but is constrained by proximity and exposure to the relevant events – manifests across space and time. The book draws on a wealth of historical and contemporary conflicts to build its case, with examples in Chapter 2 reaching back to some of the earliest days of war reporting during the US Civil War and traversing the world wars of the twentieth century, the Cold War, and the post-Cold War periods. From embedded war reporters debunking atrocity claims during WWI to frontline civilians seeing through anti-drone propaganda in contemporary Pakistan, the dangerous spread of misinformation in war and the ability of direct exposure to puncture it is clear across time.

Yet, in another sense, it is reasonable to consider how these broad patterns may evolve as they interact with situational factors that vary over time. Much of this has to do with thinking about how the book's findings are affected by technological change. In particular, the emergence of new information communication technologies – like the rise and continuing global proliferation of the Internet, smartphones, commercial satellites, and social media – has significantly changed how information from conflict settings is produced and consumed. How does the continuing march toward an increasingly interconnected, decentralized, and social-mediatized information landscape impact the fundamental dynamics identified in this book?

Careful reflection on these technologies and the dynamics of conflicts surveyed in the book before and after their emergence suggests that there may be multiple countervailing effects. On the one hand, like the rise of new and transformative mass communication technologies before them – such as the radio and the television – the spread of the Internet has in all likelihood increased the *reach* of wartime misinformation, the *speed* with which it can be shared to diverse audiences, and the visceral *impact* with which it can be conveyed. In other words, the Internet has almost certainly enabled wartime misinformation to reach broader audiences, to do so more rapidly, and to contain more immersive visual material. A social media post with a misleading and incendiary video about a contentious intercommunal incident in Sri Lanka,[7]

---

[7] See Amanda Taub and Max Fisher. "Where Countries are Tinderboxes and Facebook is a Match." *The New York Times*, April 21, 2018.

or a post showing a video of an atrocity from the Syrian civil war that is presented as if it came from Gaza,[8] can reach millions of people around the world within a matter of minutes. These effects generally work to make misinformation more dangerous, pervasive, and far-reaching in war and other fragile contexts.

And yet, on the other hand, the spread of these same technologies has also meant that more accurate frontline information about conflict is captured and shared. Armed with smartphones and Internet access, "citizen witnesses" now have a much greater capability to record and share videos, photos, and more that capture what they see and hear from the front lines of conflicts and other crises (Allan 2013). Similarly, there is a greater likelihood of at least some combatants in war using these technologies to record and share their actions and experiences, from Russian troops posting platoon selfies that betrayed their presence in Ukraine during the Donbas War[9] to Israeli soldiers recording videos of themselves smashing up shops and destroying supplies in Gaza.[10] Widespread commercial satellite coverage of conflict zones has also increased the flow of accurate visual information in war, having been used for example to provide visual evidence about events during the war in Gaza such as the heavily politicized explosion that occurred at Al-Ahli hospital on October 17, 2023.[11] In sum, there is now much more of a visual record of the front lines of war captured and shared in a decentralized way by civilians, combatants, and other actors.

The sum total might then be that moving forward, wartime misinformation is changing in multiple countervailing ways. On the one hand, those who are pushing factually biased narratives can spread

[8] See, for example, Angelo Fichera. "The Horrifying Images are Real, but They're Not from the Israel-Gaza War." *The New York Times*, November 2, 2023.

[9] See, for example, Simon Ostrovsky. "Russia Denies that Its Soldiers are in Ukraine, but We Tracked One There Using His Selfies." *VICE News*, June 16, 2015. Available at www.vice.com/en/article/ev9dbz/russia-denies-that-its-soldiers-are-in-ukraine-but-we-tracked-one-there-using-his-selfies.

[10] See Ivana Kottasová and Celine Alkhaldi. "Videos Show Israeli Soldiers in Gaza Burning Food, Vandalizing a Shop and Ransacking Private Homes." *CNN*, December 15, 2023. Available at www.cnn.com/2023/12/15/middleeast/israeli-soldiers-burningfood-gaza-intl/index.html.

[11] See Geoff Brumfield et al. "Here's the Available Evidence of What Happened at Al Ahli Arab Hospital in Gaza." *NPR*, October 18, 2023. Available at www.npr.org/2023/10/18/1206795861/heres-the-available-evidence-of-what-happened-at-al-ahli-arab-hospital-in-gaza.

wartime misinformation to wider audiences more quickly and intensively online. On the other hand, those who are on the front lines of conflict – who are shown to be a key check on misinformation in this book – can much more easily capture and share their actual experiences and observations about the realities of conflict. This makes hiding misdeeds in war more difficult. Indeed, the idea that the US government could have concealed, say, the massive expansion of the Vietnam War into Laos and Cambodia from its population – as it did for several years during the administration of President Richard Nixon – is not realistic today given the ability of civilians under bombardment to record and share their experiences. Accordingly, one interpretation of these distinct effects on the use of misinformation in conflict is that *they are making it increasingly easy to incite, but also increasing difficult to conceal in war.*

6.3.2 Lessons from the War in Gaza

The bloody October 7, 2023, surprise attack by Hamas and Israel's ensuing brutal invasion of Gaza began unfolding as the text of this book was being finalized. How does this latest and most devastating round of Israel-Hamas fighting align with the book's primary findings, and what does it suggest about the frontier of wartime misinformation moving forward?

In many senses, the latest Israel-Hamas war speaks well to the major insights in this book. There has been widespread misinformation about what is happening on both "sides" of the conflict, fueled in important ways by the factors explored in this volume.[12] Indeed, both informational and motivational biases are clearly playing crucial roles in fostering misinformation about the war and allowing it to flourish. On the informational side, the Israeli media ecosystem on the one hand, and the Palestinian and Arab media landscapes on the other have presented quite divergent pictures of events on the ground, with each side fixating on the atrocities perpetrated against their community. Israeli media for example has been saturated with a continuous stream of new bloody revelations and horrifying details about the 10/7 attacks, constantly re-traumatizing Israeli society and keeping

---

[12] See, for example, Elizabeth Dwoskin. "A Flood of Misinformation Shapes Views of Israel-Gaza Conflict." *The Washington Post*, October 14, 2023.

them focused on their own suffering.[13] In contrast, the Palestinian and Arab media environments have tended to focus little on the lurid details of 10/7, instead becoming overwhelmingly centered on the brutal consequences of Israel's heavy-handed invasion of Gaza and the civilian suffering it has produced.[14] These predictable informational discrepancies have resulted in the internalization of very different pictures of events on the ground by audiences on different sides of the dispute.

By the same token, the importance of motivated bias in shaping how people approach new information in the conflict is also palpable. Indeed, a quick perusal of some of the most influential accounts on each side of the war on Twitter reveals that many of the most hardcore and belligerent supporters of Israel have engaged in denialism about the realities of Palestinian death and suffering in Gaza, including promoting the fallacious "Pallywood" idea which alleges that Palestinian "crisis actors" are pretending to be hurt in various scenes of Gaza's destruction.[15] Similarly, some of the most hardcore pro-Palestinian supporters have engaged in persistent denialism and questioning of events on 10/7, for instance by suggesting that it was an "inside job" by the Israeli government to start the war or refusing to acknowledge the atrocities during the attack.[16] Partisans on both sides have often been clear about the "logic" that underlies their thinking, with some staunch defenders of Israel stating categorically that Hamas are liars (and thus refusing to accept any casualty numbers from the Hamas-run Ministry of Health), and some strident pro-Palestinian advocates stating that they will not believe anything that comes from the Israeli side

[13] See, for example, Tia Goldenberg. "Israeli Media, also Traumatized by Hamas Attack, Become Communicators of Israel's Message." *Associated Press,* October 29, 2023.

[14] See, for example, David D. Kirkpatrick and Adam Rasgon. "The Hamas Propaganda War." *The New Yorker,* October 30, 2023.

[15] See, for example, William Summers. "'Fake News' Claims Open Up New Front in Middle East War." *The Australian Associated Press,* December 10, 2023. Available at www.aap.com.au/news/fake-news-claims-open-up-new-front-in-middle-east-war/.

[16] See, for example, Sagi Cohen. "Denial of Hamas' October 7 Massacre is Gaining Steam Online." *Haaretz,* November 7, 2023. Available at www.haaretz.com/israel-news/2023-11-07/ty-article/.premium/denial-of-hamas-october-7-massacre-is-gaining-pace-online/0000018b-aa45-d5aa-a19f-afffabf10000.

or the Israeli Defense Forces (IDF) (which makes them reject any claims of 10/7 atrocities that are amplified or referenced by Israeli authorities). This desire to perceive the adversary as fundamentally and unqualifiedly villainous makes potential false claims about its misbehavior easy to believe, and potential true claims about its mistreatment and victimization impossible to stomach. In sum, the role of preexisting partisan orientations in the conflict in coloring people's engagement with new information and their factual beliefs is not hard to discern.

Meanwhile, there are indications that those directly exposed to the realities of the fighting at least in some cases have deviated from these patterns. To be sure, the current Israel-Hamas war is a "hard case" for the seeing-is-disbelieving argument. This is because the realities of the fighting have overwhelmingly served to *confirm and reinforce* preexisting prejudices: Hamas perpetrated brutal atrocities on 10/7 in communities in southern Israel that already overwhelmingly saw it as a hostile and even hateful force dedicated to their destruction, and Israel's heavy-handed and brutal devastation of Gaza after the 10/7 attack was directly experienced by a Gazan civilian population that already tended to see it as a cruel occupier and oppressor. The argument has its strongest potential bite where there are clear gaps or deviations between people's preexisting orientations in a conflict and the realities of it that they experience on the ground.

Yet, even in the context of the ongoing Israel-Hamas war, personal exposure to the fighting has had unexpected effects. One place where this is visible is in the context of the Israeli hostages and their families. Indeed, released Israeli hostages and the families of those still held in Gaza have not only been a powerful force pushing for a ceasefire in Gaza – in contrast to the dominant current of Israeli public opinion thus far – but they have also conveyed firsthand experiences that have been sharply at odds with Israeli propaganda. For instance, some hostages have verbally attacked Israeli government officials due to the fact that they believed they faced more of a mortality threat from Israel's reckless and indiscriminate bombing than from being killed by Hamas. For instance, one of the released hostages berated Israel's controversial Prime Minister Bibi Netanyahu and his war cabinet in an audio call, saying: "You have no information. You have no information. The fact that we were shelled, the

fact that no one knew anything about where we were ... You claim
there is intelligence. But the fact is we are being shelled."[17]

Similarly, another family member of released hostages directed
anger toward officials on the call for their ignorance of the actual
experiences of the hostages in Gaza, stating:

They were under constant threat from the IDF shelling. You sat in front
of us and assured us that it does not threaten their lives. They also roam
the street and [are] not only in the tunnels. They are mounted on donkeys
and carts. You will not be able to recognize them on the street and you are
endangering their lives. It is our duty to return them now.[18]

The mistaken killing of three hostages who were trying to surrender
in Gaza by Israeli soldiers[19] has likely compounded this issue of many
hostages and their family members not perceiving Israeli forces as liberators carefully taking out their terrorist captors but as an indiscriminate force lashing out ruthlessly in Gaza. This speaks to the power of
wartime experiences to influence beliefs about events on the ground.

There are also signs that many Gazan civilians have had some of
their beliefs challenged by the realities of the war. Notably, while
Israel's heavy-handed behavior generally seems to have confirmed
and reinforced existing Palestinian attitudes, there are reportedly
strong pockets of anger at Hamas's wartime behavior and its consequences among those experiencing it firsthand in Gaza. For instance,
there have been instances of Gazan civilians cursing out Hamas in
live press conferences[20] and yelling at reporters on live television on
friendly networks like Al Jazeera[21] about their grievances toward

[17] Irene Nasser, Tim Lister, and Richard Greene. "Leaked Audio of Heated
Meeting Reveals Hostages' Fury at Netanyahu." *CNN*, December 6, 2023.
Available at www.cnn.com/2023/12/06/middleeast/leaked-audio-of-heated-
meeting-reveals-hostages-fury-at-netanyahu/index.html.

[18] Ibid.

[19] See, for example, Yaniv Kubovich. "Investigation Into Killing of Israeli
Hostages by IDF Reveals a String of Errors and Flaws." *Haaretz*, December
21, 2023. Available at www.haaretz.com/israel-news/2023-12-21/ty-article/
.premium/investigation-into-killing-of-israeli-hostages-by-idf-reveals-a-string-
of-errors-and-flaws/0000018c-890c-d60e-afdf-ed0ec51e0000.

[20] Margherita Stancati and Abeer Ayyoub. "Gazans are Starting to Blame Hamas
for Wartime Suffering." *The Wall Street Journal*, December 21, 2023.

[21] "WATCH: Gaza Resident Criticizes Hamas on Al Jazeera, Reporter Turns
Away and Ignores Him." *Jerusalem Post*, November 15, 2023. Available at
www.jpost.com/middle-east/article-773289.

Hamas due to its inability to protect them after provoking Israel's wrath, its hoarding of desperately needed supplies, and its apparent general indifference to the terrible plight of the Gazan civilian population. This may be why polling conducted during a pause in the fighting showed that Hamas had gained much more popularity in the West Bank than in the Gaza Strip,[22] where personal experiences of the war and Hamas's role in it do not always align neatly with the organization's preferred narrative.

What about what this latest Israel-Hamas conflict suggests regarding new developments in the wartime misinformation space? One informational feature of the war that is relatively new in the history of conflict and intersects with the book's argument in intriguing ways is the widespread use of GoPros – the cameras worn by Hamas attackers on their heads to record their deeds – during the 10/7 attack. This tactic has seen growing use by some non-state violent actors in recent years, from the mass shooters in two mosques in Christchurch, New Zealand, on March 15, 2019, to the insurrectionists at the US Capitol on January 6, 2021. Attackers in these cases are seeking to record and transmit their deeds for the purposes of political messaging and propaganda. However, the use of GoPros on 10/7 shows their potential to backfire, as the footage removed from the bodies of a number of Hamas operatives proved to be a significant intelligence coup for the Israel Defense Forces and the Mossad as well as a clear empirical record of Hamas brutality to the world.[23] In the latter sense, they served much like civilian witnesses on the front lines of war, puncturing wartime misinformation and making it harder for the perpetrator to hide atrocities. This suggests their use may be disincentivized for violent non-state actors who are sensitive to political and reputational costs outside of narrow supportive constituencies moving forward.

---

[22] "Press Release: Public Opinion Poll No (90)." *Palestinian Center for Policy and Survey Research*, December 13, 2023. Available at https://pcpsr.org/en/node/961.

[23] See, for example, Emanuel Fabian. "GoPro Cameras on Hamas Gunmen Capture How Terror Group Broke into Israel." *Times of Israel*, October 18, 2023. Available at www.timesofisrael.com/liveblog_entry/gopro-cameras-on-hamas-gunmen-capture-how-terror-group-broke-into-israel/.

6.3.3 *Future Research Avenues and the Path Ahead*

This book's findings suggest several promising avenues for further research. Two of these have already been alluded to earlier: (1) exploring the generalizability of the book's argument about proximity puncturing misinformation across issue areas based on their lethality and visibility and (2) examining the diverse pathways through which accurate local information is spread in conflict to understand how the truth actually gets out in practice in wars. This section outlines three other promising avenues through which future research could fruitfully build on the book: Investigating the cognitive psychology of misinformation in war, examining genocides as a way to parse out the relative weight of the mechanisms behind the book's argument, and conducting empirical research on the efficacy of different solutions.

One important avenue for future research to examine is the role of cognitive psychology in shaping factual beliefs in war. Indeed, existing literature on social and political misperceptions is broadly split into motivational and cognitive perspectives. Motivational accounts focus on factors like partisanship and identity-based motivated reasoning in fostering endorsement of conspiracist beliefs (Nyhan and Reifler 2010, Uscinski and Parent 2014, Miller, Saunders, and Farhart 2016). Cognitive explanations stress general psychological predispositions like needs for order, certainty, and closure that lead people toward conspiratorial perceptions (Swami, Chamorro-Premuzic, and Furnham 2010, Oliver and Wood 2014). This distinction is important because, while motivational factors were a key part of the argument in this book, it did not examine the effect of psychological "need" factors. Yet it is likely that these, too, influence people's factual beliefs in war – and they may do so in different ways than in peace.

One cognitive psychological factor that may be crucial in war zones is a desire for normalcy in life. The ability of people to deny or ignore the existence of war on their doorstep can be striking. This is clear, for instance, in the accounts of villagers in war zones like Sierra Leone who ignored warning signs of the fighting approaching them, such as attacks on neighboring villages or streams of refugees telling them about what was happening (Beah 2007: 1). Likewise, many Syrians appear to have exhibited these tendencies as well, not wanting to believe their country was plunging into war for months or even years.

In the words of one, "who wants to see their country turning to war? You avoid it if you can, you avoid thinking about it. You don't want to believe it" (Di Giovanni 2016: 90). While this may reflect a sort of motivated reasoning, it may also simply be a product of peoples' underlying need for normalcy and inability to even cognitively process the notion of war touching or reaching their communities. Given that people vary in terms of their cognitive needs for things like normalcy and certainty, these traits may play important roles in shaping civilians' perceptions of what is occurring in war.

Another cognitive factor that may be important for factual beliefs in war is a perceived lack of control. Psychological studies indicate that a perceived lack of control fuels belief in conspiracy theories, illusory patterns, and other related phenomena (Whitson and Galinsky 2008). Such a lack of control is likely to be acute among civilian populations in war, as captured in the African proverb "when elephants fight, it is the grass that suffers" – which is often applied to the plight of civilians in conflict (Deng et al. 2005). In fact, the most control-starved populations may be local civilians in the line of fire – especially those with few exit options or who face seemingly random patterns of violence – which may help explain some of the misperceptions we *do* see in those communities. Indeed, one intriguing analysis of civilian behavior during violent ethnic riots in India shows that people's perceptions of control and predictability are strongly connected to their survival strategies in episodes of violent contention (Milliff in press). It is a short hop from this to thinking that such perceptions may shape their factual beliefs as well. In this way, cognitive factors such as the needs for normalcy or control may be important drivers of wartime beliefs. Moreover, these cognitive needs might also interact with situational variables like the objective complexity, uncertainty, or severity of war in ways that affect communities' ability to process it. One way in which future studies can thus build on this research is by investigating the effects of cognitive – and not just motivational – psychology in driving and shaping how people come to understand events in war.

Meanwhile, another way in which future work might build on this book is by searching for contexts in which the effects of each of our two primary mechanisms can be examined individually. Recall that the book's central argument was that *both* more direct information *and* more powerful incentives to use that information carefully help local civilians eschew lies in war. While some of the book's evidence pointed toward one of these mechanisms more directly,[24] most of its analyses were powered by both of them simultaneously. For example, results showing that people who have more experience with or live closer to the events in question tend to be less vulnerable to lies about them implicate both of these pathways. But in some situations these processes diverge, potentially impacting the conditions under which the theory applies. For example, in genocides, communities that live near the killing but are not targeted themselves by it – such as ethnic Germans living close to Jewish areas under the Nazis during the Holocaust, or Buddhists living in Rakhine State (where most Rohingya reside) in contemporary Myanmar – could be exposed to ample direct information about what is going on but not have a survival-oriented motive to understand it. Does the book's thesis apply to these individuals? In fact, there are some hints that it does, for example in anecdotes from situations like the one in Myanmar in which frontline civilians who are not at risk themselves appear to still have a better grasp of what is happening than those further removed from events.[25] But a more systematic investigation might reveal important insights about the scope of the theory's applicability and the relative influence of its two mechanisms, while teaching us something about accurate perceptions of genocide as well.

[24] For example, the analysis of Syrian interview data in Chapter 5 suggested that those with more wartime experience tended to not just have more accurate factual beliefs but to think differently, relying less on simple heuristics such as the speaker's identity when judging the veracity of rumors and more on comparisons with their personal experience. This is consistent with the idea that they are engaging in more effortful, accuracy-driven thinking rather than relying on simple and easy rules of thumb to decide what is true and false (e.g., Tetlock 1983).

[25] Indeed, while incendiary misinformation about atrocities by the Rohingya minority against the country's Buddhist majority and denialism of the brutal atrocities committed by the military against the Rohingya have found disturbingly fertile ground in Myanmar, there are indications that some of those who live within Rakhine State itself – where most of the violence has actually taken place – are more discerning. For example, one young man in Rakhine State's capital who was interviewed about the widespread (mis) information about the violence on Burmese social media dismissed false and inflammatory photos of dead Burmese soldiers as "obvious fake news" and stated that he could "usually tell the difference between real and fake news." See Annie Gowen and Max Bearak, "Fake News on Facebook Fans the Flames against the Rohingya in Burma." *Washington Post*, December 8, 2017.

Finally, a third promising pathway for future research is examining the efficacy of different solutions to the problem of wartime misinformation and misperception. Can traditional tactics used against misinformation such as factual corrections, digital literacy training, and the like ameliorate false beliefs in wars? How can they be delivered effectively and safely at scale in conflict settings? Would they gain credibility by incorporating the voices of the frontline civilian communities who have the greatest wartime experience? Can "boosting the signal" of local civilians on Twitter and other social media platforms meaningfully influence the factual balance of the conversation around a conflict? Rigorously evaluating solutions – including those that grow out of the ideas in this book – remains a pressing next step for future research as we hopefully move toward a world in which we do not just comprehend but (robustly) counter the problem.

Looking ahead, we should not be overly pollyannish about the challenges posed by factual misinformation and misperceptions in violent conflicts: They are likely to remain with us, and they can have serious consequences in triggering, aggravating, and prolonging episodes of violence and conflict around the world. But a deep understanding of why they are believed and when individuals know better shows that there are a number of potential ways to amplify accurate information from wars, from optimizing social media algorithms to prioritize local frontline posts in conflict settings to empowering high-quality war reporters and investigative organizations to helping tell the stories of refugees and soldiers with firsthand conflict experience to a broader audience. While the depths and dangers of factual misinformation in war are great, such a research-informed and multilayered approach seems promising in helping to fight them. Ultimately, with a concerted effort along these lines, one hopes that more people will begin to "see" more clearly in war.

Appendix

Expanded Discussion of Drone Strike Databases from Chapter 3

In Chapter 3, I briefly compared the three major databases on the US drone campaign in Pakistan to help establish its relatively discriminate nature. Here I provide some more background on these databases, including their methodologies and results.

One active database on US drone strikes in Pakistan is maintained by the New America Foundation (NAF), an American think tank that has developed a significant national security focus. NAF's drone database draws on major Pakistani newspapers (e.g., Dawn, The Express Tribune, The News) as well as credible international news outlets (e.g., AFP, Associated Press, Reuters) for its information. The database relies on at least two reputable sources to verify each strike, recording the number of "militant," "civilian," and "unknown" casualties in these sources and providing a range whenever there is variation. As of this writing, the database records 414 US drone strikes in Pakistan, resulting in 2,366–3,702 total casualties, with an estimated 245–303 of these listed as civilians and another 211–328 listed as unknown. If we treat all unknown casualties as civilians, this would yield a ratio of 4.6 militants for every civilian killed using the averages of the ranges provided (this goes up to roughly 9:1 if we omit all unknowns as suggested in Plaw and Fricker 2012).

Another major active strike-tracking database is maintained by the Bureau of Investigative Journalism (BIJ), a non-profit news organization based out of the UK. The BIJ database also relies on reputable Pakistani and international media reporting, supplementing these sources with leaked government documents, academic research articles, and independent fieldwork visits to Pakistan. The database uses a minimum of four different sources to verify each strike and presents narrative descriptions of each event as well as active links to all media sources used to investigate it. Overall, it is increasingly seen as the most transparent, complete, and reliable publicly available drone strike database by academics (Bauer, Reese, and Ruby 2021). To date, the BIJ database records 430 US drone strikes in Pakistan, resulting in 2,515–4,026 total casualties, of which 424–969 are civilian. This database has higher civilian casualty counts than the NAF database largely because it counts anyone reported as "tribesmen" and anyone under eighteen as civilians (meanwhile, the NAF classifies tribesmen as unknown and uses fourteen as the age of adulthood). Still, using the means of the BIJ ranges produces a similar militant-to-civilian casualty ratio of 3.7:1.

A third major active, publicly available source of drone strike data comes from the UMass DRONE Database Project, an academic data-set from the University of Massachusetts-Dartmouth. Like the other sources discussed earlier, this database uses mostly Pakistani and international media outlets, but instead of treating all credible sources as equally valid, it prioritizes the highest-quality reporting in terms of (1) level of detail, (2) range of sources, and (3) recency of publication (Plaw and Fricker 2012). Like the NAF database, the UMass Drone Database Project classifies casualties as "militant," "civilian," and "unknown," and provides ranges for each type of casualties based on the sources used. At the time of this writing, the database was currently being rebranded and moved to a new online home, but I was able to obtain its most recent figures from the individual managing that transition who graciously shared the data with me. The data-base contains 452 drone strikes in Pakistan resulting in 3,250 overall deaths, with 179 of these civilian and 486 unknown. Once again, if we (conservatively) treat all unknown individuals as civilian, this yields a militant-to-civilian casualty ratio of around 3.9:1 (or 14.4:1 if we exclude unknowns).

Finally, a fourth major source of drone strike information that was popular for many years but is no longer actively maintained is from the Long War Journal (LWJ), an online foreign policy outlet affiliated with the think tank The Foundation for the Defense of Democracies. The LWJ also relies on Pakistani and international press reports as well as its own reporting, which draws heavily on US intelligence sources. This database has limited summary statistics available online, but as mentioned earlier it is unfortunately no longer actively maintained. As

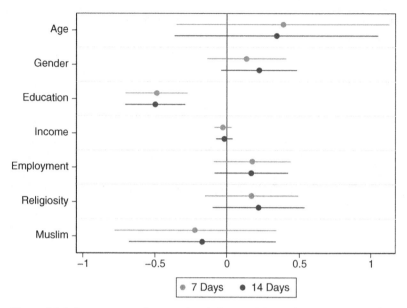

Figure A3.1 Pre vs. poststrike covariate balance with varying response windows

of May 1, 2017, when I was last able to access the database, the LWJ database recorded 392 American drone strikes in Pakistan with 2,799 militants and 158 civilians killed. The LWJ database thus provides a militant-to-civilian casualty ratio of 16.7:1, significantly greater than the NAF and BIJ estimates. Because the database is not very transparent in its methodology, is no longer active, and relies heavily on government sources, however, the estimate should be treated with appropriate caution and as an upper bound in terms of its militant-to-civilian casualty ratio.

Alternative Modeling for Analysis of Drone Support in Chapter 3

Table A3.1 replicates Chapter 3's analysis of Pakistani drone attitudes from 2009 to 12, but with ordered logistic regression models rather than ordinary least squares or linear regressions. As is clear, the sign and significance of all of the key predictors remains unchanged, with perceptions of excess collateral damage exhibiting a strong negative association with Pakistani drone support. Additionally, as in the linear

Table A3.1 *Predictors of drone support in Pakistan with ordered logistic regression*

	M1	M2	M3	M4
Attitudes				
Military necessity	0.69***	0.48***	0.42***	0.42***
	(0.09)	(0.09)	(0.10)	(0.10)
Collateral damage	−1.22***	−1.26***	−1.23***	−1.25***
	(0.16)	(0.17)	(0.17)	(0.17)
Sovereignty violation	−0.28***	−0.25**	−0.22*	−0.21*
	(0.08)	(0.09)	(0.09)	(0.09)
Pro-American		0.22***	0.21***	0.19***
		(0.05)	(0.05)	(0.05)
Pro-government		0.21***	0.20***	0.20***
		(0.05)	(0.05)	(0.05)
Taliban is threat		0.07	0.06	0.07
		(0.04)	(0.04)	(0.04)
Demographics				
Age			−0.01	−0.01
			(0.01)	(0.01)
Gender			0.47***	0.48***
			(0.10)	(0.10)
Education			−0.01	0.00
			(0.02)	(0.02)
Religiosity				0.50***
				(0.14)
Muslim				−0.63*
				(0.28)
Pashtun				−0.07
				(0.19)
Fixed Effects				
Province fixed effects	Yes	Yes	Yes	Yes
Wave fixed effects	Yes	Yes	Yes	Yes
Observations	2,976	2,693	2,678	2,675

Note: Results from ordered logistic regressions. Standard errors in parentheses. $p < 0.05$, $p < 0.01$, $p < 0.001$.

regression results, the coefficients on this variable are the largest of the three drone related items and among the largest in the models overall. To see this more clearly, I calculated different variables' average marginal effects on the probability of holding each value of the dependent variable – that is, of viewing American drone strikes as a very bad, bad, good, or very good thing. This reveals that "turning on" the collateral damage variable – that is, going from a zero to a one on the variable – increases the probability of harboring a strongly negative view of drones by 23 percentage points. In contrast, the largest shift associated with turning on the military necessity variable for any level of the DV is eight percentage points, and it is just four percentage points for the sovereignty violation variable. This is consistent with the relative sizes of the linear regression coefficients on these variables in the main text.

Supporting Information and Analyses for Chapter 4

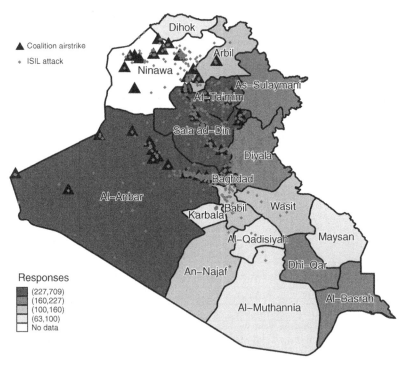

Figure A4.1 Distribution of survey responses and relevant violent events across Iraq

Table A4.1 *Comparison of sample with Arab barometer and Iraqi census projections*

	IIACSS 2016	AB 2012	AB 2013	COSIT 2014
Urban				
Urban	66.5%	71.6%	69.1%	69.7%
Rural	33.5	28.4	30.9	30.3
Gender				
Male	54.2%	52.6%	50.0%	50.9%
Female	45.8	47.4	50.0	49.1
Age				
18–24	16.7%	22.8%	25.3%	25.2%
25–34	28.0	25.9	27.4	27.0
35–44	24.2	22.8	20.0	20.4
45–54	19.0	19.1	16.8	14.1
55+	12.1	9.6	10.5	13.3
Unemployed				
Yes	14.2%	14.0%	12.5%	14.3%
No	85.8	86.0	87.5	85.7
Ethnicity				
Arab	85.8%	83.5%	83.5%	
Kurd	12.9	14.6	14.6	
Islamic Sect				
Sunni	47.6%	45.9%	44.3%	
Shi'a	52.4	53.4	51.7	

Note: Arab Barometer respondents who identified as just Muslim were split between Sunni and Shi'a proportionally for purposes of comparison. There is no contemporary census data on the country's ethnic or sectarian composition (due to the political sensitivity of these issues). COSIT is Iraq's Central Organization of Statistics, which is in charge of its census and census projections.

Table A4.2 *Descriptive statistics for all variables used in Iraq survey*

Variable	N	Mean	SD	Min	Max
Strikes target PMF	3,393	2.049	1.435	0	4
Strikes help ISIL	3,391	1.962	1.407	0	4
Shi'a Arab	3,500	0.454	0.498	0	1
Sunni Arab	3,500	0.390	0.488	0	1
Kurd	3,500	0.129	0.335	0	1
Confidence in US	3,485	0.812	1.000	0	3
Support for PMF	3,426	1.399	0.826	0	2
Iraqiyya TV	3,479	2.054	1.146	0	3
Sharqiyya TV	3,478	1.883	1.187	0	3
Rudaw TV	2,773	0.545	0.947	0	3
Lived under ISIL	3,496	0.213	0.410	0	1
Time under ISIL	743	1.688	1.258	0	4
Age	3,500	37.78	12.71	18	80
Gender	3,500	0.542	0.498	0	1
Education	3,323	2.227	1.489	0	6
Income	3,259	3.763	1.776	0	6
Urbanity	3,500	0.665	0.472	0	1
IDP status	3,498	0.144	0.351	0	1
Distance to airstrike	3,500	87.18	125.8	0.233	469.3
Support for ISIL	3,433	0.027	0.219	0	2
ISIL influence positive	3,459	0.086	0.392	0	4
Distance to ISIL attack	3,500	6.188	12.06	0.004	180.9

Note: the table shows the number of observations, mean, standard deviation, and minimum and maximum value for each of the independent variables used in the analysis.

Table A4.3 *Question wording for attitudinal survey items used in Iraq survey*

Variable	Question wording
Strikes target PMF	"*Please tell me whether you agree or disagree with the following statements regarding Coalition actions in Iraq. And is that somewhat or strongly?*" *[Coalition airstrikes mainly target PMF forces]*
Strikes help ISIL	"*Please tell me whether you agree or disagree with the following statements regarding Coalition actions in Iraq. And is that somewhat or strongly?*" *[Coalition airstrikes mainly help ISIL]*
Confidence in US	"*How much confidence do you have in the following countries to deal responsibly with problems in our region – a great deal of confidence, a fair amount of confidence, not very much confidence, or no confidence at all?*" *[The United States]*
Support for PMF	"*For each of the following groups, please tell me whether you support their goals and activities, support their goals but not their activities, or oppose them completely – or have you not heard enough to say?*" *[Popular Mobilization Forces]*
Iraqiyya TV	"*I'm going to read you the names of some news sources that people use. For each one, please tell me on average how often you use it for news and information – every day, at least once a week, less often, or never?*" *[al-Iraqiyya TV]*
Sharqiyya TV	"*I'm going to read you the names of some news sources that people use. For each one, please tell me on average how often you use it for news and information – every day, at least once a week, less often, or never?*" *[al-Sharqiyya TV]*
Rudaw TV	"*I'm going to read you the names of some news sources that people use. For each one, please tell me on average how often you use it for news and information – every day, at least once a week, less often, or never?*" *[al-Rudaw TV]*
Support for ISIL	"*For each of the following groups, please tell me whether you support their goals and activities, support their goals but not their activities, or oppose them completely – or have you not heard enough to say?*" *[ISIL]*
ISIL influence positive	"*Do you think the following organizations' influence on internal events and affairs in Iraq has been completely positive, somewhat positive, neither positive nor negative, somewhat negative, or complete negative?*" *[ISIL]*

Table A4.4 *Replication of base Iraq models, with measures of ISIL attitudes*

	Airstrikes Target PMF	Airstrikes Help ISIL
Exposure		
Time under ISIL	−0.12***	−0.13***
	(0.03)	(0.03)
Orientations		
Shi'a Arab	0.65***	0.75***
	(0.12)	(0.12)
Sunni Arab	0.07	0.22
	(0.12)	(0.11)
Confidence in US	−0.32***	−0.24***
	(0.03)	(0.03)
Support for PMF	0.18***	0.25***
	(0.05)	(0.05)
Information		
Iraqiyya TV	0.11***	0.05
	(0.03)	(0.03)
Sharqiyya TV	−0.20***	−0.12***
	(0.03)	(0.03)
Rudaw TV	−0.27***	−0.28***
	(0.04)	(0.04)
ISIL attitudes		
Support for ISIL	−0.10	−0.08
	(0.12)	(0.12)
ISIL influence positive	0.06	0.14*
	(0.06)	(0.06)
Distance to ISIL attack	−0.00	−0.00
	(0.00)	(0.00)
Constant	2.27***	1.88***
	(0.17)	(0.17)
Observations	2,218	2,219
R^2	0.33	0.31

Notes: Results from linear regressions. Demographic factors (age, gender, education, income, urbanity, IDP status) not shown. Standard errors in parentheses. ***$p < 0.001$, **$p < 0.01$, *$p < 0.05$.

Table A4.5 *Placebo test: Impact of exposure on concerns about PMF abuses vs. ISIL*

	PMF will punish	PMF will displace
Exposure		
Time under ISIL	0.09	0.04
	(0.05)	(0.05)
Orientations		
Shi'a Arab	−4.71***	−5.65***
	(0.54)	(0.74)
Sunni Arab	−0.67**	−0.86***
	(0.24)	(0.23)
Confidence in US	−0.44***	−0.38***
	(0.08)	(0.08)
Information		
Iraqiyya TV	−0.81***	−0.84***
	(0.07)	(0.07)
Sharqiyya TV	0.54***	0.42***
	(0.08)	(0.08)
Rudaw TV	0.36***	0.40***
	(0.09)	(0.10)
Constant	−0.90*	−0.22
	(0.38)	(0.38)
Observations	2,214	2,211

Notes: Results from logit regressions. Demographic factors (age, gender, education, income, urbanity, IDP status) not shown. Standard errors in parentheses.
*** $p < 0.001$, ** $p < 0.01$, * $p < 0.05$.

Additional Analyses for Chapter 5

Table A5.1 *Predictors of discernment confidence with alternate measure of temporal experience*

	Discernment confidence	Discernment confidence
War exposure		
No. days pre-displacement	0.00***	
	(0.00)	
No. event types witnessed		0.48**
		(0.22)
Other factors		
Wasta	0.13	−0.51
	(0.53)	(0.47)
Education	−0.05	−0.09
	(0.19)	(0.18)
Anti-Assad	−0.66	−0.44
	(0.58)	(0.55)
Constant	0.02	1.12*
	(0.89)	(0.67)
Observations	113	108

Note: Results from logistic regression models. Standard errors in parentheses.
***$p < 0.01$, **$p < 0.05$, *$p < 0.1$.

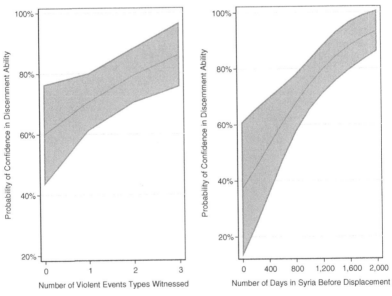

Figure A5.1 Predicted probability of discernment confidence with alternate measure of temporal experience

References

Aberbach, Joel D., and Bert A. Rockman. 2002. "Conducting and Coding Elite Interviews." *Political Science & Politics* 35(4): 673–76.

Adena, Maja, Ruben Enikolopov, Maria Petrova, Veronica Santarosa, and Ekaterina Zhuravskaya. 2015. "Radio and the Rise of the Nazis in Prewar Germany." *The Quarterly Journal of Economics* 130(4): 1885–939.

Airwars. 2017. "US-Led Coalition in Iraq & Syria Conflict Data." *Database*. Available at https://airwars.org/conflict-data/?belligerent=coalition&country=iraq%2Csyria

Akcinaroglu, Seden, and Efe Tokdemir. 2020. *The Battle for Allegiance: Governments, Terrorist Groups, and Constituencies in Conflict*. Ann Arbor: Michigan University Press.

Allan, Stuart. 2013. *Citizen Witnessing: Revisioning Journalism in Times of Conflict*. Cambridge: Polity.

Amos, Deborah. 2010. "Confusion, Contradiction, and Irony: The Iraqi Media in 2010." Joan Shorenstein Center, Discussion Paper #D-58. Available at http://nrs.harvard.edu/urn-3:HUL.InstRepos:4421401

Ansari, Neha. 2022. "Precise and Popular: Why People in Northwest Pakistan Support Drones." War on the Rocks. Available at https://warontherocks.com/2022/08/precise-and-popular-why-people-in-northwest-pakistan-support-drones/

Arias, Sabrina B., and Christopher W. Blair. 2023. "In the Eye of the Storm: Hurricanes, Climate Migration, and Climate Attitudes." *Working Paper*. Available at https://papers.ssrn.com/sol3/papers.cfm?abstract_id=4440111

Arjona, Ana. 2016. *Rebelocracy: Social Order in the Colombian Civil War*. Cambridge: Cambridge University Press.

Arraf, Jane. 2016. "How Iraqi Forces Drove ISIS from Ramadi." Newsweek. Available at www.newsweek.com/2016/03/04/iraqi-forcesfighting-isis-ramadi-fallujah-mosul-430042.html

Baddeley, Alan, and Graham Hitch. 1993. "The Recency Effect: Implicit Learning with Explicit Retrieval?" *Memory & Cognition* 21(2): 146–55.

Badrinathan, Sumitra. 2021. "Educative Interventions to Combat Misinformation: Evidence from a Field Experiment in India." *American Political Science Review* 115(4): 1325–41.

Balcells, Laia. 2017. *Rivalry and Revenge: The Politics of Violence During Civil War*. Cambridge: Cambridge University Press.

Batailler, Cedric, Skylar M. Brannon, Paul E. Teas, and Bertram Gawronski. 2022. "A Signal Detection Approach to Understanding the Identification of Fake News." *Perspectives on Psychological Science* 17(1): 78–98.

Bauer, Vincent, Michael Reese, and Keven Ruby. 2021. "Does Insurgent Selective Punishment Deter Collaboration? Evidence from the Drone War in Pakistan." *Journal of Conflict Resolution* 66(2): 297–326.

Baum, Matthew. 2013. "The Iraq Coalition of the Willing *and (Politically) Able*: Party Systems, the Press, and Public Influence on Foreign Policy." *American Journal of Political Science* 57(2): 442–58.

Beah, Ishmael. 2007. *A Long Way Gone: Memoirs of a Boy Soldier*. New York: Sarah Crichton Books.

Becker, Ernest. 1973. *The Denial of Death*. New York: The Free Press.

Bellingcat. 2014a. "Revealed: Around 40 Russian Troops from Pskov Died in the Ukraine, Reinforcement Sent In." Available at www.bellingcat .com/news/mena/2014/08/27/revealed-around-40-russian-troops-from-pskov-died-in-the-ukraine-reinforcement-sent-in/

Bellingcat. 2014b. "Origin of the Separatists' Buk." Available at www .bellingcat.com/wp-content/uploads/2014/11/Origin-of-the-Separatists-Buk-A-Bellingcat-Investigation1.pdf

Benabou, Roland. 2013. "Groupthink: Collective Delusions in Organizations and Markets." *Review of Economic Studies* 80: 429–62.

Berlinski, Nicholas, et al. 2021. "The Effects of Unsubstantiated Claims of Voter Fraud on Confidence in Elections." *Journal of Experimental Political Science* 10(1): 34–49.

Berman, Eli, Joseph H. Felter, and Jacob N. Shapiro. 2018. *Small Wars, Big Data: The Information Revolution in Modern Conflict*. Princeton, NJ: Princeton University Press.

Bisgaard-Martin. 2015. "Bias Will Find a Way: Economic Perceptions, Attributions of Blame, and Partisan-Motivated Reasoning During Crisis." *Journal of Politics* 77(3): 849–60.

Blainey, Geoffrey. 1973. *The Causes of War*. New York: The Free Press.

Blattman, Chris. 2022a. *Why We Fight: The Roots of War and the Paths to Peace*. New York: Penguin Random House.

Blattman, Chris. 2022b. "Lecture 6: Intangible Incentives & Misperceptions." *Teaching Why We Fight: Undergraduate & Master's Classes, 2–4 Week Unit Lecture Slides*. Available at https://secureservercdn.net/45.40.150.136/af4.cf3 .mwp.accessdomain.com/documents/teaching/6.%20Misperceptions.pdf

Bohnet, Heidrun, Fabien Cottier, and Simon Hug. 2018. "Conflict-Induced IDPs and the Spread of Conflict." *Journal of Conflict Resolution* 62(4): 691–716.

Box-Steffensmeier, Janet M., John R. Freeman, Matthew P. Hitt, and Jon C. W. Pevehouse. 2014. *Time-Series Analysis for the Social Sciences.* Cambridge, UK: Cambridge University Press.

Boyle, Michael. 2013. "The Costs and Consequences of Drone Warfare." *International Affairs* 89(1): 1–29.

Braman, Eileen, and Thomas E. Nelson. 2007. "Mechanism of Motivated Reasoning? Analogical Perception in Discrimination Disputes." *American Journal of Political Science* 51(4): 940–56.

Brooking, Emerson T., and Peter. W. Singer. 2018. *LikeWar: The Weaponization of Social Media.* Boston, MA: Houghton Mifflin Harcourt.

Bueno de Mesquita, Ethan. 2005. "The Quality of Terror." *American Journal of Political Science* 49(3): 515–30.

Buhaug, Halvard, and Scott Gates. 2002. "The Geography of Civil War." *Journal of Peace Research* 39(4): 417–33.

Byman, Daniel. 2013. "Why Drones Work: The Case for Washington's Weapon of Choice." *Foreign Affairs* 92(4): 32–43.

Bytwerk, Randall L. 2004. *Bending Spines: The Propagandas of Nazi Germany and the German Democratic Republic.* East Lansing: Michigan State University Press.

Campbell, Troy H., and Aaron C. Kay. "Solution Aversion: On the Relation Between Ideology and Motivated Disbelief." *Journal of Personality and Social Psychology* 107(5): 809–24.

Capps, Ron. 2014. *Seriously Not All Right: Five Wars in Ten Years.* Tucson, AZ: Schaffner Press.

Carson, Austin. 2015. "Facing Off and Saving Face: Covert Intervention and Escalation Management in the Korean War." *International Organization* 70(1): 103–31.

Cioppa, Thomas M. 2009. "Operation Iraqi Freedom Strategic Communication Analysis and Assignment." *Media, War & Conflict* 2(1): 25–45.

Cohen, Dara Kay. 2016. *Rape During Civil War.* Ithaca, NY: Cornell University Press.

Condra, Luke, and Jacob Shapiro. 2012. "Who Takes the Blame? The Strategic Effects of Collateral Damage." *American Journal of Political Science* 56(1): 167–87.

Corstange, Daniel. 2019. "The Syrian Conflict and Public Opinion Among Syrians in Lebanon." *British Journal of Middle Eastern Studies* 46(1): 178–200.

Cronin, Audrey Kurth. 2013. "Why Drones Fail: When Tactics Drive Strategy." *Foreign Affairs* 92(4): 44–54.

Danzger, M. Herbert. 1975. "Validating Conflict Data." *American Sociological Review* 40(5): 570–84.

Davenport, Christian, and Patrick Ball. 2002. "Views to a Kill: Exploring the Implications of Source Selection in the Case of Guatemalan State Terror: 1977–1995." *Journal of Conflict Resolution* 46(3): 427–50.

De Vries, Catherine, Sara B. Hobolt, and James Tilley. 2018. "Facing Up to the Facts." *Electoral Studies* 51: 115–22.

Deng, Alephonsion, Benson Deng, Benjamin Ajak, and Judy Bernstein. 2005. *They Poured Fire on Us from the Sky: The True Story of Three Lost Boys from Sudan.* New York: Public Affairs.

Di Giovanni, Janine. 2016. *The Morning They Came for Us: Dispatches from Syria.* New York: Liveright Publishing.

Djankov, Simeon, Carlee McLiesh, Tatiana Nenova, and Andrei Shleifer. 2003. "Who Owns the Media?" *Journal of Law and Economics* 46(2): 341–81.

Driscoll, Jesse, and Daniel Maliniak. 2016. "Did Georgian Voters Desire Military Escalation in 2008? Experiments and Observations." *The Journal of Politics* 78(1): 265–80.

Druckman, James N., and Kjersten R. Nelson. 2003. "Framing and Deliberation: How Citizens' Conversations Limit Elite Influence." *American Journal of Political Science* 47(4): 729–45.

Druckman, James N., and Mary C. McGrath. 2019. "The Evidence for Motivated Reasoning in Climate Change Preference Formation." *Nature Climate Change* 9: 111–19.

Earhart, David C. 2008. *Certain Victory: Images of World War II in the Japanese Media.* Armonk, NY: M. E. Sharpe.

Engel, Stefanie, and Ana Maria Ibañez. 2007. "Displacement due to Violence in Colombia." *Economic Development and Cultural Change* 55(2): 335–65.

Fair, C. Christine. 2004. "Militant Recruitment in Pakistan." *Studies in Conflict and Terrorism* 27(6): 489–504.

Fair, C. Christine, and Ali Hamza. 2016. "From Elite Consumption to Popular Opinion: Framing of the US Drone Program in Pakistani Newspapers." *Small Wars & Insurgencies* 27(4): 578–607.

Fair, C. Christine, Karl Kaltenthaler, and William Miller. 2014. "Pakistani Opposition to American Drone Strikes." *Political Science Quarterly* 129(1): 1–33.

Fazio, Lisa K., et al. 2015. "Knowledge Does Not Protect Against Illusory Truth." *Journal of Experimental Psychology* 144(5): 993–1002.

Fearon, James D. 1995. "Rationalist Explanations for War." *International Organization* 49(3): 379–414.

Feldman, Lauren, Edward W. Maibach, Connie Roser-Renouf, and Anthony Leiserowitz. 2011. "Climate on Cable: The Nature and Impact of Global Warming Coverage on Fox News, CNN, and MSNBC." *The International Journal of Press/Politics* 17(1): 3–31.

Ferber, Robert. 1966. "Item Nonresponse in a Consumer Survey." *Public Opinion Quarterly* 30(3): 399–415.

Filson, Darren, and Suzanne Werner. 2002. "A Bargaining Model of War and Peace: Anticipating the Onset, Duration, and Outcome of War." *American Journal of Political Science* 46(4): 819–37.

Fleeson, William. 2004. "Moving Personality Beyond the Person-Situation Debate: The Challenge and the Opportunity of Within-Person Variability." *Current Directions in Psychological Science* 13(2): 83–87.

Fownes, Jennifer R., and Shorna B. Allred. 2019. "Testing the Influence of Recent Weather on Perceptions of Personal Experience with Climate Change and Extreme Weather in New York State." *Weather, Climate, and Society* 11(1): 143–57.

Furr, Michael R., and David C. Funder. 2021. "Persons, Situations, and Person-Situation Interactions." In O. P. John and R. W. Robins (eds.), *Handbook of Personality: Theory and Research*, pp. 667–685. New York: The Guilford Press.

García-Ponce, Omar, and Benjamin Pasquale. 2015. "How Political Repression Shapes Attitudes Toward the State." Working Paper. Available at https://omargarciaponce.com/wp-content/uploads/2013/07/GarciaPonce_and_Pasquale_2014.pdf

Garrison, James. 2017. "Popular Mobilization Messaging." International Center for Counter-Terrorism, Research Paper. Available at https://icct.nl/publication/popular-mobilization-messaging/

Gärtner, Lea, and Harald Schoen. 2021. "Experiencing Climate Change: Revisiting the Role of Local Weather in Affecting Climate Change Awareness and Related Policy Preferences." *Climatic Change* 167: 31.

Gartzke, Erik, and James Igoe Walsh. 2022. "The Drawbacks of Drones: The Effects of UAVs on Escalation and Instability in Pakistan." *Journal of Peace Research* 59(4): 463–77.

Gelber, Yoav. 2006. *Palestine 1948: War, Escape, and the Emergence of the Palestinian Refugee Problem*. Eastbourne, UK: Sussex Academic Press.

Gentzkow, Matthew A., and Jesse M. Shapiro. 2004. "Media, Education, and Anti-Americanism in the Muslim World." *Journal of Economic Perspectives* 18(3): 117–33.

Gerner, Deborah J., Philip A. Schrodt, Ronald A. Francisco, and Judith L. Weddle. 1994. "Machine Coding of Event Data Using Regional and International Sources." *International Studies Quarterly* 38(1): 91–119.

Getmansky, Anna, and Thomas Zeitzoff. 2014. "Terrorism and Voting: The Effect of Rocket Threat on Voting in Israeli Elections." *American Political Science Review* 108(3): 588–604.

Graham, Matthew H., and Omer Yair. 2022. "Expressive Responding and Trump's Big Lie." *Working Paper*. Available at https://m-graham.com/papers/GrahamYair_BigLie.pdf

Granger, Clive W. J. 1969. "Investigating Causal Relations by Econometric Models and Cross-Spectral Methods." *Econometrica*, 37(3): 424–38.

Greenberg, Jeff, Tom Pyszczynski, and Sheldon Solomon. 1986. "The Causes and Consequences of a Need for Self-Esteem: A Terror Management Theory." In R. F. Baumeister (ed.), *Public Self and Private Self*, pp. 189–212. New York: Springer-Verlag.

Greene, Ciara M., and Gillian Murphy. 2021. "Quantifying the Effects of Fake News on Behavior: Evidence from a Study of COVID-19 Misinformation." *Journal of Experimental Psychology: Applied* 27(4): 773–84.

Greenhill, Kelly, and Benjamin Oppenheim. 2017. "Rumor Has It." *International Studies Quarterly* 61(3): 660–76.

Guay, Brian, Adam J. Berinsky, Gordon Pennycook, and David Rand. 2022. "How to Think about Whether Misinformation Interventions Work." *Online Working Paper*. Available at https://psyarxiv.com/gv8qx

Guess, Andrew, et al. 2020. "A Digital Media Literacy Intervention Increases Discernment Between Mainstream and False News in the United States and India." *The Proceedings of the National Academy of Sciences* 117(27): 15536–45.

Hale, Henry E. 2022. "Authoritarian Rallying as Reputational Cascade? Evidence from Putin's Popularity Surge after Crimea." *American Political Science Review* 116(2): 580–94.

Hanna, Martha. 2014. "War Letters: Communication Between Front and Home Front." *International Encyclopedia of the First World War*. Available at https://encyclopedia.1914-1918-online.net/article/war_letters_communication_between_front_and_home_front

Heflick, Nathan A., and Jamie L. Goldenberg. 2012. "No Atheists in Foxholes: Arguments for (but not Against) Afterlives Buffer Mortality Salience Effects for Atheists." *British Journal of Social Psychology* 51(2): 385–92.

Hemingway, Ernest, ed. 1942. *Men at War: The Best War Stories of All Time*. New York: Crown Publishing.

Henry, Vincent E. 2004. *Death Work: Police, Trauma, and the Psychology of Survival*. New York: Oxford University Press.

Hogg, Robert, Nkala Busisiwe, Janan Dietrich, Alexandra Collins, Kalysha Closson, Zishan Cui, and Steve Kanters et al. 2017. "Conspiracy Beliefs and Knowledge about AIDS Origins among Adolescents in Soweto, South Africa." *PLOS One* 12(2): e01650.

Hoover Green, Amelia. 2018. *The Commander's Dilemma: Violence and Restraint in Wartime.* Ithaca, NY: Cornell University Press.

Hughes, Heather, and Israel Waismel-Manor. 2021. "The Macedonian Fake News Industry and the 2016 US Election." *PS: Political Science and Politics* 54(1): 19–23.

Hyun, Ki Deuk, and Soo Jung Moon. 2016. "Agenda Setting in the Partisan TV News Context." *Journalism & Mass Communication Quarterly.* 93(3): 509–29.

International Committee of the Red Cross (ICRC). 2009. *Interpretive Guidance on the Notion of Direct Participation in Hostilities Under International Humanitarian Law.* Geneva: ICRC.

Jessop, Donna C., Ian P. Albery, Jean Rutter, and Heather Garrod. 2008. "Understanding the Impact of Mortality-Related Health-Risk Information: A Terror Management Theory Perspective." *Personality and Social Psychology Bulletin* 34(7): 951–64.

Johnson, Dominic, and Simon Levin. 2009. "The Tragedy of Cognition: Psychological Biases and Environmental Inaction." *Current Science* 97(11): 1593–603.

Johnston, Patrick B., and Anoop K. Sarbahi. 2016. "The Impact of US Drone Strikes of Terrorism in Pakistan." *International Studies Quarterly* 60(2): 203–19.

Jolley, Daniel, and Karen M. Douglas. 2015. "The Social Consequences of Conspiracism: Exposure to Conspiracy Theories Decreases Intentions to Engage in Politics and to Reduce One's Carbon Footprint." *British Journal of Psychology* 105: 35–56.

Jones, Edgar, Robin Woolven, Bill Durodie, and Simon Wessely. 2004. "Civilian Morale During the Second World War: Responses to Air Raids Re-examined." *Social History of Medicine* 17(3): 463–79.

Jones, Seth G., James Dobbins, Daniel Byman, Christopher S. Chivvis, Ben Connable, Jeffrey Martini, Eric Robinson, and Nathan Chandler. 2017. "Rolling Back the Islamic State." *RAND Research Report.* Available at www.rand.org/pubs/research_reports/RR1912.html

Jong, Jonathon, Jamin Halberstadt, and Matthias Bluemke. 2012. "Foxhole Atheism, Revisited: The Effects of Mortality Salience on Explicit and Implicit Religious Belief." *Journal of Experimental Social Psychology* 48(5): 983–89.

Kenneth R. M. Short, ed. 1983. *Film & Radio Propaganda in World War II.* Knoxville, TN: The University of Tennessee Press.

Kenrick, Douglas T., and David C. Funder. 1988. "Profiting from Controversy: Lessons from the Person-Situation Debate." *American Psychologist* 43(1): 23–34.

Kahan, Dan. 2017. "Misconceptions, Misinformation, and the Logic of Identity-Protective Cognition." *Cultural Cognition Project Working Paper Series No. 164.* Available at https://papers.ssrn.com/sol3/papers.cfm?abstract_id=2973067

Kalb, Marvin, and Carol Saivetz. 2007. "The Israeli-Hezbollah War of 2006: The Media as a Weapon in Asymmetrical Conflict." *International Journal of Press/Politics* 12(3): 43–66.

Kallis, Aristotle A. 2005. *Nazi Propaganda and the Second World War.* Basingstoke, UK: Palgrave and MacMillan.

Kaltenthaler, Karl, William Miller, and C. Christine Fair. 2012. "The Drone War: Pakistani Public Opposition to American Drone Strikes in Pakistan." *Working Paper.* Available at http://papers.ssrn.com/sol3/papers.cfm?abstract_id=2193354

Kalyvas, Stathis N. 2006. *The Logic of Violence in Civil War.* Cambridge: Cambridge University Press.

Kalyvas, Stathis N., and Matthew Adam Kocher. 2007. "How 'Free' Is Free Riding in Civil Wars?" *World Politics* 59(2): 177–216.

Kan'ana, Sharif, and Nihad Zaytuwi. 1987. "Deir Yassin," *Destroyed Palestinian Villages Documentation Project, Monograph No. 4.* Ramallah: Bir Zeit University Research and Documentation Center.

Kaplan, Oliver. 2017. *Resisting War: How Communities Protect Themselves.* Cambridge: Cambridge University Press.

Kerhsaw, Ian. 1987. *The Hitler Myth.* New York: Oxford University Press.

Khan, Shehryar, and Naheed Akhtar. 2016. "Operation Zarb-e-Azb: An Analysis of Media Coverage." *Strategic Studies* 36(1): 114–27.

King, Gary, Robert O. Keohane, and Sidney Verba. 1993. *Designing Social Inquiry: Scientific Inference in Qualitative Research.* Princeton, NJ: Princeton University Press.

Klein, Gary A. 1998. *Sources of Power: How People Make Decisions.* Cambridge, MA: MIT Press.

Knightley, Phillip. 1975. *From the Crimea to Vietnam: The War Correspondent as Hero, Propagandist, and Myth-Maker.* New York and London: Harcourt Brace Jovanovich.

Knightley, Phillip. 2004. *The First Casualty: The War Correspondent as Hero and Myth-Maker from the Crimea to Iraq.* Baltimore: Johns Hopkins University Press.

Knuppe, Austin. 2024. *Surviving the Islamic State: Contention, Cooperation, and Neutrality in Wartime Iraq.* New York: Columbia University Press, 2024.

Koppes, Clayton R., and Gregory D. Black. 1990. *Hollywood Goes to War: How Politics, Profits, and Propaganda Shaped World War II Movies.* Berkeley: University of California Press.

Kose, Talha, Mesut Ozcan, and Ekrem Karakoc. 2016. "A Comparative Analysis of Soft Power in the MENA Region: The Impact of Ethnic, Sectarian, and Religious Identity on Soft Power in Iraq and Egypt." *Foreign Policy Analysis* 12(3): 354–73.

Kramer, Alan. 2009. *Dynamic of Destruction: Culture and Mass Killing in the First World War*. Oxford, UK: Oxford University Press.

Krause, Jana. 2018. *Resilient Communities: Non-Violence and Civilian Agency in Communal War*. Cambridge: Cambridge University Press.

Kunda, Ziva. 1990. "The Case for Motivated Reasoning." *Psychological Bulletin* 108(3): 480–98.

Landau, Mark J., Sheldon Solomon, Tom Pyszczynski, and Jeff Greenberg. 2007. "On the Compatibility of Terror Management Theory and Perspective on Human Evolution." *Evolutionary Psychology* 5(3): 476–519.

Laughlin, Benjamin. 2018. "Information Cascades and Refugee Crises: Evidence from Kosovo." *Working Paper*. Available at www.benjamin-laughlin.com/refugee_cascades.pdf

Leach, John. 1994. *Survival Psychology*. Basingstoke, UK: Palgrave MacMillan.

Leach, John. 2004. "Why People 'Freeze' in an Emergency: Temporal and Cognitive Constraints on Survival Response." *Aviation, Space and Environmental Medicine* 75(6): 530–42.

Lelkes, Yphtach, Gaurav Sood, and Shanto Iyengar. 2016. "The Hostile Audience: The Effect of Access to Broadband Internet on Partisan Affect." *American Journal of Political Science* 61(1): 5–20.

Levin, Dov. 2023. "How Low Can You Go: The Effects of Low Credibility False Flag Incidents on International and Domestic Approval for Interstate Wars." *Paper Presented at the 2023 Meeting of the American Political Science Association*.

Lifton, Robert J. 1991. *Death in Life: Survivors of Hiroshima*. Chapel Hill: University of North Carolina Press.

Liosky, Joanne M., and Jennifer Henrichsen. 2009. "Don't Shoot the Messenger: Prospects for Protecting Journalists in Conflict Situations." *Media, War & Conflict* 2(2): 129–48.

Lister, Charles R. 2016. *The Syrian Jihad: Al-Qaeda, the Islamic State, and the Evolution of an Insurgency*. Oxford: Oxford University Press.

Lucas, Caleb. "Mere Puffery or Convincing Claims? Rebels News and Civilian Perceptions of Group Strength." *International Studies Quarterly*, in press.

Lyall, Jason. 2009. "Does Indiscriminate Violence Incite Insurgent Attacks? Evidence from Chechnya." *Journal of Conflict Resolution* 53(3): 331–62.

Lyall, Jason. 2010. "Are Coethnics More Effective Counterinsurgents? Evidence from the Second Chechen War." *American Political Science Review* 104(1): 1–20.

Lyall, Jason. 2019. "Civilian Casualties, Humanitarian Aid, and Insurgent Violence in Civil Wars." *International Organization* 73(4): 901–26.

Lyall, Jason, Graeme Blair, and Kosuke Imai. 2013. "Explaining Support for Combatants during Wartime: A Survey Experiment in Afghanistan." *American Political Science Review* 107 (4): 679–705.

Mansour, Renad, and Faleh A. Jabar. 2017. "The Popular Mobilization Forces and Iraq's Future." Carnegie Endowment for International Peace, Carnegie Middle East Center. Available at https://carnegieendowment .org/files/CMEC_63_Mansour_PMF_Final_Web.pdf

Marlin, Randal. 2002. *Propaganda and the Ethics of Persuasion.* Peterborough, Ont.; Orchard Park, NY: Broadview Press.

Matanock, Aila M., and Natalia Garbiras-Diaz. 2018. "Considering Concessions: A Survey Experiment on the Colombian Peace Process." *Conflict Management and Peace Science* 35(6): 637–55.

McAllister, Daniel W., Terence R. Mitchell, and Lee Roy Beach. 1979. "The Contingency Model for the Selection of Decision Strategies: An Empirical Test of the Effects of Significance, Accountability, and Reversibility." *Organizational Behavior and Human Performance* 24: 228–44.

McCarthy, John D., and Clark McPhail and Jackie Smith. 1996. "Images of Protest: Dimensions of Selection Bias in Media Coverage of Washington Demonstrations, 1982 and 1991." *American Sociological Review* 61(3): 478–99.

Miller, Joanne M., Kyle L. Saunders, and Christina E. Farhart. 2016. "Conspiracy Endorsement as Motivated Reasoning: The Moderating Roles of Political Knowledge and Trust." *American Journal of Political Science* 60(4): 824–44.

Milliff, Aidan. "Making Sense, Making Choices: How Civilians Choose Survival Strategies During Violence." *American Political Science Review*, in press.

Milton, Joyce. 1989. *The Yellow Kids: Foreign Correspondents in the Heyday of Yellow Journalism.* New York: HarperCollins Publishers.

Morris, Benny. 2005. "The Historiography of Deir Yassin." *The Journal of Israeli History* 24(1): 79–107.

Morris, Jonathon S. 2005. "The Fox News Factor." *The International Journal of Press/Politics* 10(3): 56–79.

Mueller, Carol. 1997. "International Press Coverage of East German Protest Events, 1989." *American Sociological Review* 62(5): 820–32.

Navarette, Carlos D., and Daniel M. T. Fessler. 2005. "Normative Bias and Adaptive Challenges: A Relational Approach to Coalitional

Psychology and a Critique of Terror Management Theory." *Evolutionary Psychology* 3: 297–325.

New America Foundation. N.D. *Drone Wars Database*. Available at http://natsec.newamerica.net

Nilsson, Maria. 2019. "An Ethics of (Not) Showing: Citizen Witnessing, Journalism, and Visualizations of a Terror Attack." *Journalism Practice* 14(3): 259–76.

Nyhan, Brendan, and Jason Reifler. 2010. "When Corrections Fail: The Persistence of Political Misperceptions." *Political Behavior* 32(2): 303–30.

Nyhan, Brendan. 2021. "Why the Backfire Effect Does Not Explain the Durability of Political Misperceptions." *The Proceedings of the National Academy of Sciences* 118(15): 1–7.

Oberg, Magnus, and Margareta Sollenberg. 2011. "Gathering Conflict Information Using News Resources." In Kristine Hoglund and Magnus Oberg (ed.), *Understanding Peace Research: Methods and Challenges*, 47–73. New York: Routledge.

Oliver, J. Eric, and Thomas J. Wood. 2014. "Conspiracy Theories and the Paranoid Style(s) of Mass Opinion." *American Journal of Political Science* 58(4): 952–66.

Orwell, George. 1943. *Looking Back on the Spanish War*. London, UK: New Road.

Osmundsen, Mathias, Alexander Bor, Peter Bjerregaard Vahlstrup, Anja Bechmann, and Michael Bang Petersen. 2021. "Partisan Polarization is the Primary Psychological Motivation Behind Political Fake News Sharing on Twitter." *American Political Science Review* 115(3): 999–1015.

Otto, Sabine. 2013. "Coding One-Sided Violence from Media Reports." *Cooperation and Conflict* 48(4): 556–66.

Pak Institute for Peace Studies (PIPS). N.D. *PIPS Security Database*. Available at www.pakpips.com

Paoline III, Eugene A. 2003. "Taking Stock: Toward a Richer Understanding of Police Culture." *Journal of Criminal Justice* 31: 199–214.

Parker-Stephen, Evan. 2013. "Tides of Disagreement: How Reality Facilitates (and Inhibits) Partisan Public Opinion." *Journal of Politics* 75(4): 1077–88.

Pearlman, Wendy. 2016. "Narratives of Fear in Syria." *Perspectives on Politics* 14(1): 21–37.

Peffley, Mark, Jon Hurwitz, and Paul M. Sniderman. 1997. "Racial Stereotypes and Whites' Political Views of Blacks in the Context of Welfare and Crime." *American Journal of Political Science* 41(1): 30–60.

Peffley, Mark, Marc. L Hutchinson, and Michal Shamir. 2022. "Terrorism and Political Tolerance Toward 'Fellow Travelers.'" *Journal of Conflict Resolution* 66(7–8): 1208–34.

Pennycook, Gordon, and David G. Rand. 2019. "Lazy, Not Biased: Susceptibility to Partisan Fake News is Better Explained by Lack of Reasoning than by Motivated Reasoning." *Cognition* 188: 39–50.

Pennycook, Gordon, and David G. Rand. 2021. "The Psychology of Fake News." *Trends in Cognitive Sciences* 25(5): 388–402.

Pennycook, Gordon, Tyrone D. Cannon, and David G. Rand. 2018. "Prior Exposure Increases Perceived Accuracy of Fake News." *Journal of Experimental Psychology: General* 147(12): 1865–80.

Petersen, Michael Bang, Mathias Osmundsen, and Kevin Arceneaux. 2023. "The 'Need for Chaos' and Motivations to Share Hostile Political Rumors." *American Political Science Review* 117(4): 1486–505.

Petraeus, David H., and James F. Amos. 2009. *U.S. Army U.S. Marine Corps Counterinsurgency Field Manual.* ed. John C. McClure. Kissimmee, FL: Signalman Publishing.

Pew Research Center. N.D. *Global Attitudes Project Public Opinion Datasets (Pakistan).* Available at www.pewglobal.org/category/datasets/

Plaw, Avery, and Matthew Fricker. 2012. "Tracking the Predators: Evaluating the US Drone Campaign in Pakistan." *International Studies Perspectives* 13(4): 344–65.

Ponsonby, Arthur. 1928. *Falsehood in War-Time: Containing an Assortment of Lies Circulated Throughout the Nations During the Great War.* London, UK: Garland Publishing Company.

Popkin, Samuel. 1979. *The Rational Peasant: The Political Economy of Rural Society in Vietnam.* Berkeley: University of California Press.

Porter, Ethan, and Thomas J. Wood. 2022. "Political Misinformation and Factual Corrections on the Facebook News Feed: Experimental Evidence." *Journal of Politics* 84(3): 1812–17.

Porter, Ethan, Yamil Velez, and Thomas J. Wood. 2022. "Factual Corrections Eliminate False Beliefs about COVID-19 Vaccines." *Public Opinion Quarterly* 86(3): 762–73.

Posen, Barry. 2013. "Pull Back: The Case for a Less Activist Foreign Policy." *Foreign Affairs* 92(1):116–28.

Powers, Shawn, and Ben O'Loughlin. 2015. "The Syrian Data Glut: Rethinking the Role of Information in Conflict." *Media, War & Conflict* 8(2): 172–80.

Qazi, Shehzad. 2011. "Rebels of the Frontier: Origins, Organization, and Recruitment of the Pakistani Taliban." *Small Wars and Insurgencies* 22(4): 574–602.

Radnitz, Scott. 2021. *Revealing Schemes: The Politics of Conspiracy in Russia and the Post-Soviet Region.* Oxford: Oxford University Press.

Rathje, Steve, Jon Roozenbeek, Jay J. Van Bavel, and Sander van der Linden. 2023. "Accuracy and Social Motivations Shape Judgements of (Mis)information." *Nature Human Behaviour* 7: 892–903.

Redlawsk, David P., Andrew J. W. Civettini, and Karen M. Emmerson. 2010. "The Affective Tipping Point: Do Motivated Reasoners Ever 'Get It'?" *Political Psychology* 31(4): 563–93.

Reese, Michael J., Keven G. Ruby, and Robert A. Pape. 2017. "Days of Action or Restraint? How the Islamic Calendar Impacts Violence." *American Political Science Review* 111(3): 439–59.

Revkin, Mara R. 2021. "Competitive Governance and Displacement Decisions Under Rebel Rule: Evidence from the Islamic State in Iraq." *Journal of Conflict Resolution* 65(1): 46–80.

Rincker, Meg, Ghazia Aslam, and Mujtaba Ali Isani. 2016. "Crossed My Mind, But Ruled It Out: Political Ambition and Gender in the Pakistani Lawyers' Movement 2007–2009." *International Political Science Review* 38(3): 246–63.

Robinson, Sarita, and Nikola Bridges. 2011. "Survival – Mind and Brain." *The Psychologist* 24: 30–33.

Roozenbeek, Jon, et al. 2020. "Susceptibility to Misinformation About COVID-19 Around the World." *Royal Society Open Science* 7: 1–15.

Ross, Lee, and Richard E. Nisbett. 1991. *The Person and the Situation: Perspectives of Social Psychology*. New York: McGraw-Hill.

Rossino, Alexander 2003. *Hitler Strikes Poland: Blitzkrieg, Ideology, and Atrocity*. Lawrence: University of Kansas Press.

Rowling, J. K. 2003. *Harry Potter and the Order of the Phoenix*. London: Bloomsbury Publishing.

Rozenas, Arturas, and Denis Stukal. 2019. "How Autocrats Manipulate Economic News: Evidence from Russia's State-Controlled Television." *Journal of Politics* 81(3): 982–96.

Ryan, Camille D., et al. 2020. "Monetizing Disinformation in the Attention Economy: The Case of Genetically Modified Organisms (GMOs)." *European Management Journal* 38: 7–18.

Schon, Justin. 2020. *Surviving the War in Syria: Survival Strategies in a Time of Conflict*. Cambridge, UK: Cambridge University Press.

Schutte, Sebastian. 2015. "Geography, Outcome, and Casualties: A Unified Model of Insurgency." *Journal of Conflict Resolution* 59(6): 1101–28.

Sexton, Renard, and Christoph Zürcher. 2023. "Aid, Attitudes, and Insurgency: Evidence from Development Projects in Northern Afghanistan." *American Journal of Political Science*, Early View. Available at https://doi.org/10.1111/ajps.12778

Shah, Aqil. 2018. "Do US drone Strikes Cause Blowback? Evidence from Pakistan and Beyond." *International Security* 42(4): 47–84.

Shapiro, Jacob N., and C. Christine Fair. 2010. "Understanding Support for Islamist Militancy in Pakistan." *International Security* 34(3): 79–118.

Shapiro, Jake N. 2013. *The Terrorist's Dilemma: Managing Violent Covert Organizations*. Princeton, NJ: Princeton University Press.

Sharkey, Patrick. 2010. "The Acute Effect of Local Homicides on Children's Cognitive Performance." *Proceedings of the National Academy of Sciences* 107(26): 11733–8.

Sheets, Penelope, Charles M. Rowling, and Timothy M. Jones. 2015. "The View from Above (and Below): A Comparison of American, British, and Arab News Coverage of US Drones." *Media, War & Conflict* 8(3): 1–23.

Silverman, Daniel. 2019. "What Shapes Civilian Beliefs about Violent Events? Experimental Evidence from Pakistan" *Journal of Conflict Resolution* 63(9): 1460–87.

Silverman, Daniel. 2020. "Too Late to Apologize? Collateral Damage, Post-Harm Compensation, and Insurgent Violence in Iraq." *International Organization* 74(4): 853–71.

Silverman, Daniel, Karl Kaltenthaler, and Munqith Dagher. 2021. "Seeing is Disbelieving: The Depths and Limits of Factual Misinformation in War." *International Studies Quarterly* 65(3): 798–810.

Smith, Crispin, and Michael Knights. 2023. "Remaking Iraq: How Iranian-Backed Militias Captured the Country." *Just Security*. Available at www.justsecurity.org/85566/remaking-iraq-how-iranian-backed-militias-captured-the-country/

Soroka, Stuart N., Dominik A. Stecula, and Christopher Wlezien. 2015. "It's (Change in) the (Future) Economy, Stupid: Economic Indicators, the Media, and Public Opinion." *American Journal of Political Science* 59(2): 457–74.

South Asia Terrorism Portal. N.D. "Fatalities in Terrorist Violence in Pakistan, 2003-2016." Available at www.satp.org/satporgtp/countries/pakistan/database/casualties.htm

Stack, Megan K. 2010. *Every Man in this Village in a Liar: An Education in War*. New York: Anchor Books.

Stevens, Tim. 2013. "Book Review: Neville Bolt, The Violent Image: Insurgent Propaganda and the New Revolutionaries." *Media, War & Conflict* 6(1): 93–4.

Stewart, Greg L., and Murray R. Barrick. 2004. "Four Lessons Learned from the Person-Situation Debate: A Review and Research Agenda." In B. Schneider and D. B. Smith (eds.), *Personality and Organizations*, pp. 61–85. Mahwah, NJ: Lawrence Erlbaum Associates Publishers.

Stout, Michael J. 2011. "The Effectiveness of Nazi Propaganda During World War II." Master's Thesis, Eastern Michigan University. Available at https://commons.emich.edu/theses/314/

Stratfor. 2009. "Special Report: U.S.-NATO, Facing the Reality of Risk in Pakistan (with STRATFOR Interactive Map)." Online Report. Available at https://worldview.stratfor.com/article/special-report-us-nato-facing-reality-risk-pakistan-stratfor-interactive-map

Sunstein, Cass. 2003. "Terrorism and Probability Neglect." *Journal of Risk and Uncertainty* 26(2–3): 121–36.

Swami, Viren, Tomas Chamorro-Premuzic, and Adrian Furnham. 2010. "Unanswered Questions: A Preliminary Investigation of Personality and Individual Difference Predictors of 9/11 Conspiracist Beliefs." *Applied Cognitive Psychology* 24(6): 749–61.

Taber, Charles S., and Milton Lodge. 2006. "Motivated Skepticism in the Evaluation of Political Beliefs." *American Journal of Political Science* 50(3): 755–69.

Taj, Farhat. 2010 "The Year of the Drone Misinformation." *Small Wars & Insurgencies* 21(3): 529–35.

Tandoc, Edson, Zheng Wei Lim, and Richard Ling. 2018. "Defining 'Fake News': A Typology of Scholarly Definitions." *Digital Journalism* 6(3): 1–17.

Tellez, Juan Fernando. 2019. "Worlds Apart: Conflict Exposure and Preferences for Peace." *Journal of Conflict Resolution* 63(4): 1053–76.

Tesler, Michael. 2018. "Elite Domination of Public Doubts about Climate Change (Not Evolution)." *Political Communication* 35(2): 306–26.

Tetlock, Philip E. 1983. "Accountability and the Perseverance of First Impressions." *Social Psychology Quarterly* 46: 285–92.

The BFRS Political Violence in Pakistan Dataset. N.D. Available at https://esoc.princeton.edu/data/bfrs-political-violence-pakistan-dataset

The Bureau of Investigative Journalism (BIJ). 2017. Covert US Drone Warfare Investigation. Available at www.thebureauinvestigates.com/category/-projects/drones/drones-pakistan/

The Islamic State of Iraq and the Levant (ISIL). 2014. "The Failed Crusade." Dabiq Magazine. Available at http://clarionproject.org/docs/islamic-state-isis-magazine-Issue-4-the-failed-crusade.pdf

The United States Strategic Bombing Survey (USSBS). 1947. *The Effects of Strategic Bombing on German Morale*. Washington, DC: Government Printing Office.

Thompson, Mark. 1999. *Forging War: The Media in Serbia, Croatia, Bosnia, and Herzegovina*. Luton, UK: University of Luton Press.

Toft, Monica, and Yuri Zhukov. 2015. "Islamists and Nationalists: Rebel Motivation and Counterinsurgency in Russia's North Caucasus." *American Political Science Review* 109(2): 222–38.

Tugwell, Maurice. 1986. "Terrorism and Propaganda." *Journal of Conflict Studies* 6(2): 5–15.

Uscinski, Joseph E., and Joseph M. Parent. 2014. *American Conspiracy Theories*. New York: Oxford University Press.

Vraga, Emily and Leticia Bode. 2020. "Defining Misinformation and Understanding its Bounded Nature: Using Expertise and Evidence for Describing Misinformation." *Political Communication* 37(1): 136–44.

Vultee, Fred. 2009. "The Second Casualty: Effects of Interstate Conflict and Civil War on Press Freedom." *Media, War & Conflict* 2(2): 111–27.

Walsh, James Igoe. 2013. *The Effectiveness of Drone Strikes in Counterinsurgency and Counterterrorism Campaigns*. Carlisle, PA: US Army War College Press.

Webster, Steven W., and Bethany Albertson. 2022. "Emotion and Politics: Noncognitive Psychological Biases in Public Opinion." *Annual Review of Political Science* 25: 401–18.

Wedeen, Lisa. 2015. *Ambiguities of Domination: Politics, Rhetoric, and Symbols in Contemporary Syria*. Chicago, IL: University of Chicago Press.

Wedeen, Lisa. 2019. *Authoritarian Apprehensions: Ideology, Judgment, and Mourning in Syria*. Chicago, IL: University of Chicago Press.

Weidmann, Nils B. 2015. "On the Accuracy of Media-Based Conflict Event Data." *Journal of Conflict Resolution* 59(6): 1129–49.

Weinstein, Jeremy. 2006. *Inside Rebellion: The Politics of Insurgent Violence*. Cambridge: Cambridge University Press.

Weiss, Jessica-Chen. 2013. "Authoritarian Signaling, Mass Audiences, and Nationalist Protest in China." *International Organization* 67(1): 1–35.

Whitson, Jennifer A., and Adam D. Galinsky. 2008. "Lacking Control Increases Illusory Pattern Perception." *Science* 322(5898): 115–17.

Williamson, Vanessa. 2018. "Public Ignorance or Elitist Jargon? Reconsidering Americans' Overestimates of Government Waste and Foreign Aid." *American Politics Research* 47(1): 152–73.

Wood, Thomas, and Ethan Porter. 2019. "The Elusive Backfire Effect: Mass Attitudes' Steadfast Factual Adherence." *Political Behavior* 41(1): 135–63.

Wood, Thomas J., and J. Eric Oliver. 2014. "Conspiracy Theories and the Paranoid Style of Mass Opinion." *American Journal of Political Science* 58(4): 952–66.

Yanagizawa-Drott, David. 2014. "Propaganda and Conflict: Evidence from the Rwandan Genocide." *Quarterly Journal of Economics* 129(4): 1947–94.

Young, Lauren. 2015. "Preying on the Poor: The Impact of Repressive Violence on Citizen Behavior." *Working Paper*. Available at www.laurenelyssayoung.com/wp-content/uploads/2016/02/Young-Intimidation-of-the-Poor-Dec-2015.pdf

Yusuf, Huma. 2011. "Conspiracy Fever: The US, Pakistan and its Media." *Survival* 53(4): 95–118.

Zeitzoff, Thomas. 2017. "How Social Media is Changing Conflict." *Journal of Conflict Resolution* 6(9): 1970–91.

Zhukov, Yuri. 2017. "External Resources and Indiscriminate Violence." *World Politics* 69(1): 54–97.

Zhukov, Yuri M., and Matthew A. Baum. 2016. "Reporting Bias and Information Warfare." *Presented at the Annual Meeting of the International Studies Association*, Atlanta, GA, March 16–19.

Index

Made in United States
North Haven, CT
02 January 2025

63918532R00114